Best wns

David Brown

PLAYING FOR ENGLAND

BY DAVID BLACK

© Copyright David Black 2011

ISBN: 978-1466377714

Published in Paperback by CreateSpace
Cover design by David Black Books

2

Also by David Black:

The Great Satan

Siege of Faith

Eagles of the Damned

http://www.david-black.co.uk

Summary

David Black served in the British army for more than 15 years.

From the ugly, war-torn streets of Londonderry in the early 1970s, to the ranks of a Territorial regiment of the now famous Special Air Service, until the mid-eighties. When not serving part-time with the Regiment, he worked as a fully qualified London black cab driver. Because of the security implications with the SAS, David has waited over twenty years before writing anything about his many military adventures. Names have been changed, because even now; ex-members of the Regiment (and their families) are potential targets for the more rabid elements of the terrorist world. David holds many memories of life and experiences in the British army and particularly the Special Air Service Regiment; happy, sad, funny, outrageous and sometimes, downright dangerous. This book covers his early military years, and culminates with a detailed look at his SAS selection and Continuation training course. He holds the old saying "I wouldn't change a moment" close to his heart... and means every word of it!

Authors Notes
Introduction

When I decided to write this book, it wasn't planned to be an exposé or whistle blower of sensitive British military missions. If that disappoints a potential reader, I suggest looking in the fiction sections of good bookshops to get their fix.

I wanted to put down on paper the incredible experience of cracking a selection process which for one reason or another failed more than 90% of the applicants who initially started the course. Phrases like: 'The pain barrier' and 'Utter exhaustion' don't do justice to a physical experience of SAS selection in the lonely wilderness of the Welsh mountains, which few men attempt and even fewer pass

I've included some experiences of my earlier military years before embarking on SAS selection, because I firmly believe that they were an important part of maturity and my physical and mental toughening process. Those experiences were at least part of my eventual decision to try out for the reserve SAS Regiment. I know the full story, but I'll leave the reader to make up his or her own mind on what it really takes to make the necessary grade.

Forward

The vast majority of British soldiers carry two secret wishes within themselves.

The first is to win a Victoria Cross, and the second is to serve in the Special Air Service Regiment. The main problem with their initial desire is that unfortunately, the recipient of the Victoria Cross normally dies during the process of winning it. There have of course, been a few brave and lucky men who have lived to tell the tale, but they are sadly, very few in number. There is also a problem with opportunity. Given that wars (declared or otherwise) are few in number, the odds against being in the correct place at the exact time are considerably worse than winning the jackpot in the Euro lottery. British soldiers tend by nature to be brave men, especially when their backs are to the wall, or if their friends are in trouble, but the chances are, they will not be putting V.C. after their name. They simply don't get the chance to win Gt. Britain's highest military award for valour in the face of the enemy, during their term of military service.

Given an overall strength of perhaps 175,000 men serving in the British Regular and Territorial Army in the 70s, probably less than 700 would have been serving in the combined regular or reserve SAS Regiments at that time.

The greatest barrier to serving within the SAS is that before joining its exclusive ranks the prospective candidate must pass the hardest physical and mental selection process ever devised by any military organisation. It is entirely an individual effort; no advantage is given to any man, whatever his previous social or military background.

The initial mental selection process begins long before the first start line on the Brecon Beacons. There are plenty of soldiers who fancy their chances; especially over a few beers in the NAAFI; but when the time comes, they can think of at least a dozen good reasons why it is suddenly not quite such a good idea to try. There are also those who know in their heart of hearts they would never reach the Olympic fitness standards required by the Regiment. They often think hard about it for a few moments, then shrug their shoulders, head off to the NAAFI to munch happily on a mid-morning bacon sandwich. Surprisingly, another obstacle is the military establishment its-self. In the British army, a potential applicant must seek permission from his Colonel to attempt Special Forces selection, and Colonels do not like to lose their best men to another unit, even the SAS If a senior N.C.O. or Commissioned officer holds an important position in a battalion, he would find it an uphill struggle to get the go-ahead to even take a shot at selection. If he was a motivated junior rank - private, lance corporal or even full corporal he may well have the potential to become a first class senior Non-Commissioned Officer one day. These are not the men any sensible Colonel would happily release. It is normally a case of being a real pest, until the big Boss finally OKs the attempt at SAS selection.

Given the fact that service with the Regiment is a life-changing decision, where the applicant's future will be affected forever, the vast majority of British soldiers never get to the stage of attempting selection; humping an extremely heavy bergan backpack, rifle and belt kit over the rugged mountains of South Wales. While of course they are attracted the popular image of cruising ghostlike across the battlefield in a heavily armed Land Rover, or being a military version of 007, they fail to make the final decision to go for it. No discredit to any of them, they are all good men, they just do not make it happen during their window of military opportunity.

My right of passage into the SAS happened for a number of diverse reasons. Everyone faces crossroads during their lives; mine eventually led to the now famous Special Air Service Regiment.

During my time in the SAS, I had the privilege of serving with some of the hardest, toughest men the United Kingdom has to offer. Their spirit, training and uncompromising attitude towards the enemies of this country make them a truly formidable fighting force.

My military service ranged through the 70's and 80's, at the height of the Cold War. I had already accrued four years' experience of the Military before reaching Special Forces, and some of the character building experiences, which helped me through selection, are detailed in this book. This is the true story of my journey, which eventually led me into the secretive world of the reserve SAS…

PHASE ONE

CHAPTER 1

The arduous journey, which ultimately led to the exclusive ranks of the SAS began when I first joined the army way back in 1972. It was at my local Territorial Army infantry drill hall in Edgware, North London. I had only recently celebrated my 17th birthday and was still at school, studying hard for my "O" levels.

Ever since I was little I had never followed the usual pattern of boyhood dreams of becoming an engine driver or fireman; I just wanted to be a soldier.

My family had enjoyed a long tradition of military service, and I was brought up hearing occasional stories of their deeds, and of course, my dear old dad's national service. He had served for two years in an Airborne (Parachute) company with the Royal Army Service Corps – the forerunner of the Royal Corps. of Transport. Exciting tales of his operational duties in Palestine fighting Jewish terrorist groups back in the latter half of the 40's touched an adventurous nerve somewhere deep inside, and I felt drawn to his stories of comradeship, adventure and the general lifestyle in the military. Because was I was still at school, I thought it a sensible first step to try out army life and join the part-time military: The Territorials.

The initial introduction was pretty painless. My first Territorial Army unit; 'A' Company, 6th Battalion, The Queen's Regiment (v) had only been recently (then) been formed under a Conservative Government decree, which greatly expanded the regular army reserve, due to the ongoing cold war and the growing threat from the Communist Empire which stretched far beyond their side of the Iron Curtain.

I must admit that it was enormous fun as a young lad, serving once a week for a couple of hours on drill nights and sometimes at weekends with my new friends. They brought a wealth of colourful stories and life skills into my newly grown-up world. The only drawback I can remember was that as I was under 18, the army classed me as a boy soldier. I did the same physical training, weapon handling and so on but just received half pay. It really bit home when a pay parade was held months later during my first two week annual camp, where I only received 50% of the army pay the other guys in my unit received. No one joins for the money, but after stoppages, I only received about eleven pounds for two-weeks hard work.

Our annual camp was held at Shorncliff army barracks on the Kent coast. As I remember it, it was cold and wet, but brilliant fun for a lad of my tender age. Faces blackened and armed to the teeth, we learnt to creep quietly around the countryside at night, while silently practising patrolling and ambushing missions. We fired all sorts of weapons on the military ranges by day; assault rifles, machine guns and semi-automatic pistols. Route marching, assault courses, early-morning physical training and hours on the drill square made the days, and nights fly by.

The two weeks of intensive training culminated with a big battalion parade in front of some Defence Ministry bigwigs and a large posse of Brass hats (senior officers). It went smoothly enough, until my friend Mike's toecap fell off.

Covered in minute leather blisters, our newly issued military DMS boots had to be burnt with a hot spoon to flatten them before we could bull (polish) them up to the required standard. The parade was our Battalion's first serious attempt at a spit and polish affair, and naturally, we all wanted to make a good impression. The evening before the big parade, one of our ex-regular sergeants showed us how to burn off the bubbly surface of the heavy boots with a spoon heated over a candle flame. Once completed, we could then polish the resulting smooth leather into a sleek glass finish, and as a result, look absolutely immaculate on the forthcoming parade. Unfortunately, Mike wasn't paying enough attention to detail, got his spoon far too hot, and accidentally incinerated the stitching holding his toecap to the rest of his boot. He didn't notice the damage at the critical moment and both his boots looked outstanding after he had built up numerous layers of polish over the now invisible and badly scorched stitching. In fact, our Sergeant displayed Mike's finished boots to the rest of us as a glowing example of first class spit and polish.

Mike's problems only began the next morning, after our Battalion had carefully formed up on the parade square. When boots have been diligently bulled, the operation builds up dozens of layers of black polish and results in a high-gloss mirror finish. We had to march very carefully onto the parade square, so that the layers of dry polish didn't crack too soon, and ruin the overall effect. When the entire Battalion was neatly formed up by Companies, and the dignitaries had duly arrived, the Regimental Sergeant Major cleared his throat and roared.

"Parade...Shun!"

600 army boots crashed into a position of attention; however, unfortunately, that's when it happened. The impact of smartly coming to attention caused Mike's toecap to part company with the rest of his boot; except for a thin lifeline of undamaged stitching. The toecap hung limply to one side, and there was absolutely nothing Mike could do about it; except stand perfectly still. To make matters worse, he had a large hole in his sock, and his big toe was sticking through it.

"You bloody idiot Jones," whispered the Corporal next to him. Mike didn't know what to do. It didn't help when several loud sniggers erupted around him. "Shut up and stand still!" hissed the Corporal out of the side of his mouth. The Big Wigs got out of their convoy of staff cars and mounted the review podium.

"Why me?" whispered Mike miserably.

When the Minister and his VIPs were ready, the unsuspecting R.S.M. roared out the order "Battalion will move to the right in threes............RIGHT TURN!"

All 600 members of the battalion executed a smart pivot on their right heel and turned. It not only looked good, but also sounded crisp and military. Well actually 599 men sounded perfect. Mike, distressed as he was, added a popping sound as his toecap flipped shut - More sniggers from the soldiers surrounding him.

"The Battalion will advance in review order....QUICK MARCH!" R.S.M Shinn bellowed. The battalion's band launched into a lusty rendition of 'Soldiers of the Queen' our Regimental quick march, as every soldier on parade stepped smartly off with his left foot. Crunch, Crunch, Crunch, our boots hit the ground in time to the beat of the band's big bass drum. Mike unfortunately was beating a strange tattoo of his own. Crunch, flip, crunch, flop, crunch flip and so on, as we all marched smartly around the parade square. There is a lot of tension during a big parade, as no-one wants to make a mistake and reflect badly on his Regiment. It's difficult to keep in step, make sure you are in exactly in the right position, hold your rifle at the correct regulation angle and listen for the next order over the sound of the band and all those crunching feet. It's even more difficult as 95% of us had never taken part in a large military parade before. I suppose it's a natural reaction to focus on someone else's misfortunes, and the nervous release came with a bad case of stifled mirth, which rippled through our entire marching company. When the eyes' right was successfully completed, and we finally reached our original starting point, the R.S.M. bellowed.

"Battalion.........HALT!" ......"Battalion will advance...Left TURN!"

As one, we carried out the order, and the Battalion was exactly back where it started. The only casualty was Mike's toecap, which chose the last drill movement to finally part company with his rest of his boot. It lay about 6 inches from his big toe, which still poked proudly through the hole in his sock.

"Now we're really in it," hissed the Corporal "The old bugger's going to inspect the troops!"

Sure enough, after saying a few kind words to our Colonel on the podium, the Minister was ushered to the head of our Company where he walked slowly along its ranks, stopping occasionally to chat with the boys, who were still standing smartly to attention.

"Do you think he might push off before he gets to us?" Whispered Mike hopefully.

"Not a hope in hell," said someone at the back.

"Quiet" hissed the Corporal, "Here he comes!"

Moments later, the Defence Minister, followed by the huge posse of Brass hats, dignitaries' and the local Mayor, etc. arrived at our file. The old boy was giving each soldier a quick once over, and he seemed genuinely impressed. He stopped in front of Mike. He slowly looked down at Mike's big toe and raised his head. There was a puzzled look on his face.

"Bit of trouble with your boot, I see?"

"Eh… Yes Sir!" Spluttered Mike, half expecting to be shot out of hand.

The Minister smiled, and said to our dumfounded and utterly horrified Colonel.

"It's been a very smart parade. Shouldn't penalise the lad's for trying too hard, what?"

This last comment probably did save Mike from summary execution behind the toilet block, as all the entourage smiled, because his eminence, the Minister had smiled. Well, that's not quite true; the Regimental Sergeant Major didn't smile. As the Minister and his gang sloped off for a drink and lunch in the Officer's Mess, the R.S.M. put his face about half an inch from Mike's, as if to forever burn Mike's ashen image into his memory. Regimental Sergeant Major Shinn's face was puce, boiling with a terrible rage as only R.S.M.'s can. It twitched as a vein throbbed ominously on the side of his head.

A shower of spit hit Mike as the R.S.M. fought to resist disembowelling him with his Regimental pace stick. There was only one phrase uttered, which said it all.

"You, you … 'ORRIBLE little man!"….

Chapter 2
In at the deep end

Having finally stopped laughing at Mike's misfortune, and really having developed a taste for military life with the Territorial's it was a natural progression to start thinking about transferring to the regular infantry. By now, I'd passed my exams, scoring four good 'O' level grades, and a handful of high-grade C.S,E.s.

When I left school, I started working in the Westminster Bank; and hated every single moment of it. The same tedious 9 to 5 routine, repetitive paperwork day after day and due to lack of interest, a disappointing report from Head Office after my first boring six months really made the decision for me. I had done the work required of me by the Bank, but it was so mind numbingly dull; and my heart, frankly, just wasn't in it. I'm ashamed to say that it was the only time in my life, that I've ever thrown a sicky, on just one occasion, and pretended to be ill, rather than turn up for work.

The national news was full of Northern Ireland really starting to get ugly. Scenes of burning rows of terraced houses, riots and sectarian hatred filled the T.V., radio and newspapers. British troops had been deployed on the streets to quell the violence. Here at last was my chance for some real action and adventure. I think I'd have lost the plot and lumped my branch Sub- Manager if I'd stayed much longer in the employ of the Bank. He was a miserable old bastard with a tin leg; whose mind was locked in 'the good old days' when junior bank clerks were seen and not heard. He had a fit one morning, while I was quietly sitting at my desk, filling in some longwinded report forms. A relief clerk came into our branch wearing a pink shirt under his suit. This poor young guy might just a well have been caught taking a dump on the Manager's desktop. The Sub-manager turned puce, and he screamed at the lad to get home and change. The shocked relief clerk's mortal sin of wearing a coloured shirt instead of a white one finally confirmed my conviction that I was definitely a square peg in a round hole, and needed to make a serious career change.

During my time with them, I had made a good friend in the Territorials called John Griffin. He was studying for an apprenticeship with British Telecom, but like me, felt he needed an injection of action into his life. We talked at great length about signing on for a stretch in the regular infantry, and finally announced to our respective families that we were off to take the King's shilling. It's only now, with a son of my own, that I can appreciate just how my parents must have felt. They knew I was very unhappy working in the bank and probably felt an equal share of pride and fear for me. Young soldiers were dying in Northern Ireland at an alarming rate, and my mum and dad naturally worried for my safety. My older sister and little brother were not too chuffed about the idea, but I just had to go and do it – it was something that had to be done!

Off John and I went to the recruiting office, passed the entrance tests with flying colours, and signed up. Following a medical, the date arrived to report to the Bassingbourne infantry depot in Royston, Hertfordshire, to begin basic infantry training. After much tearful hanky waving, and not a second thought or regret on my part, off we both went, each armed with a small suitcase, and a military travel warrant to exchange at a London's St. Pancras Railway station, for a ticket for Royston, and the beginning of a new life.

When we arrived at the depot, our fit and rather wolfish looking training corporals were waiting for us. They immediately marched the assembled recruits down to the barbers for a serious (and very short) haircut. The army likes its young trainees to have pretty much shaved heads, so that should one of them abscond; the Military Police could easily spot and arrest them at the local bus or railway station. The rest of our first day was taken up with military orientation lectures, kit issues, learning how to lay out our equipment in our big iron lockers (for inspection purposes) and how to make a bed block. To this day, I have never really fathomed why we had to spend about 10 minutes every morning during basic training folding our sheets, blankets and pillow cases into a fiendishly difficult square block. The tension had to be just right, so that the training platoon Sergeant could bounce a coin on the top of the finished block of tightly folded bedding. It had to be perfectly formed, or the whole thing looked like a sack of shit. I guess it was just one of those irritating sickeners, which enforce military discipline on raw young soldiers. God help any poor lad that rushed making a bed block because they were running a bit late before morning inspection. Our thirty man barrack room was on the first floor of the building, and during early-morning room inspections, I soon lost count of the bed blocks that were hurled out of the upstairs open window by our angry Sergeant and Corporals, occasionally followed headfirst by their unlucky owners.

The camp bugler lustily blew reveille on the camp's parade square at 5.30am every morning. As he let rip with the first couple of notes, our duty corporal would flick on the lights and crash in through the barrack room door banging a dustbin lid with a pickaxe handle. Anyone who had not leapt out of bed, by the time he had reached the end of the 40-foot room could expect his bed to be overturned, with him still in it, and a swift kick in the butt for good measure. We had to quickly dress into P.T. (Physical Training) kit and rush downstairs and parade outside, ready for our early-morning 5-mile run. When it was finished, we would come back completely knackered, then whizz off to the washroom for a shit, shower and shave. Next, it was into fatigues, ready to be marched to breakfast by

13

the ever-attentive duty Corporal. I only made the mistake of asking for an extra sausage once, and had to endure a loud and very serious balling out from one of the cooks, in front of the entire depot, who were also having their breakfast in the cookhouse at the time.

March back to the block, quick scrub of washroom and barracks (and make our bloody bed blocks), and stand to attention at the end of our beds, ready for room inspection. Our training platoon officer or Sergeant usually carried out the inspection. If either of them found a tiny piece of paper, dust or anything else, which should not have been there, we would all be doing another inspection a 10pm that night, and again at 11pm and so on until the place finally gleamed. If someone's locker was not exactly squared off, the whole locker went out of the window, and the luckless recruit would be cleaning out the toilets with a toothbrush (once he had carried and dragged his locker back upstairs of course).

For the first six weeks we were not allowed to wear civilian clothes. They had been locked in a storeroom in the barrack block, probably to make it harder to escape, should someone wish to make a break for it. At any time during that initial period though, a young trainee soldier could ask for voluntary discharge and simply leave the army.-finish, out and gone, and no hard feelings. Of thirty-six recruits on day one, about 8 had gone in the first week. They were the soft mummy's boys who would cry in their beds at night. It wasn't what they had expected; just not their scene. Another one went AWOL, that's did a bunk in army speak. God knows why, what a pratt; he only had to ask to leave! They brought him back, processed his discharge, and slung him out on the next train home.

There was one particular lad called Brittain in our recruit platoon, who always tried to act like the tough nut. He made it widely known that he was related to the Kray brothers. The Kray's had run London's East end crime scene for many years and had committed numerous murders and vicious attacks on other crooks on or near their dingy Shoreditch manor. Brittan acted the hard man, and always tried to throw his weight around, bullying the smaller lads whenever he could. On about the fourth week, our training platoon marched off to the grenade range to practice throwing dummy hand grenades. Just for a joke, I let some air out of Corporal Sinclair's bicycle tyres. This, I should point out, by the way, was a very, very daft thing to do, but at seventeen, you do not always think of the consequences. It was just a lark, a prank; a bit of fun and youthful devilment. Brittan thought it was hilarious and completed the job. We finished our practice on the grenade range and were marched back to the cookhouse for tea. The duty corporal was reading out some notices to us afterwards as we paraded outside our accommodation block, when along came Corporal Sinclair, pushing his bike, which now had two very, very flat tyres. I had never seen anyone who actually looked purple with rage before, and didn't know, at the time, of his history of Grievous Bodily Harm. He had been busted down from Sergeant to corporal twice before, - pretty serious stuff; it takes a Court Marshal or Brigadiers signed order). Both times he had been busted for being too ready to use his fists on junior ranks.

As he drew level with the platoon, he picked up the bicycle, and threw it clear over our heads. Not a mean feat, as we were three ranks deep at the time.

"Who dared do this?" he roared at us in his thick Geordie accent. Understandably, no one moved, as he stood before us, literally shaking with anger. "I'll fucking back squad all of you unless the guilty man steps forward." He hissed at us through clenched teeth. Now this suddenly had become a bloody serious situation. Back squading meant starting again from scratch or even being binned (thrown out). I couldn't let my mates in the platoon suffer for what I had done, it was time to do the decent thing.......so like an idiot I stepped forward.

"Err, it was me Corp, sorry." I said.

" SORRY! SORRY! I'll give you SORRY!" He screamed, and landed a savage punch to the side of my head. I wasn't expecting it, and didn't see it coming. The impact knocked me clear of the front rank, and now he had room; he really laid into me. I took a flurry of punches and kicks, and he seemed to grow even angrier because I wouldn't fall to the ground. It may sound daft now, but I didn't retaliate; it was already ingrained in me. I couldn't ever hit an N.C.O. After a minute or so (I think), having heard the commotion the other platoon corporals arrived at the run and pulled him off me. They quickly fell the platoon out, and dragged him away.

I was in a pretty banged up way the next morning, bruised and battered; and sporting a black eye and a scabby cut on my bottom lip. The platoon Sergeant inspected us before we went off for our early-morning run. Although I had cleaned myself up as best I could; I still looked terrible. He didn't say a word to me until the platoon inspection was finished.

"The block is in a right state" he said, "Black, fall out and mop out the toilets."

I complied without a word, as I didn't fancy the run, because of the severely battered state I was in. The duty corporal doubled the boys away, and I slowly and painfully climbed the stairs to start my latrine duties. The platoon Sergeant, a tough Irishman named Delaney stopped me at the head of the stairs.

"Are you going to make a fuss, Black?"

I winced as I did my best to straighten up and face him; my bloody ribs were killing me, where Cpl. Sinclair had kicked them. I looked Sgt. Delaney in the eye, shook my head and simply said.

"No Sergeant, no fuss."... I was there to learn to soldier, and a beating from a punchy Geordie wasn't going to stop me. Delaney stared hard at me for a moment, and nodded.

"Good lad" he said, "Now piss off and sort out the bogs."

Of course, although I was guilty of committing a pretty stupid act, the real culprit was Brittan. He had frozen with fear while I was beaten up, and had said nothing. This broke an unspoken code between us recruits. The boys in the platoon knew what had really happened, and it wasn't long before our training corporals knew too. I had told Brittan what a useless, cowardly prat he was, but that's all I said to anyone. We had a very serious lecture on upholding the traditions of the Regiment that morning, playing the game, and sorting out problems internally, etc. Our Platoon Officer, who gave the lecture, clearly knew all about the assault, but the whole thing taught me that the army looks after its own. Within a week, Brittan was gone. The training staff had trumped up a series of charges against him, and he was summarily thrown out of the army.

Strangely enough, years later, I bumped into a bloke who had also crossed Cpl. Sinclair's path. Sinclair later was caught stealing recruit's kit and secretly selling it back to them, rather than formally charging them with being deficient. He was Court-martialed again, found guilty and did some porridge time at the Military Prison in Colchester. His military pension was revoked; and he was given a dishonourable discharge. Nice. The whole thing was definitely not politically correct, but it all balanced out in the end. I have often wondered what the bleeding hearted, politically-correct liberals would make of the whole incident, if it happened now, and went public. Newspaper headlines, questions in the House, and bags of shit for everyone!

A week or so after Brittan had gone, the dust had settled, as my ribs healed and my black eye faded. The whole business was glossed over, and we all soldiered on. The end of our initial phase of training loomed, and we would shortly be granted a weekends leave. As it was our first break in six weeks, we were all really looking forward to it. Our only hurdle was that we first had to "Pass off the Square."

Not some strange Masonic ritual, we simply had to pass various basic military tests, based on what we had learnt thus far, and finish with a drill parade to show the world we could march in a military fashion, salute, and perform other simple drill movements; both individually and as a platoon. We had all cracked the training, so the tests shouldn't be any real problem. We had a young Yorkshireman in our platoon called Buttle. If I describe him as thick, he and his Mum might have been offended, but no-one else on the planet who knew him would argue the point. He always boasted he knew the drill book backwards, but didn't have a clue when it came to marching in step with the rest of the platoon. It takes a lot of effort to march swinging the left leg and arm at the same time, but Buttle was a natural, in fact, he was a master at it. He looked like a gorilla with haemorrhoids when he marched. My buddy John and I spent the last few hours of daylight before the next morning's all important 'passing off' parade trying to coach young Buttle.

"Nay, lad, you just don't know what you're talking about," said Buttle when we tried to explain and demonstrate exactly what was required of him on the drill square. It was hopeless, and the training staff knew it. They back-squadded him an hour before the parade began because they knew he would screw it up for the rest of us. As a result, the parade passed off without incident and at last, we were free for the weekend. I went home and slept for most of it but was then, reluctantly trooped around various Uncles and Aunties...

"Here is David, he's on leave from the army."

I'd never really defied my dad before, but when it was time to go back to the depot, I put him in the picture. It didn't ever happen again.

One of the important aspects of military training is the development of focused aggression. Not the aggression often seen in a bar on a Saturday night, when some drunken lout thinks he's a hard man because he's had 7 or 8 pints of strong beer. The army develops controlled aggression, so that it can be switched on and off as required. The Physical Training Instructors (PTIs) at the depot gymnasium warned us early on during our training that we would have to demonstrate our grasp of controlled aggression in the boxing ring. The army, in its infinite wisdom calls this 'Milling'. The Parachute Regiment makes a big thing of this aspect of aggression training, but it's really just a glorified punch up, and all infantry depots did it, irrespective of Regiment. On the afternoon of our milling bout, we marched smartly down to the gym in our P.T. kit. Our Corporals handed us over to the Physical Training Instructors. They paired us off according to size and weight. The senior PTI informed us that the three- minute bouts would be held under the Marquis of Queensberry's rules. Biting, kicking or rabbit punching was strictly forbidden. Boxing gloves would be worn when fighting, and we were to back off smartly when the order 'break' was given by the referee. I was paired with a lad called Sam Barley. Sam and I had become good mates, and we both agreed that we would make it look good, but not set out to really damage each other. The first few bouts were good fun to watch, guys flailing away, throwing haymakers and uppercuts, with the odd cut lip and black eye to show for their violent efforts. Gradually, the numbers diminished, and it was our turn. The referee ordered us both into the middle of the ring and gave us the standard pep talk.

"Right lads, you both know what to do, when the bell rings, come out fighting. And I want to see some genuine aggression!"

We went back to our corners and appeared to be waiting for the bell. When it rang we assumed the classic hunched boxing position; fists

17

up, head down, and bobbed and weaved towards each other. Maybe it was because I was still a bit wet behind the ears, or perhaps I just trusted Sam too much, but I didn't expect, or see, his straight right punch that thumped me on the nose. I recoiled across the ring. "Bastard!"

Sam grinned at me; he was really going for a win. I stepped back and shook my head. What Sam didn't know, was that my dad had taught me to box a few years previously. I didn't want to hurt Sam, but the goalposts had moved, and I certainly wasn't going to let him beat me.

I tucked my head tighter into my gloves, and made a move on my opponent. I ducked his next wild swing and hit Sam hard twice in the stomach. I danced away and checked the results. He looked winded, so I pressed home my attack with a couple of good jabs to his head. The whole platoon was getting into this bout. They were yelling and hooting their support, with lots of shouts, pugilistic advice and loud whistles. After a couple of minutes of hard boxing, I clearly had the better of my opponent, but I hadn't knocked him out. His eyes were looking quite glazed, but he just wouldn't go down. By now, my blood was up, and I really wanted to win with a big finish. Just before I could deliver the final blow the bell went to loud cheers from the crowd. The referee immediately raised my right hand. Poor old Sam was looking pretty stunned and groggy, as I helped him out of the ring. Grinning broadly, we both sat down together on an exercise bench and got our breath back, while the referee set up the last fight.

The biggest bloke in our platoon was 'Tonka' Thompson. He was 6' 4", very broad-shouldered and looked what he was; an ex-coal miner. 'Tonka' was a good bloke, but built like the proverbial brick shithouse. Because he was as broad as he was tall he didn't have a partner for his milling bout, and the only other guy left was the weediest in the whole platoon. There was one other pair left to fight. The PTI thought for a moment, and then spoke.

"Thompson, you can fight the last three!" Tonka grinned, but his three opponents looked absolutely horrified. One of them said nervously to the PTI.

"You must be joking Staff; he'll kill us all!"

This was going to be a bout to remember, providing you were watching safely from outside the ring. Tonka jumped over the ropes, and started limbering up. Two of his opponents climbed reluctantly through the ropes; the third, was pushed into the ring by two grinning Corporals, despite his loud protests. The referee called them all into the centre. He didn't give the usual pre-fight talk. He just looked up at Tonka and said.

"You're not allowed to kill anyone Thompson, understand? "

Tonka punched his gloves together and grinned wolfishly. The colour drained out of the faces of the three little lambs, as they herded together and walked slowly and miserably back to the temporary safety of their corner. We were all laughing and yelling so much, we nearly missed the opening bell.

Ding!

Round One. When the bell clanged, the big mouth of the unlucky three, climbed straight out of the ring. Only dire threats from our laughing Corporals, of being instantly back-squaded got him back in again. The other two were doing their best to stay away from their massive opponent. Tonka swung his huge fists, but fear was giving his opponents wings. They all ducked and dived, frantically trying to avoid being clobbered. The first thirty seconds had ticked by, before Tonka managed to corner all three; and from then on, it was just horrible, but hilarious too. With such a huddle of cowering targets it was impossible for him to miss. Although Tonka was clearly enjoying himself, he was the only combatant who was. It was a slaughter. The first guy took a massively powerful blow to the head and dropped to the floor in a crumpled heap. The second took an uppercut and flew across the ring, hitting the opposite ropes with a loud twang. He fell face forward onto the deck and lay still. He may only of have been feigning death, but as far as he was concerned, that was the end of his chance for the title. The last little lamb had jumped on Tonka's back and wrapped his arms around the giant's neck. Tonka flailed his arms as he spun around and round, bellowing like a mad bull while trying to shake the poor devil loose. The referee eventually decided to show some mercy, and rang the bell to end the fight. No-one disputed the result.

Controlled aggression, you can't beat it.

The routine of physical training, weapon handling, map reading and field craft ground on for weeks before the tenth week when Sgt. Delaney held a drill parade during the hottest day of the year. He was a bit of a bastard on the quiet, ex-SAS and hard as nails with it. None of us knew much about the shadowy SAS, but we knew they were tough blokes that our Corporals spoke of with unconcealed awe. Delaney seemed to have a sadistic streak in him, and it showed during the drill parade. It must have been in the high nineties on the parade square, but he kept us out in the hot sun for several hours, practising a particularly complicated drill movement called a Right Form. It took a fair bit of practice getting it right, but we eventually cracked it. When done properly this involved and very complicated drill movement looks smart and professional. The Brigade of Guards does it every year when they Troop the Colour on the Queen's birthday, and it's magic. Delaney kept us doing the same practice over and over, while he stood on the edge of the parade square under the cool shade of a tree, smoking his pipe. We all felt sick with too much sun when he finally finished his lesson, and handed us over to our profusely sweating Corporals, who would fall us out. As I mentioned earlier, things

19

have a habit of balancing, because when he tapped his pipe on his boot to shed the hot spent tobacco, he didn't get all the glowing embers out. He put the pipe in his trouser pocket and marched smartly away from the square for a pint in the Sergeant's mess. To our collective joy, the fluff in his back pocket ignited and smoke began to billow from his trousers. He probably managed ten more paces before it took hold, and he felt the heat. He jumped into the air, frantically slapping his thigh, shouting "Oh Jesus; I'm on fire!" A good hot burn on his arse made up for our painful sunburn, any day.

We had a week out on the huge military training area in Thetford, honing our newfound infantry skills. There were night and day patrolling exercises, laying ambushes, and lots of digging in. Now in the infantry, when you stop out in the countryside, you have to dig in. What that means is you must dig a slit trench, about six feet long and about chest deep. You have to do this as a matter of routine, because there is always the danger on a real battlefield that the enemy has seen you, and calls in an artillery barrage on top of your position. As the shells rain down around you, they explode, sending out a lethal high-velocity spray of red hot, razor-sharp chunks of shrapnel. If troops are caught out in the open the shrapnel will literally cut them into pieces. To avoid being slaughtered, soldiers dig in and hide at the bottom of their trenches if an enemy barrage arrives without warning. Years ago, some bright spark caught on to the fact that if you had overhead protection, you would be even safer. The British army's Infantry Research Establishment designed a thing called a "KIP," which stood for Kit Individual Protection. Using one, involved digging an angled extension to the end of the trench and laying a lattice of pegged parachute cord over the new part of it. Then thick green plastic sheet is laid over the para. cord lattice, and the whole lot was covered with a couple of feet of compacted earth. It worked really well, but was tricky to set up, especially in the dark.

We used to dig slit trenches in pairs, one picking and one shovelling. It was much quicker that way. The finished trench was plenty room enough for two guys to stand in or crouch down. If you had a KIP fitted, one could sleep in the extension while the other stood guard, or if he was off duty, slept in the bottom of the open part of the trench. Now, it doesn't take a brain surgeon to work out that each man should have his own KIP, so that everyone in the eight-man patrol or section had his own, individual overhead cover. Just add a new section to either end of your trench and hey presto, everyone's happy, snug and safe. Maybe it was defence cuts, or they just issued one between two during training, but we were stuck with one KIP per trench. Our task within the overall exercise was that we had to dig a formal defensive platoon position inside the edge of a wood, where there was plenty of cover from view. The recruits set to, late one afternoon, and after an hour or two we were dug in, and snug in our trenches. Of course, it had to be done tactically; which meant as quietly as possible. Everyone spoke in whispers, and no lights were to be shown after dark. We had been briefed that there was an active enemy patrolling the general area trying to find us. Everyone had to be very careful not to accidentally give the platoon's location away by banging a metal object against a rifle or even coughing too loud. When it got dark, we all settled down for the night. Each trench did a two-hour stretch on guard within each section, so we all had a good chance of some decent sleep for a change. John and I were in the same trench and we copped the middle of the night; twelve 'till two shift. It passed by without incident. At 2 a. m., while I remained on guard, John crawled over to the adjacent trench and woke the next two guys, ready for their stint (or stag, as it was known). He quietly came back and reported that they were up and ready. A muffled cough from their trench confirmed they were awake, and on stag. We were now off duty. I'd already whispered to John that I needed a crap, so now seemed a good time.

"Got any bog paper left?" I quietly enquired.

"Sorry Dave, I'm out mate." Came the whispered reply.

This is not good news but being an inventive lad; I'd manage, somehow. To avoid being accidentally shot by our own side, we were trained to never go forward of, or outside the perimeter of our trenches, so I climbed out of my trench and slowly and carefully crawled towards the rear of our position, where I could have a jolly good crap in peace. It was a moonless overcast night, and without night-vision aids, inside a wood it's as black as your hat. When I was about 20 feet from the trench, I slowly stood up and walked carefully deeper into the wood. If you take your time, and move really slowly, you make hardly a sound. I found a spot and slowly and quietly scraped a shallow hole. I felt the depth of the hole; perfect. I was surrounded on three sides by thick bushes. I assumed the position, and did the business, trying hard not to make too much noise. When it's that quiet, the slightest fart can sound like a thunderclap. It wasn't long before I'd finished, but now came the tricky part. I need to wipe my arse, and the only available material was leaves. OK, not a problem, I was surrounded with them. I grabbed a big handful of leaves from the bushes to my right...

"AHHHH, MY ARSE, OH JESUS CHRIST!" I yelled. My arse was on fire, and I couldn't stay tactical. It felt like some bastard had lit a blow torch and shoved it up my bum. Sweet Jesus, I'd never felt burning pain like it. I was hopping up and down with my camo. trousers around my ankles yelling like a banshee. All hell broke loose in our carefully prepared position. Shouts of "What's going on?" and "Who the hell was that?" Came out of our defensive perimeter. A torch flicked on, and someone yelled. "QUIET!" Whoever had the torch ran over with to me.

"Black, you wanker, what are you doing?" It was Corporal Kennedy, one of the training staff.

"Jesus, it's my bloody arse Corporal!"

"Pipe down, you idiot, we're on tactical alert." The pain had subsided a little, and I managed to pull my strides up.

"You idiot, look behind you." The cause of my pain was instantly identified. I had chosen the biggest bunch of stinging nettles in the world to wipe my arse on.

"Fill that hole, and get back to your trench." He hissed. "And don't let me hear another peep out of you, or I'll come over there and shoot you myself!"

"Yes, Corporal." I said meekly. I did as I was told, and then beat a hasty and not too tactical retreat. I carefully eased myself onto the ground at the bottom of my trench and tried to get comfortable. John lay in his sleeping bag; snug inside the KIP extension. His muffled voice whispered.

"Good shit; was it?"

Next morning, we left our defensive position, and marched a couple of miles over to the river which meanders slowly through the training area. We halted next to an ancient wooden jetty.

"Ok ladies, fall out and get your butts onto the riverbank. Not you Black....Come here." Corporal Kennedy had an ominous grin on his face. "Put this on," he said, giving me a bright orange life jacket. "Come on, hurry up, and then double over to the front of the platoon."

Once again, I did as I was told and ended up standing at the end of the jetty. My eyes were drawn to the murky water ten feet below me. It was covered with a thick scum of bright green pond weed.

"Today, my lucky lads, we are going to practice river crossings in a steel assault boat. You will all wear a life jacket while in the boat, just in case you fall in." This was better than I expected, just modelling the latest fashion in military Mae Wests. "You have all passed your basic swimming test, but just to assure you the life jackets will save you"...

The next thing I knew was a hard shove in the small of my back, and I was somersaulting through the air. I hit the water with a huge splash but quickly bobbed to the surface, thanks to my life jacket. I coughed up a couple of pints of scummy river water as I wiped pond weed off my face.

"There you are lads, no problem. They work a treat.... Arse feeling a bit cooler now, Black?"

When the assault boat training was finished, we marched back to our defensive position. We had to cook our evening meal on our little individual Mexi solid fuel stoves. Because training dictated that we should always work in pairs, one man from each trench cooks both meals, while the other stands guard. The army calls this the buddy-buddy system. Food is always known as 'scoff' in the Army; presumably, because you scoff it down. When scoff was finished, we had a briefing by the Platoon Officer. There is a set way of briefing troops, which is very thorough, as forgetting something can get you killed. Our officer outlined an imaginary scenario, which put us in the front line of a small war in Fantasia. The local communist party cell had stirred up an insurrection against the legitimate Fantasian government, and they had asked HMG for British troops to help sort the rebels out. It turned out that intelligence reports had filtered through that the bad guys were having a tough time against us professional British soldiers. What was left of their rag-tag mob was planning an attack soon. They would punch through our front line, then melt away and regroup, ready for the next uprising when conditions were better, and the time was right. We had been tasked to stop them.

The enemy were expected to probe our defences during the night, and launch an all-out attack around dawn. They were well equipped, having pinched large amounts of weapons and ammo. from the Fantasian army depots, prior to our arrival. When the briefing was over, we set to cleaning our weapons and made sure that everything was ready. At last light, several of us crawled forward and set up trip flares, in front of our position. These were tricky bits of kit to set up, involving stringing out about thirty yards of near invisible ultra thin black wire. The wire was pegged out at about knee height, and attached to a big brown plastic-coated flare. The idea was simple enough. The enemy blundered into the wire during the night, which set off the flare. This gave us warning they were close, and plenty of light to shoot them. When the last team reported back, we were set for the night. As we were on a heightened state of alert, each trench kept one man on guard throughout the night. Two hours on and two hours off, and so on, until first light.

As the dark hours dragged by, an occasional shot rang out from enemy territory. The Yanks call this 'Reconnaissance by fire'. We were trained to ignore these random shots, as to return fire would identify our exact position. One of our flares went off in the middle of the night, causing a full platoon 'stand to'. It involved everyone quickly coming into a position of readiness, to repulse the impending attack, but as in the nature of military operations...nothing happened. We spent the next forty minutes straining our eyes and ears, but couldn't see anything, and all we could hear was the wind rustling through the trees above us. Eventually, the order to 'stand down' was whispered throughout our trench network, and our guard duties resumed. While I stood in the trench during one of my stags, I could not help but think about something our officer had said last night, at the end of his briefing.

"Stay sharp, and always expect the unexpected!" I pondered his last sentence; what exactly, I wondered, did he mean by that?

This phase would come to haunt me, later in my military career, but more of that later. The long night dragged by, until shortly before first light. Our Corporal crawled around the various trenches whispering "Stand To." Those lucky enough to be still asleep received a sharp kick on their boot from their partner in the trench, and within a couple of minutes, the whole platoon was stood to, weapons at the ready. After fifteen minutes, the first glow of the coming day appeared on the horizon. The breaking morning was bitterly cold. As the light slowly increased, a thick white mist began to roll towards us, from the direction of the enemy. Early morning mist is not uncommon on the training area, but this looked different. It didn't show the thin wispy tendrils that we had seen on numerous occasions before, it looked thicker somehow. The guys in the machine-gun trench off to our left were closest to it. As the white fog floated over them, they reacted suddenly.

"GAS, GAS, GAS" they yelled at the top of their lungs. Immediately, everything went completely pear shaped. Every young trainee soldier frantically reached for their S6 gas mask. The masks were always carried on the left-hand side of our belt, so we could easily find them in the dark. One of the training staff was frantically banging a couple of mess tins together, another standard warning of an impending gas attack. A few seconds later, the first 2" mortar bomb landed about twenty yards short of our trenches. It didn't explode, just hissed out great gouts of thick white smoke, adding to the recruits' confusion. More bombs fell, closer than before.

One of the staff yelled. "INCOMING, TAKE COVER!"

No one needed telling twice; everyone ducked down, and tried to get into their KIP shelters. We could hear the mortar bombs whistling towards us, and they impacted with a really loud thud, within yards of our trenches. I was lying on top of John, jammed into the narrow bay. Between the crumps of the mortar bombs' landing, all I could hear was my own laboured breathing through my gas mask. I turned my head as best I could and looked up, and behind me. Thick oily clouds of off-white smoke and tear gas were billowing into and over the trench, where we had so bravely stood moment's ago. My heart was pounding; this was almost too real!

After a minute someone outside blew long blasts on a whistle and screamed. "Stand to, here they come."

Diving into a KIP on top of your mate is easy, wriggling out again, isn't. Luckily, I was pumped up full of adrenaline and managed a pretty close impression of Harry Houdini at his best. John quickly followed and we assumed our ready positions, standing in our fire trench. We all still wore our gas masks, as the-all clear hadn't been given. The machine gun on our left opened fire first, firing wicked scything bursts of 7.62mm blank ammunition towards the enemy; that were appearing like ghosts in front of us through what was left of the smoke. Several other riflemen opened fire. As the enemy ran closer, they started throwing thunder flashes at our trenches. Simulating grenades, Mk. 8 thunder flashes are like supercharged bangers, which detonate with a brilliant flash and a fantastically loud bang. They really added to the general din and chaos of the attack.

"I hope they haven't got a bloody flamethrower!" yelled John through his gas mask as he let go with a couple of shots.

"Yeah, right!" I yelled back, while I changed magazines on my rifle. The bad guys were dropping like flies under our concentrated fire until the last one, rather theatrically, keeled over and played dead. After a minute's pause, the Corporal moved some of us forward to check the 'dead' enemy. We had practiced this drill, over and over, earlier in our training. One man points his rifle straight at the 'corpse' and the other guy carefully pulls the dead (or wounded) enemy soldier over, to check for weapons. If the corpse comes back to life with a gun in his hand, you put a couple of bullets into him, pronto. Once the enemy were declared 'clean' we nipped back to our trenches.

"ALL CLEAR, ALL CLEAR!" Yelled one of the training staff, and we thankfully pulled off our gas masks. Sweat and dirt streaked our faces, but we all stood around grinning like Cheshire cats.

"Get back in your trenches, you idiots!" yelled a corporal and we broke up and dived back into our foxholes. When the training staff was happy with everything, they gave us the order we had all been waiting for. 'End-Ex'. This made it official; the exercise was over.

"Get your weapons clean and get some scoff on.

Ah, deep joy, hot food time, and a brew. While John started cleaning his rifle, I lit our little Hexi stoves. They burned a two-inch square of Hexamine, which was a bit like a slow-burning firelighter. Pop a water-filled mess tin on top, and start cooking the scoff. Once we had finished weapon cleaning and our very welcome breakfast, one of the boys called us over to his trench. Half-buried in the earth, about two inches from the edge of the slit where he stood, was a spent mortar bomb. Because they were carrying smoke, and not high explosive, they remained intact on impact.

"That was a bit too close!" he said, "Missed my bloody head by a couple of inches, I couldn't get into the KIP!" The dead bomb just sat there, but the guy was right, a couple of inches the other way, and he would be sporting a two-inch hole through his skull.

Three weeks before our basic infantry training was over Sgt. Delaney called me and John into his small office in our accommodation block. He was being sent on a Guard's Division drill course and would be leaving the depot, next day. It was a tradition at the depot, that the recruits in each training platoon would buy their platoon Sergeant a small tankard to commemorate the passing of his fully trained platoon into their respective regular battalions. It was a sort of "Class of 72" idea; I suppose. By this stage, Delaney had pissed off everyone in the platoon; he was not Mr. Popular with the recruits, or the Corporals.

"You're to buy my mug at the jewellers, don't buy that cheap crap from the camp's NAAFI shop." Delaney scowled. "And get it engraved for me: I want it to say - To the best Sergeant in the depot" he commanded. "I'll be back off my drill course a couple of days after you have gone to your battalion, so I'll drive into Royston and pick it up myself from the shop."

We were standing smartly to attention, a necessity when addressing a member of the training staff.

"Yes Sergeant," we both said together. He handed me a four-hour pass, which gave us temporary permission to leave the depot.

"Now get away and sort out my mug."

We about turned and left smartish. As we marched towards the main gate an idea was forming in both our minds.

"David, I've had an idea," said John rather formally.

"Yes mate, me too." I replied, with a wink. We stopped at the guard room and explained our mission to the Corporal of the guard. I handed him my freshly signed pass. When he had looked it over, he handed it back to me.

"All right, off you go lads" he said with a scowl. "And don't be late; or else."

We got the bus into town, and easily found the jewellers. We explained that we needed the best and most expensive tankard he had in stock. His eyes lit up, and he disappeared into the back of the shop. He quickly returned, still unwrapping a solid and pretty impressive gold-plated tankard. When he had finished assuring us that it was the best he had, we agreed to take it.

"We will need quite a bit of engraving done," said John.

"With our Regimental badge, and a message too." I chipped in. The Jeweller assured us that he could reproduce the required cap badge on the tankard, and he wrote down the long message we wanted inscribed. We explained that our beloved Sergeant was off on a drill course, and that he would pick it up in person, in three weeks time. This sort of thing wasn't uncommon, and the Jeweller didn't bat an eyelid. He started to calculate the total bill, and when he had finished the cost of the tankard, and all the engraving, it was just short of thirty quid – a fortune to us.

"Are you sure you want to spend that much?" The Jeweller asked suspiciously.

"You bet; he's a great bloke" I said, trying my best to sound like I meant it. Thirty quid was a lot of money back in 1972, John and I were only being paid twelve pounds a week as recruits.

"Is it OK if we leave a deposit of a fiver, because we have to collect the rest from the boys, and give it to the Sergeant in a sealed envelope, so he can pay the balance when he comes in?"

"Can't you drop it in yourselves?" asked the Jeweller. We explained that we were off for our big final exercise, a two-week battle camp in Warcop the following day, and we just didn't know if we would have time afterwards, what with our final passing out parade close on its heels. The Jeweller thought for a moment and agreed. We collected the final bill, and thanking him profusely, left. That evening, making sure the coast was clear, we explained in great detail what we had done, to the other long suffering boys in the platoon. The best bit, having split the fiver deposit between all of us, was when we placed the jeweller's bill with great ceremony in an empty fire bucket, and burnt it.

"He is going to go completely barmy when he gets the bill, and we've all gone," said one of the boys.

"I'd give my pension to see his face," said another, and our barrack block echoed with our delighted and expectant laugher.

The next morning, we paraded outside the block with our kitbags, webbing and weapons. The coach arrived at 08.00 hrs., ready to take us to distant Warcop, far off in Cumbria for our final phase battle camp. Delaney was there to see us off in his best dress uniform.

"Off to the Guards depot at Pirbright in a minute," he puffed. "Got to look smart!" He called me over and said quietly. "Did you sort things out Black?"

"Yes Sergeant, it's a thing of golden beauty. You're going to be well chuffed!"

"Good lad, now fall back in with your mates."

I exchanged knowing grins with my co-conspirators. We stowed our kitbags and webbing into the luggage compartments on the coach and climbed aboard. The coach was ancient, and managed to envelop Delaney in a cloud of black smoke when the driver started the tired old diesel engine. Our last sight ever of Sgt. Delaney was him appearing out of the black toxic cloud of exhaust smoke, coughing his lungs up.

Warcop Battle Camp is located down a long winding country lane, in a little valley, high in the Cumbrian Mountains. It is used as a finishing school by all the infantry depots around the country, where the now fully trained recruits put it all together, for their last two weeks of basic training. We had been told that we were not to march during our stay at Warcop; we had to jog at the double, everywhere. The resident training staff were a pretty mean looking bunch, and they left us in no confusion about our current situation.

"You are here to work, Gentlemen, and work hard," were the first words our fearsome looking camp Regimental Sergeant Major said to us. "Her Majesty, the Queen, God bless her, has invested a lot of money in turning you into the country's latest batch of professional killers, and here and now is where you start really earning your pay!" We all exchanged apprehensive looks at each other. "You are all fitter, harder and better than you have ever been in your lives so far," he continued "So don't screw up all your hard work in getting here." He paused for a moment to let that sink in, and then continued... "The local pub Gentlemen; the Chumley Arms, is strictly off-limits to all of you, and if I catch any of you in there, I will personally lock you up! I will now hand you over to Colour Sergeant Price, who will explain how Warcop Battle Camp works." His initial pep talk over; the R.S.M. turned and marched smartly away, with his head up, and his pace stick clamped firmly and horizontally under his left arm.

The next two weeks were a blur of action packed training. Live firing exercises were the name of the game at Warcop, where vast military training areas in the Cumbrian mountains gave us plenty of scope to put all our training to good use. Close quarter battle shoots, live firing section attacks, all with real ammunition. The first week of the exercises finished with a set piece live firing section attack, in front of the senior battle camp staff, who would grade our efforts. Each of our three sections had to be tested, and my section went first. I had been nominated as the gun controller, a job usually done by an infantry section second in command (Lance Corporal). His job is to control the section's light machine gun, the GPMG (General Purpose Machine Gun). The 'Jimmpy' as it is unofficially known is a rugged, belt-fed machine gun, which gives supporting fire onto the target when the infantry section attacks. The gun commander has a key role in a successful attack. He must suppress the enemy's fire, and sweep past the target, laying down a barrage of bullets on the other side of the enemy's position when the friendly attacking force reaches the objective. He also must watch the ammunition consumption, as 900 rounds per minute eats the gun's ammunition supply in no time. He has himself, the Gunner and an ammunition bearer in his team, and can call on the bearer to put shots down on the target with his rifle, when necessary to conserve ammo. John was acting as ammo. bearer and a guy called Paul Merton was my Gunner. The Jimmpy is classed as a light machine gun but at twenty-five pounds (plus ammo.) it's really bloody heavy. Paul was also the best shot with the GPMG in our platoon. John was always very switched on, a natural soldier and I was lucky to have them both as my gun team (known as a gun group). We had a range safety officer attached to us, who acted as an observer and would only interfere if something went wrong, and lives were put at risk by a mistake made by any one of us.

The attack began when a member of the directing staff threw a thunder flash. The complete infantry section, including my gun group had shaken out in an extended line, and were advancing towards a low hill, about two hundred yards distant. When the explosion went off, we all hit the dirt, and crawled into whatever cover was available. The Corporal yelled out. "Can anyone see the enemy?" One of the boys had spotted the targets on the hill as he ducked, and yelled out directions, which zeroed us into the target. The patrol commander made a quick assessment and made his attack plan.

"Gun group, right flanking, rifle section RAPID FIRE!"

That was my signal to double the gun group up a slight rise and into some dead ground, which led us closer to the target but gave us the benefit of good cover. We doubled fifty metres forward, gaining about ten metres in height. As soon as we moved, the infantry section put rounds down on the target to give us some covering fire. I spotted a good final position, which gave us a commanding view, while offering the most protection. It took seconds to set up and start firing the machine gun. As soon as it opened up, the infantry section started to move towards the enemy. They did this by pepper potting. In simple terms, half the section fire at the enemy while the other half runs forward. When they have zigzagged 15-20 feet, down they go and start firing. That's the other half's signal to get up and double forward past their prone mates, hit the dirt and open fire. My gun group were spraying bursts of 3-5 rounds into the target all the while. Our job was to stay put, and keep firing. Ammo. was going fast, so I told the Gunner to stop firing, and John to put some rapid rounds down with his assault rifle. This conserved belted machine gun ammunition. When he had banged off about fifteen rounds, I ordered him to stop firing and fired at the targets myself. The infantry section had manoeuvred to within fifty yards of the target, and I ceased fire and ordered Paul to start firing the Jimmpy again. The patrol commander ordered. "Fix bayonets!" The signal for the final assault was the infantry section throwing thunder flashes (simulating grenades) onto the target. When they detonated that was my time to order rapid fire into the enemy strong point. Long bursts until the last possible moments are fired into the assaulted position then the command. "Switch RIGHT!" I ordered Paul to sweep right, firing past the position, in case an enemy reserve was hiding behind the assaulted area. When our rifle section had swept through the enemy camp and were clear, I ordered Paul to stop firing, and shouted - 'Watch and shoot'. If a target appeared and Paul saw it first, he was clear to open fire without waiting for my fire order. The range safety officer fired a red very light into the area ahead of the rifle section, which was the signal to stop, unload all weapons, as the assault was over. I ordered Paul and John to unload, did the same myself, and we doubled down to join the rest of the section.

The safety officers had a quick chat, compared notes, did a bit of nodding, and then came over to de-brief us on the attack. The safety officer following the infantry section spoke first, going through the attack stage by stage; picking up points as he went. Overall, he was quite pleased with the section's performance and made sure they knew it. Now it was our turn. Our safety officer, who hadn't said a word during the assault, looked at us and nodded.

"Not bad boys, you were bloody good" This was praise, real praise. In fact, it was the first proper pat on the back any of us had received since our very first day of basic training. "I would say, overall, that was the best gun group I've seen at this camp. You were all slick, professional and spot on with your drills. I've agreed with the other D.S. (Directing Staff) that the three of you get an R.S.M.'s medal, when you get back to camp."

We didn't have a clue what he was talking about. "Err, sorry Staff, what's that?" I figured that as I had been gun controller, it was my duty to make a prat of myself and ask."

It's a good night out on the beer, laddie, in the Chumley Arms!" The three of us looked at each other in disbelief. He told us that the Battle School R.S.M. had authorised a special 'goody' award for outstanding performance during training. The medal wasn't real; you just got a pass to go out to get pissed.

The three of us took some serious stick from the boys in the platoon as we gratefully climbed aboard the four tonner (lorry), which was taking us back to camp. There were plenty of comments about brown nosers and sucking up to 'Sir', but we ignored it. Just a bunch of jealous twats, as far as the three of us were concerned. As it happened, our platoon had pulled camp guard duty that night, so we had scored a double whammy; a night out on the beer, and no guard duties. We finally arrived back in camp, cleaned and returned our weapons to the armoury, and grabbed some scoff at the cookhouse. The boys had been ordered to report to the guardroom at 18.00hrs, prior to mounting guard for the night. John, Paul and I had been told to be on duty at 06. 00hrs the next day, or the wrath of almighty God would descend on us. Having showered, and changed into civvies, we waited until the boys had mounted guard, and then took great pleasure in reporting to the guardroom clutching our magic pass. The guard corporal nodded us through, and under a barrage of obscene gestures and comments from our boys on guard, we nipped out quickly, before the bubble burst, and we got recalled.

The Chumley Arms is a tiny quaint old country pub, about 100 metres from the main gate of Warcop Battle Camp. We said hallo to the busty barmaid when we found the oak beamed snug, and showed her our pass, so that we could get served. All went well for the first hour or so, lots of chat and laughter between the three of us; all washed down with plenty of pints of nutty brown ale. The pub had been nearly empty when we arrived, except for a couple of wizened old sheep farmers, sitting in a corner snug by the fire which warmed us from the hearth. It had got dark outside, and we were just starting to feel the warm glow of the local ale taking effect. Suddenly, there was a commotion at the door, and in streamed dozens of big hairy blokes. Luckily, Paul had just got his round in, because the counter was soon packed with guys loudly demanding pints of beer. They were all clearly from a Scottish Regiment judging by their accents; we only caught about one word in five. It turned out later, that they were from a Territorial Battalion of the Black Watch, a famous Scottish Regiment with a long and proud military history. They had been dug in on a hillside, out in the dank and cold Cumbrian Mountains for a week, and were now off duty, and in need of some serious refreshment. As regular recruits, we were under different orders concerning what was normally out of bounds. The jocks didn't seem to be too worried; they just needed BEER! The biggest (and hairiest) of them heard us talking, lent over and growled.

"English?"

We all looked at him, and I simply enquired.

"Yes mate, Scottish?"...

He thought about it for a moment, grinned and said. "Aye."

Introductions done, we all got back to the serious business of drinking. One of the things about lots of beer and good company is that it can bring on serious bouts of singing, particularly when everyone's pissed. As closing time approached the jocks were busy singing a very loud medley of Scottish ballads. Regimental pride, and too much beer got involved, and they all decided it was time for the bastard English to sing. The three of us stood up and belted out a pretty good rendition of 'Maybe it's because I'm a Londoner,' and honour was satisfied. We all left the pub, vowing eternal international brotherhood between our two proud nations, and headed back to camp. We decided it had been a brilliant night out. We walked into our empty barrack block. All our mates were on guard, so they were sleeping in the guardhouse, when they were not on duty. I was just coming out of the bogs, when John leapt out of his bunk. "There's something in my bloody pit!" He yelled, rubbing his leg. We were all pretty pissed, but sure enough, there was something moving under John's covers.

"What is it?"...."

"God knows, go on, have a look." John pulled back his blankets, and there was the biggest hedgehog we had ever seen.

The poor thing looked half asleep, but promptly curled up into a ball when it was disturbed.

"Better put it outside, before it shits in your bed." I suggested helpfully.

John shrugged his shoulders, hic-coughed and carefully picked the beastie up, and released it outside. It seemed that the military sense of black humour was being honed, as well as our military skills. At breakfast next morning, our boys came in, having finished their guard duties and immediately launched into David Attenborough impressions.

"And here, we have the biggest, smelliest hedgehog in Warcop," said one.

"And if you look carefully, you can see hundreds of fleas on it," said another"

"Fuck off!" Grunted John, absently scratching a tiny bite on his arm.

Our two-week battle camp at Warcop finished with a twenty five mile road march over the Cumbrian Mountains. We were all dreading it, although we were young and pretty fit, twenty-five miles in full kit is a hard slog in anyone's money. When the lorries dropped us at the start line, we fell in on the lay-by. Two guys were fitted with orange jackets and briefed to march fifty metres in front of the column and two kitted out and briefed to follow up in the rear. All our training corporals were with us, and they led us off, at a brisk pace. No one wanted to screw this march up; it was the end of our basic training, and an individual was automatically backsquaded if they fell out, and failed to complete the march within the set time. The human body develops a rhythm on long marches, and the first twenty miles, although hard, went quickly. Like in the marathon, there is a 'wall' at about 20 miles, when the pain really kicks in. The bad news was that we had just arrived at the bottom of Tan Hill. It boasts the highest pub in England, which sits at the summit like the cherry on top of a cup cake. We were promised a quick shandy at the top, if we hit the summit within an hour. The killer on Tan Hill, is that it's not a hill at all, but a bloody great mountain. It rises in a series of false summits, where you think you can see the top, only to reach it, and see another above you. We sweated and laboured our way up that damned road, which ran up the mountain and just didn't seem to be getting any closer. Suddenly though, there it was, the pub at the top.

"With our luck, it's probably closed for redecoration."

The voice of doom didn't need to worry though, it was open, and we got our pint; probably the best we had ever tasted. After a fifteen-minute break, we fell back in, and marched away from our haven of rest. When you stop marching, your body looses the rhythm. Starting tired muscles takes ages and hurts like hell. Most of us had blisters, and they were really starting to burn. The Jimmpy was a section weapon, so we all took our turn carrying it. Sharing the machine gun wasn't so bad, as we changed every couple of miles. It came around to my turn again, and I hefted the gun onto my shoulder and marched on. The boys were starting to flag, and when the Corporal shouted the change at the end of my stint, no-one volunteered to take over. I didn't feel too bad; I'd got my second wind early, so I kept it. That turned out to be a big mistake, as I ended up with the bloody thing until the end of the march. We finally finished the last five miles, rounded a corner, and there, finally, was the assault course. It was the army's last test. Once over the assault course, fire ten live rounds on the target range and finish. We were all limping by now, and were pretty shagged, but we went around the long assault course anyway. Bang off the required ten shots and that was it. Game over, or so we thought.

When we arrived back at camp in the lorries, we were told to get to our bed spaces for foot inspection. We could all do with getting our boots off, so everyone hobbled painfully into the block, dumped our boots and socks, and lay face up on our bunks, as ordered. Our Corporals came into our barrack room, each carrying a medic pack. Now this was a real service, our Corporals, who had bullied and shouted their way through our 14 weeks of basic training were finally going to do something decent for us and tend our blistered, and in several cases, bleeding feet. We should have known better. The nearest corporal stood at the end of my bed and looked at my feet. Probably, 40% of the soles of my feet were badly blistered; the biggest was almost the size of a cigarette packet. "Hmmm, this might hurt a bit!" With that, he opened the medic pack, withdrew a hypodermic and fitted a brand-new needle. "Hold still, Black," he ordered and stuck the needle into the blister. "I'm drawing off the fluid," he told me. "It promotes rapid healing!" As he went sideways into the blister, it only pulled a bit as he broke the skin. I winced but it was nothing, compared with the last twenty-five miles. "Good lad," he said withdrawing the needle and squirting the fluid from the hypo. into a small surgical kidney bowl. What I didn't realise was that he was going to replace the fluid from the blister with pure iodine. He inserted the hypo needle into a large bottle of purple fluid, flicked the now full hypo to expel any small air bubbles and reinserted the needle into the flat blister. The pain felt like standing on a sea of fire. I hissed with the agony of it, until he'd finished. The Corporals went from bed to bed administering the same treatment to all of us.

"OK lads; take the rest of the evening off." Walking on big blisters hurts; walking on iodine filled blisters hurts more, much more. To this day, I've never found a medical book which recommends that method of treating badly blistered feet. Ah well, we were off to join our battalion shortly, and let's face it, if you can't take a joke, you shouldn't have joined.

Chapter 3
The Emerald Isle (1)

Having happily said our fond farewells to the Queen's Division depot at Bassingbourne, John and I got the train back to London. We had a week's leave, then a week's attachment to the North London army Recruiting Team. The army ran a 'Satisfied Soldier' scheme where they picked a couple of newly qualified recruits to help man recruiting stands on local High Streets. John had got the 'Best Recruit' prize the day we left the depot; he'd pipped me by a couple of points because he'd bulled up the soles of his boots, daft bastard. Anyhow, our weeks leave over, we duly reported to the same recruiting office we had signed up at, months earlier in Finchley, North London. Dressed in uniform, we marched in and banged our feet together in best regimental fashion at the Recruiting Sergeant's desk, and stood rigidly to attention. He was sitting reading a paper, and jumped out of his skin.

"Fuck me lads, relax! Take it easy! ......You from the depot?"

"Yes Sergeant," we said together.

"OK, chill out lads; you're not at the depot now. We do things a bit differently here." We spent the week on slack time, on the recruiting stands during the morning, and in the pub at lunchtime. This may not have been real soldiering, but it made a nice change from being beasted by hard-hearted corporals at the depot. Our new battalion: 2nd Battalion The Queen's Regiment, had deployed on a four-month emergency tour in Northern Ireland two months earlier; and that's where we were bound, at the end of our quick stint with the recruiting team. We arrived at Kings Cross B.R. Station and exchanged our travel warrants for tickets to Liverpool. We caught the train by the skin of our teeth, found a seat and relaxed. The journey was uneventful, and on arrival at Liverpool's mainline station, John and I loaded our kit into a taxi and headed off to the docks, to catch the ferry over the Irish Sea to Belfast. We were dressed in civilian clothes, and no-one took the slightest notice of us. The crossing was pretty uneventful and when we docked, we reported to the army Movements Office. We expected to be picked up and taken to our Battalion in Londonderry, but as with all things military no-one knew anything about two new guys needing a lift. The bored looking clerk scratched his face with his biro and said he would give our Battalion H.Q. a ring. We sat down on our kit and waited. Eventually, after about four hours, a lance corporal wearing a Queen's Regiment cap badge in his beret and a thick flak vest over his uniform, arrived at the counter and spoke with the duty clerk. The clerk pointed in our direction, and the lance corporal sauntered over.

34

"You the nigs (new boys) from the depot?" He enquired. We stood up quickly.

"Yes Corporal" I replied.

"You're a fucking week late boys, and in serious trouble!" Our jaws both dropped.

"But we're bang on time." I stammered. I quickly explained about the satisfied soldier scheme.

"OK, it ain't up to me matey, let the orderly room sort it out." He told us to pick up our kit and follow him. We went out into the ferry terminal car park and climbed into an army Land Rover, which was covered in drab green slabs of plastic armour. We sat quietly in the back as the armed escort climbed in. He was wearing a dog-eared flak jacket over his uniform and sat with his rifle pointing out of the rear door, watching for snipers. His beret looked a bit battered, much like the rest of him, for that matter. The journey through Belfast was a real shock. Rows of burnt out terraced houses, army checkpoints and plenty of armoured vehicles on the roads made us feel, for the first time, that we really were in a war zone. We finally arrived at Battalion Headquarters in Londonderry ('Derry for short). The main gate had a long-arm barrier which raised as we drove in. Beside the gate was a heavily sandbagged blockhouse with a Jimmpy barrel poking out of a slit window. When the Land Rover finally came to a stop, the lance corporal opened his door, climbed out and walked around to the back of the Land Rover. "Right then, grab your kit and follow me," he said. We did as he ordered, and walked into a heavily guarded building. Having climbed several flights of stairs, we finally reached an office door marked 'Orderly Room'. The young lance corporal knocked and slid inside. The door opened moments later, and he told us to come in. We entered what looked like an office, with several clerks sitting typing out forms. A fat Sergeant stood up and yelled.

"Where the fucking hell have you two been? We were expecting you a fucking week ago!" He then spent the next minute thoroughly bollocking us, without giving us a chance to get a word in edgeways and explain. The noise must have had some effect, as an older head appeared around the door.

"What's all the noise Sgt. Collet?"

"It's the two missing nigs from the depot Sir; they've finally turned up."

"Why are you so late?" He asked sternly, coming into the room. Now we were for it; it was the Regimental Sergeant Major, the most senior Non-Commissioned Officer in the Battalion, or 'God' for short.

"But we're not late Sir." I jabbered, and quickly explained our short tour with the North London recruiting team. The R.S.M. exhaled slowly.

"Hmmm, sounds like a paperwork cock-up to me, Sgt. Collet, get it sorted."

"On it right now Sir," said Collet a bit too fast for my likeing. Fat brown-nosing office bound twat, if ever I'd seen one. "Wait outside, you two." Collet snapped at us. We did as we were told, and after a minute or two of hanging around in the corridor, a fit looking Captain walked by. We saluted smartly, as he stopped and enquired.

"Who are you two then?" We explained that we had just arrived, and he said, "you're been missing for a week, haven't you?"

Fuck me, I thought, we were going to have to explain this load of old bollocks to every bloke in the battalion. John explained our story, and the Adjutant shrugged.

"OK, Sgt. Collet will sort it out, no doubt," and with that he wandered absently off. After about half an hour, Collet poked his head around the door and said.

"Right, you're both in the clear, get downstairs and wait for your transport. Griffin, you're going to 'C' Company here at Piggery Ridge, and you Black; you're going off to 'A' Company at Blighs Lane." With that he closed the door in our faces.

"Right then, off we go." Said John. We picked up our kit, and headed back downstairs. The lance corporal who had first picked us up at Belfast docks was waiting inside the front door.

"Right, who's going where?" He asked. We told him, and I shook hands with John.

"Good luck mate, see you..."

"Take care wanker, keep your head down," he said. "I'd better go and find 'C' Company then."

"Straight down the corridor, out through the doors and follow your nose to the blue portacabin, they'll sort you out," said our lance corporal to John.

"Cheers then, matey." Farewells made, I walked down the steps to the Land Rover.

"Right, 'A' Company at Blighs Lane it is," and off we went.

The drive to Blighs Lane didn't take long. We drove inside the corner entrance, of what looked like a municipal park. It's difficult to get your bearings when you are looking backwards out of a half closed rear door. We were driving along a tarmac road inside a park, complete with flower beds on either side. The driver took a hard right and put his foot down.

"This next part is a wee bit open," said my grinning escort. "We're a sitting duck on the next stretch if the Paddies kick off. Hold on to you nuts!"

He braced himself, but before I could even get close to following his example, we hit a bloody speed ramp. I shot up in the air and banged my head on the roof, then landed like a sack of spuds on the hard Land Rover floor.

"You've got to watch that bump; it's more likely to kill you than the Provos! (Provisional IRA)" Laughed the driver, as he continued to floor the accelerator. We drove through another raised barrier, past the same sort of sandbagged blockhouse we'd see earlier. The lads on guard waved as we passed them. Dressed in standard army camo. Suits, they were also clad in flak vests, but wore steel helmets, instead of berets. This was looking more like real sharp end stuff! Having unloaded my kit, I was directed towards the Company office, inside what looked like an old council office building. Admittedly, it sported a couple of sandbag blast walls outside, and plenty of barbed wire, but it still had the feeling of the council about it. I knocked on the door marked 'A Coy. Office'. A loud "Come in!" was called from within, and I entered. A big bloke, with a silver crown on his forearm was talking to a little guy with a single stripe on his arm. He looked at me and raised an eyebrow.

"I'm Sgt. Major Ormrod."

"Err, Black Sir, from the depot"

"Ah, yes, we've been expecting you...You're late."

Settling into 'A Company' was a doddle. The blokes were friendly and showed me the ropes without slagging me off too much. I'd drawn a flak vest & rifle from the company stores which was easy enough, but I found a small dog in my bed when I arrived at my new section's portacabin. The mutt growled at me when I tried to shift it. One of the section's young private soldiers, a guy who I later found out was called 'Blacky Blackwell' cautioned me.

"Watch it mate, that's Butch, and he'll bite you!"

. "Oh cheers," I replied, feeling like a helpless tosser. I stood beside the iron bed for a moment, not knowing what on earth to do, when someone came into the portacabin behind me.

"You the new bloke?" I turned and sprang to attention.

"Yes Sergeant." I replied, staring straight ahead, as I had been taught.

"All right son, relax, this isn't the depot and life's a bit different here." This was Pete Washouse, my new platoon Sergeant. A short stocky bloke of about 35. That's pretty ancient to a green kid of just 18, but he looked calm and experienced. Someone else stood just behind him.

"This is Corporal Clarke, your new section commander. Listen to him, and do exactly what he tells you. You've got a lot to learn quickly. And for Christ's sake someone, get that bloody dog out of his bed!"

He had a point about needing to learn quickly, as the only internal security training I had received at the depot was firing my rifle wearing my respirator (gas mask) once, on the range. That evening, I queued up at the pay-phone inside our main building and rang my folks at home to let them know I was OK. I told them some old rubbish about being attached to a training company for the next few weeks, but I don't think they believed a word of it. I had been right about the building being an ex-Council; our cookhouse was downstairs in the cellar, in the municipal morgue; charming! Pete Washouse took me out for an orientation ride around the area next morning in a lightly armoured Land Rover. He explained that there were normally two sections out on patrol at any one time, one mobile (split between two Land Rovers) and one on foot. Our patrol area was the Creggan, a tough Catholic area, and staunchly IRA with it. Sgt. Washouse explained to me that most people in the Creggan were decent God-fearing people, but there was a hard core of Republicans, who ruled the area with a rod of iron. If a riot started, they would expect everyone out and God help anyone who didn't come to the party. If a local girl got too friendly with the young soldiers, she would be grabbed by these hardliners one night, have her head shaved, then be tarred and feathered. A cruel punishment to her, and a strong warning to any other lass with a wandering eye. 'Stay away from the Brits'. From time to time, he told me, a front door would be opened a crack as a foot patrol went by, and a warning would be whispered.

"Don't go down so and so street, the boys are waiting!"...

"They aren't all bad" he said. "Just trapped by the troubles". He carried on with his briefing as the vehicle sped around the Creggan. "This corner is a bit lively sometimes." ...BANG! A stone hit the side of the Land Rover. I jumped out of my skin.

"Bloody kids," he said absently; and calmly lit a cigarette.

I did my first couple of patrols on foot and in the Land Rovers, with my heart in my mouth. Pete Washouse had said that I should copy the example of the experienced soldiers in the section, and listen carefully for Corporal Clarke's orders. The most seasoned senior privates were referred to as 'old sweats'. They usually had at least 8-10 years of service under their belts. A platoon (three sections of eight men each) was lucky if it boasted more than four or five 'old sweats'. My section didn't have any, but all the boys had some time in. They looked out for me, although they were, in most cases only a year or two older. My section's radio call sign was one-two-Charlie. This unique call sign was used to identify our section on the army radio network when we were out on patrol. You get to know guys quickly on active service, and I soon knew everyone well enough. Bill Simpson, from Birmingham was our driver; he drove the section's tracked 15 ton 432 armoured personnel carrier when the battalion was deployed at its NATO base at Werl, West Germany. Eaton Gail, a strapping West Indian lad from Deptford, South London was the section's Jimmpy Gunner. Steve Broad and Mick Collins also hailed from different parts of London. Our section second in command was lance corporal Vic. Manning, born just down the road from me in Childs Hill, North London.

With Blacky Blackwell and Cpl 'Nobby" Clarke, that was our section complete. One of the first lessons they all drummed into me was never to get separated while out on foot patrol. A young Royal Anglian in Belfast missed a move on signal, and become separated from his patrol. An angry crowd had cornered him in a garage, and the IRA shot him dead. It was a bad mistake, not to be repeated. Army foot patrols moved together in a 'brick' formation. Although we were spread apart, on both sides of the road, we always stayed in visible contact. If something needed checking around a corner, or whatever, you always went with a mate, who would cover you.

Sleep was a major luxury, and was always in short supply in Ulster. Because manpower was always stretched, we had to put extra hours into every single day. Three or four hours sleep out of each twenty-four was the norm, and that was usually fully dressed with our boots on. When a section was on a 24-hour patrol period; we would be out for 2-3 hours on foot, then back to base for a short break and tea, and back out for another few hours on patrol. This routine went on for eight hours, and then we swapped with the other section and used the Land Rovers. The vehicle-mounted section also acted as a fast backup, if the foot patrol got into trouble. As each platoon had three sections, the spare section acted as a reserve, on immediate standby in the guardroom, back at base. When on standby, you snatched sleep when you could. As the Creggan was a major 'hot-spot' in Londonderry, at least one call per standby duty was quite normal. At the end of the 24-hour patrol period, the platoon went straight onto guard duty. Our camp had a big perimeter and needed plenty of guarding. Four hours on guard in a cold and boring sandbagged pillbox or Sanger, then four hours off in the section 'basher' (with boots on) having a kip, or in the Company's TV room watching any rubbish to relieve the boredom. While I was there, the Sun newspaper ran a big campaign to raise funds to buy some decent television sets for the troops in Ireland. A big, brand new colour TV arrived at our Battalions Headquarters at Piggery Ridge a week later, which was promptly pinched by the Officer's Mess. We got a black-and-white set at Blighs Lane, but thank you; Sun readers in 1972, it was much better than nothing.

If our platoon wasn't on patrol or guard, we would be on admin. detail. This entailed doing any odd jobs within the camp, or helping out in the cookhouse. The odd jobs included replacing old sandbags, clearing rubbish or scrubbing out the showers and toilets. Working on this three-day routine, there wasn't such a thing as a day off, throughout the emergency four-month tour.

Rifle sections had to gather information while on patrol, which was fed through the system to our Battalion's intelligence cell. They would then collate the information and try to form an overall picture of what was happening on the terrorist side, within our area. If a particular house seemed a bit too busy on several nights, the int. boys would get excited, and put it under surveillance, or task a platoon to carry out a house search. We tended to do our house searches at night, normally at about 2am, when hopefully, the occupants of the target house were all fast asleep. When someone's door is battered down in the middle of the night, and the house suddenly fills up with heavily armed soldiers, resistance as they say is futile. My first house search, as it turned out, was nearly my last. A building had been identified as a possible safe house for the IRA, and one-two-Charlie was given the task of the exterior guard, during the search. If you set up an outer cordon before the search team goes in, you are in a position outside to catch any suspect having it away, on his toes, when the front door goes in. I was under the wing of Blacky Blackwell, as back garden outer guard. The raid was timed to go in at 0200 hours, and was aimed at grabbing the local Provisional IRA commander. We all blacked up our faces with camouflage cream, searched each other for anything noisy in our pockets (keys, small change, etc.). We checked our weapons and spare ammunition and climbed aboard two Saracen wheeled armoured personnel carriers. The search team took one, and we were in the second. The Saracens were much loved by the troops who rode in them. Driven properly, they were quite fast for their size, and offered excellent protection from small-arms fire and shrapnel. The Saracen gearbox gave out a loud and very distinctive ghostly whine when the driver changed up through the gears. When you have heard it once, you never forgot the sound. The Saracens dropped us off several streets away from the target house, and we crept slowly and very quietly through the adjoining gardens of the estate, until we were all safely in position. Apart from a dog barking a street or two away, all was quiet. The street lights were shining brightly, but the rear gardens were silent and cloaked in darkness. The target house showed no lights, and not a sound could be heard from inside. The back garden was quite long, seventy feet of so, but there was nowhere to hide in ambush close to the house. Blacky whispered for me to follow him further down the garden, almost to its far end where there were some thick bushes to hide in.

We had been given plenty of time to get into position and we both sat tucked in the bushes, kept very still, and waited. At exactly 0200hrs our two Saracens roared down the target street and screeched to a halt outside the suspected safe house. The search party leapt out of the back of the first Saracen and ran into the front garden. CRASH! The front door was suddenly history, and the searchers swarmed into the house. A woman started screaming somewhere inside the house, and a baby cried. Now all this noise had woken the neighbours. The first few came out onto the street, having grabbed their iron dustbin lids. They started banging the lids on the road, making a terrible racket. This was a signal that there was army trouble, and EVERY resident must come out and fend off the Brits. There was the sound of a growing crowd shouting obscenities and defiance at our guys in the front. Add to that, the sound of bottles thrown by the crowd, smashing in the road, it sounded like all hell had broken loose in front of number 49! Blacky and I sat silently in our bush listening to the battle waging out of our sight, at the front of the house. It seemed to go on for ages. Blacky stirred, and whispered in my ear.

"This ain't right Dave; something's gone wrong!"

The words had hardly left his mouth, when we heard the roar of the Saracens over the din of the crowd.

"Christ, they're fucking off without us!" shouted Blacky "Come on Dave, RUN!"

We broke cover and legged it to the top of the garden, then down the darkened side of the house. We burst through the front garden into the street. Smashed glass and rocks littered the roadway, and an old woman was still screaming obscenities and banging her bin lid on the pavement opposite. There must have been a couple of hundred civilians, men, women and children yelling and screaming no more that twenty metres to our left. It was unreal, almost like a Keystone Cops comedy. They saw us come tearing out of the garden, and their surprise stopped them screaming. But only perhaps, for just three short heartbeats. Then, with a mighty roar of anger and hatred, they surged after us, waving hurly sticks, pickaxe handles and broken bottles. We were now running for our lives, if they caught either of us in the fired-up state they were in, we were dead men. The Saracens were only about thirty metres ahead of us, pulling away.Luckily, it was our Saracen in the rear. I could see Vic Manning sitting at the rear door, frantically screaming into the front of the armoured wagon. The crowd was getting closer, judging by the noise behind us. We were carrying flak vests, belt kits, rifles and spare ammo. Added to all the gear, we were running in bloody awful DMS boots. Christ knows what the Paddies had on, but I bet it didn't weigh much. The Saracen's brake lights suddenly flicked on, and it slowed to a crawl. It was the edge Blacky, and I needed. He was first to reach the door and dived headfirst through it. I arrived moments later and followed his lead. I remember several pairs of hands grabbing my webbing as I entered the vehicle horizontally, and I landed with a crash on top of an already winded Blacky. The angry mob behind us screamed in frustration, but they were too late; our driver floored the gas pedal, and we were gone. Someone probably got a good bollocking, but the target had been successfully lifted, and Blacky and I were just happy to be in alive, and still in one piece.

One of the problems with patrolling big civilian estates is that they contain substantial amounts of small children. Catholics are told from the pulpit to be fruitful, and have large families, and that's what they do. We always tried to be friendly to the kids, dishing out packets of spangles and polo mints whenever the chance arose. It wassimple; a grass roots exercise in hearts and minds. We couldn't very well launch into a football match with the kids, but once in early December 1972, we got involved in a serious snowball fight. I can't remember who started it, but soon there were dozens of kids chucking snowballs at us, and us returning the same. Plenty of laughter and everyone's having a bit of fun. A snowball whizzed past my ear, and slapped against the wall behind me. I don't know why I chose to look at its remains, but I'm glad I did. There was a razor blade embedded in it. I shouted to Nobby Clarke (who was just a couple of metres in front of me) and pointed. He saw the blade, and we stopped playing, called it a draw, and pissed off quick. On another occasion, I was standing in a doorway, giving cover while the section did a snap road block. A beautiful little girl of no more than two toddled up to me. She had masses of golden hair in flowing ringlets and lovely blue eyes. I smiled at her and said gently. "Hallo, what's your name?" She turned her angelic little face up at me, and spat on my knee... It's not the sort of thing that happens to most people in a lifetime, and no amount of training can prepare you for it, but it made a good story to tell the boys afterwards.

Late one night, we had just arrived back at base, after a long, uneventful foot patrol. Having unloaded our weapons, we headed straight for the cookhouse for a warming cuppa, and a fried egg banjo (sandwich). We were standing around the hotplate chatting, and frying up some eggs, when suddenly there was an almighty BOOM! outside. We all charged up the stairs, and spilled out into the courtyard at the rear of the building. There was lots of hot dust and black smoke floating around, and a powerful smell of burnt explosive. Our patrol commander Nobby Clarke had been in the Company Ops. room, being debriefed on the earlier patrol.

"Blast bomb!" he shouted, "Anyone hurt?" We quickly checked the area, and thankfully, there were no bodies, or bits of bodies lying anywhere. It turned out that the IRA had somehow found a blind spot in the perimeter and had slung a milk bottle full of gelignite over the twenty-foot wall, which covered that side of the building. You had to hand it to the bastards, because they did exactly the same thing the very next night. An identical bomb came sailing over the wall in the middle of the night, but once again, thankfully, didn't cause any casualties. There was a big oak tree on our side of the wall, roughly in the middle of the two Sangers which guarded it. Eaton Gail was sent up into the tree on the next night, to cover the blind spot. His rifle was fitted with a starlight scope, a cunning device for seeing clearly through the rifle's sights, even on the darkest night. Perhaps the Provos had decided third time unlucky, because they didn't come back for another attempt. Poor Eaton froze his nuts off, all night up that tree, for nothing.

We were once tasked to escort a Parachute Regiment Intelligence section vehicle from Londonderry to Aldergrove Airport, just outside

Belfast. The small convoy was due to leave in an hour, so we all had some time to kill. I got chatting to one of the Parachute. Regiment drivers, and he told me a typical Para story. He and the rest of his section had been out on patrol a few weeks previously in the Crumlin Road area of Belfast. As they patrolled on foot through an alleyway at the back of some shops, they found a body. The dead guy was kneeling in what looked like a praying position, with what was left of his head pressed hard against a brick wall. It was a classic terrorist execution. Kneel the man down, and give him a quick bullet in the back of the head, no messing. The patrol commander quickly checked the body for booby traps, and then searched the dead man's pockets, looking to identify him. The only thing he found was a wallet, with fifty quid in it. The Para. grinned with glee as he told me that the Para. Corporal pinched the money. "Spoils of war, mate" laughed the Corporal. The R.U.C. (Royal Ulster Constabulary) arrived shortly after the murder had been reported via the patrol's radio. The big Irish copper walked over to the corpse. He looked around, taking in the blood and brain splattered scene. Then he spotted the wallet, lying on the ground. Picking it up carefully by the corners he checked for contents "Jesus Christ, they robbed him as well" exclaimed the policeman. "Bastards!" Said the Para Corporal, sadly shaking his head.

One of the most vivid things I remember about Northern Ireland was the smell. Peat was burnt in the hearths of countless homes in the Creggan and the distinctive aroma of this cheap; readily available fuel is to me, Ulster's fingerprint. The other overwhelming memory is how cold and wet the place was. Waterproof clothing was almost unknown to the British army at the time, and if it rained hard, you got wet. Not just a bit damp, but really soaked through. Ireland has a very high annual rainfall because next to it, of course, is the mighty Atlantic Ocean. Huge weather fronts are generated way out to sea, and slam across the Emerald Isle on an all too regular basis. Once, during a particularly heavy rainstorm, I was sitting in the back of a Land Rover, in the rear-guard position. We were driving on the very edge of our area, patrolling down the road which divided the Creggan and the Bogside strongholds of the IRA. We passed a foot patrol of very wet and pissed off looking Royal Green Jackets who were on the edge of their (Bog side) area. The R.G.J., or Black Mafia as they are nicknamed, are a first class Regiment, renowned for their sharp shooting and drill at the double. The last guy in their patrol looked pretty soggy and forlorn, but I caught his eye and he gave me a very dejected two fingered 'peace-man' 'V' sign, which I happily returned from inside my snug, dry Land Rover.

One afternoon, shortly before my first two-month tour in Ireland ended I was ordered to the 'A' Company's Office. I walked into the building, and knocked on the office door. L/Cpl Moggy Moore, the Company's clerk, called me in, and told me he had some good news.

43

Because I had joined the Battalion on active service, and had completed the second part of their four-month tour, I was going on an extended leave to England for Christmas. The battalion missed out on most of its annual leave that year. I had expected to fly back to Germany and join the Battalion's rear detail, and spend Christmas doing endless guard duty. The powers that be in the Company had taken the view that I'd done time in the shit, and like the others, deserved some decent leave.

When the battalion left Northern Ireland, we paused for a couple of hours over in Fort George, on the other side of 'Derry. Parked in a distant corner of the camp was what looked like a large pile of scrap metal. With nothing better to do, a couple of us wandered over to have a look. Another Regiment had a pair of Land Rovers blown up, after they drove over a big bomb hidden in a countryside culvert. Because of the high rainfall, there are countless roadway culverts, to drain away the excess rainwater. The patrol in question were just unlucky; they chose to drive over a culvert with a beer keg packed with 100lbs of explosive. The blast from the bomb blew a hole in the road thirty feet wide, and had nearly bent one of the Land Rover chassis in two, so that the front and back axles were almost touching. I didn't know what happened to the crew ... but I could guess.

Chapter 4
Achtung – Germany !

In 1973 Germany was still split into two parts; Communist controlled East Germany, and Democratic West Germany. After WW2, all the counties 'liberated' from Nazi Germany by the Russians were forced into forming a military alliance called the Warsaw Pact. To counter the threat of a possible Communist 'Warsaw Pact' invasion, the Western European countries, backed by the U.S.A. formed their own military alliance called 'Nato.' Tension between the two huge power blocks was at an all-time high when I arrived in West Germany in the early 70s. The Russian army was; we were told, well equipped, trained and motivated. They had over a million men stationed on or near their side of the Iron Curtain, which acted as an artificial border between the Communists and the NATO alliance.

The Russians had erected the Iron Curtain (also known as the I.G.B. - Inner German Border) in 1961, as a physical barrier between East and West. It was 1,378 kilometre long, five kilometres deep, and guarded by over 1.3 million mines, sown to catch any unwary escapee. The I.G.B was guarded by thousands of heavily armed K.G.B. (secret police ministry) troops. To further increase their security, the East German K.G.B. troops used fierce, powerful guard dogs during their patrols, and had wicked explosive anti-personnel booby traps installed along thousands and thousands of miles of coiled barbed wire. These directional 'mines' were packed with tiny metal cubes, specifically designed to inflict more severe injuries than ball bearings. Watch towers were set at regular intervals along their side of the border, always with at least two K.G.B. guards. They had a minimum of two sentries, because the Communist theory was brutally simple. Should one guard try to defect to the west, the other was there to shoot him.

We were briefed that it had been originally built by the Russians to stop people moving out of their sphere of influence, and living in the west. Sadly, over 350 civilians were killed, trying to escape through the I.G.B., to the west. The minds which created the Iron Curtain, belonged to the same people who now cast their envious eyes over prosperous Western Europe.

My infantry Battalion was stationed a few kilometres outside Werl (pronounced Verl), in West Germany. Werl was a typical West German town, clean, neat and prosperous. It was a small provincial town, 30 kilometres west of Dortmund, and about 160 kilometres from the I.G.B. The West Germans didn't want British troops on their soil, but took the view that at least we put money into their economy, and didn't interfere too much with their lives. The alternative was maybe the 101st Soviet motor rifle division, who certainly would upset their cosy way of life. We all arrived back at camp after a long six-week Christmas leave, having been coached all the way from England. It had been a good break over Christmas, as it had been a busy 7/8 months previously, what with basic training and Northern Ireland. Now, we new boys had to learn to settle into Battalion life in Germany. Our daily routine was quickly established. Up at 7.00, wash shave etc., then down to the cookhouse for breakfast until about 07.50. Nip back to the barrack block (known as a 'basher') and clean out our rooms, ready for room inspection. The Battalion had struck it lucky, when they were posted to Werl several years earlier. The camp had been originally built for a Canadian Battalion after WW2. It was made up of smart, single story blocks; each divided into four-man rooms. The Company's Corporals and Lance Corporals had their own rooms within each basher. The married men lived with their wives and children in separate married quarters in Werl itself. When room inspections were completed, each Company paraded at their Company 'Lines', and jobs, notices and instructions were handed out for the coming day. Once Sgt. Major Ormrod had finished his muster parade, we dispersed, and went about our respective duties. Usually, this entailed going over to the vehicle park, where our carriers were parked. As a fully mechanised infantry battalion we were equipped with the 432 Armoured Personnel Carrier, a 15 ton tracked vehicle. There were always plenty of odd jobs to do on them, and our mornings were usually spent helping our driver sort them out. If there were a serious problem, the R.E.M.E. (Royal Electrical and Mechanical Engineers) were called in. They dealt with the more complicated parts of our carriers: engines, gearboxes and transmissions and so on. In the afternoons, we did various military training, much the same as in the depot. To keep sharp, it was necessary to keep practising our skills because we were pretty close to the I.G.B. This meant, should the balloon go up and the Russians invade, we could be in action within a matter of hours.

We had to be ready to go almost at once, and in order to be at the highest state of readiness, we spent about two weeks out of each month out on exercise. It involved assuming practise wartime positions deployed in the German countryside, along with our tanks and artillery, which made up an armoured battle group. We would then be moved about by our Brigadier while he fought the 'battle', from his H.Q. When 'end-ex' came, we would drive in long armoured convoys back to our Werl barracks, clean the 432, and perform any necessary maintenance, ready for the next exercise. We had most evenings off, unless tasked for guard duties, and weekends were mostly free, if we weren't away on exercise or again, on guard. After a few months, I had settled in well with life in Germany. It was hard work sometimes, but good fun. I had stayed with one-two-Charlie, and was becoming great friends with all the boys in the section.

Once a week, we had an afternoon of sport. We could play squash, use the gym, or go running, if no formal physical training had been planned by the Company office. I often trained with Eaton Gail, a Jamaican born lad, whose nickname was 'Muscles'. As our Jimmpy Gunner, he had to be pretty fit and strong anyway, but he liked hard physical circuit training and so did I. The only bad thing I can say about Eaton was his ability to drink vast amounts of rum, and then stay on his feet. He didn't drink often, but when he did, we all took a little extra care. On one occasion, he had gone out with several West Indian mates on a Friday evening and didn't re-appear until late Saturday night. The rest of us in the section had been watching an England International football match on the television room in the NAAFI. Our national team had just been stuffed, and as we headed back to our basher, we bumped into one of Eaton's drinking buddies. Apparently, there had been an incident in a bar in Werl, and Eaton's sense of honour had been offended. Bearing in mind he was extremely pissed at the time, he decided that the only way to sort out his disagreement was to chop off the other bloke's head with a machete. He was now prowling around the camp, in the dead of night, searching for his victim. We quickly agreed that we had to find him, before he did something really stupid.

"Phasers on stun, Captain?" Said Blacky.

"I don't think that would stop him," said Mick, nervously looking over his shoulder. We searched the camp for the best part of an hour, but drew a blank. Eaton hadn't been arrested by the guard, and wasn't locked up in the guardhouse (I'd checked). We met up in our basher; and were trying to think what to do next, when in staggered Eaton. Dressed like Shaft, in a long black leather coat and a big black hat, Eaton looked pissed. No, he looked very, very pissed. He had a half-empty bottle of Rum in one hand, and a wickedly sharp-looking machete in the other. As he lurched down the corridor towards us, someone softly muttered "Oh Fuck!"

When Eaton got to within ten feet of us, Steve, who always had too much to say for himself, spoke first.

"Hallo Eaton, what's up mate?" Eaton stopped. He swayed as he tried to focus on who had just spoken to him.

"I'm looking for Glen Toffrey; I'm goner kill him!" growled our Gunner.

"What happened Eaton?" asked Mick.

"He called me a black bastard, and I'm going to chop his fucking head off!" Said Eaton, drunkenly slicing through the air with his machete.

"The guy's a total tosser, and he can't talk to one of us like that," said Steve. "Let's have a drink, and then we'll all go and kill him." Eaton didn't move.

"Yeah, good idea," said Blacky, who was the first to cotton on. "Come on Eaton, give us a drink, mate." By now, the penny had dropped

47

for all of us, and we wandered around Eaton muttering what a waste of oxygen Toffrey was. Eaton passed the bottle around, and we finished it quickly.

"I've got a bottle of schnapps in my locker; I said. "We'll do that before we do Toffrey."

Someone muttered what a good idea that was, and we shepherded Eaton towards my room. I quickly opened my locker, and pulled the bottle down off the shelf. Once it was open, I raised the bottle and said, "Death to Toffrey!" Talking a long swig, I passed the bottle to Eaton.

"Death to Toffrey," he growled and also took a long pull from it. Another bottle appeared from somewhere and was passed the other way. It didn't take too long to finish it, but we were all starting to feel the effects. Luckily, Steve's plan worked. We were all sitting on the beds' drinking when Eaton's tanks finally clocked full, and he passed out. Mick picked up the machete and disappeared with it. He came back a minute later, without the weapon.

"He'll never find it," he laughed. "let's get this idiot into his own bed; I want to get my head down too." We picked up our now happily snoring machine Gunner and carried him down the corridor to his own pit. Leaving him fully dressed, lying on his side in the recovery position, we called it a night.

Boredom was a serious enemy in Germany. Blokes would go out on the beer, get into trouble and end up doing a week locked in a cell in the guardhouse. A guy from 'C' Company accidentally got locked inside a bar one night, in Werl. He'd had far too much to drink, and fell asleep sitting on one of the toilets. The owner didn't check the loos before he locked up for the night. When the guy woke up in the early hours, he wandered around the bar, looking for a way out. As he was still pretty pissed, it seemed like a good idea to help himself to some bottles of booze, from behind the bar. When he arrived back at camp in a taxi, he still clutched his stolen bottles, complete with optics. A mate of his was on guard, and looked the other way as he staggered through the gate. His buddies in the 'C' Company block were none too happy however, being awoken at 3am by a pissed up twat offering free drinks in his room, which he announced proudly was now the new Company bar.

We had just finished a weeks battle training, and our convoy of 432s arrived back at the vehicle park. Having unloaded all our kit, and hosed down our vehicle, we headed for the armoury to lock away our weapons. It was a bright sunny afternoon, and after a final company parade, we were fallen out for the day. You get pretty dirty and smelly after a week out in the cuds (countryside) and we all hit the showers. I was running slightly behind, as I had to report to the Company office, to be told that my application to go on an Assault Pioneer course had been turned down. Each Battalion in the British army had a platoon which was dedicated to combat engineering. Not big jobs like building Bailey bridges, or large-scale large-scale minefield clearance. Those skills belonged to the Royal Engineers. The Assault Pioneers did lots of cool stuff, laying mines, demolitions, booby traps and the like. I was very keen to learn these skills, but Sgt. Major Ormrod simply said.

"No Black, if you go on the course, they'll want to keep you."

I was pretty pissed off about it, but you don't argue with the Company Sergeant Major. I miserably trudged back to the block, took off my dirty kit and headed for a shower. Everyone else had finished, so the shower room was empty. The hot stream of clean water was a real pleasure. I was just rinsing off the soap when the fire alarm sounded. The drill was very simple. Stop what you are doing, grab something to fight the fire, and double down to the Battalion parade square for an emergency parade. Our blokes were running down the corridor and the Corporals were yelling.

"Come on, move yourselves!"

One of them saw me and yelled. "Shift it Black! Grab your towel and get down to the parade square." Not being one to disobey an order, I did exactly that. I wrapped my green army towel around my waist, grabbed a fire bucket full of sand and did my best to run in flip flops down to the rest on the Battalion on the square. I fell in with my platoon amid howls of delight from the boys.

"Sorry to get you out of the bath, Black."

"Washed behind your ears yet, wanker?" The Colour Sergeant was handing out steel helmets. He had managed to scrounge up some old tin hats from somewhere and had got the Company store man to paint them red, and stencil FIRE on each of them. He walked up to me and shook his head.

"Sometimes, I don't think you take things too seriously Black," he said. He handed me his last steel hat.

"I was in the showers, Colours, honest!" More sniggers and laughter around me. The R.S.M. marched onto the parade square and announced this was just a drill. Then he roared out the order.

"Battalion 'SHUN!."

In my haste, I'd made a bit of a mess wrapping my towel around myself, because as I banged my flip-flopped heels together, and came to attention, the bloody thing fell off. I stood rigidly still, naked as the day I was born. A lot more sniggers from my mates erupted around me. Our Sgt. Major inspected his troops. It was the first time I'd ever seen him laugh on parade. I suppose you couldn't blame him. I didn't exactly look like a lean mean fire fighting machine. Not with just a fire bucket full of sand, a pair of flip-flops and a red tin hat with 'Fire' written on it.

"Put your towel back on Black," was all he said.

49

As part of our continuing rigorous training, we had to pass an annual small arms proficiency test. This involved firing all the normal infantry weapons, including the belt-fed General Purpose Machine Gun. The weapons' test was held at the military ranges at Sennelager. On this occasion, all went well until we got to the grenade range. We were issued with some of the last wartime stock of the old 36 Mills bombs. They called it a 36, because when Mr. Mills designed the grenade, it was supposed to explode into thirty-six iron fragments. I'll take his word for it, as I'm glad to say that I never got close enough to count, when the bloody things went off. Before we could use the grenades, it was necessary to remove the grease, which preserved them during storage and prevented the entrance of moisture. Having carried out the correct cleaning process, I joined the queue and threw my two grenades, when my turn came. They both went off with a very loud and satisfying bang. One of my section, Steve Broad had somehow managed to scrounge up a spare grenade, but couldn't be bothered to throw it. He passed it to me, and I happily joined the end of the queue again to use it. When it finally came to my second visit to the throwing bay, I presented myself to the Sgt. in charge. I told him I'd scrounged a spare grenade, and assumed the upright throwing position. When the officer controlling the range gave the all clear, my Sgt. ordered me to throw it. Clutching the heavy grenade tightly, I pulled the safety pin, and lobbed the bomb into the detonation area. The grenades had an inbuilt five-second delay, before they exploded. We were trained to watch where the grenade landed, and then duck smartly down behind cover, and await the explosion...But nothing happened. We stayed in a crouched position for about a minute, until the officer declared a miss-fire. The grenade range Sgt. immediately swore at me, and told me to report to the Sgt. Major. I presented myself smartly to Dave Ormrod, who also gave me a serious mouthful of colourful Anglo Saxon. In his hand, he had a small red steel box with 'DANGER - EXPLOSIVES' stenciled on it.

"I've got to blow the bloody thing up, and you Black, are coming with me!"

The range was deathly quiet, as we both walked into the detonation area. As I had watched the dud grenade land before ducking, I knew roughly where it was. The grenade lay on its side, looking very sinister and dangerous. In its current condition, it might go off at the slightest touch, so it had to be destroyed, where it lay. We both stood back about ten feet from it, while the Sgt. Major prepared the demolition charge. When he was ready, he held a plastic explosive charge, about the size of a cricket ball. The explosive was fitted with a two-minute delay fuse.

"Come on Black, if I'm going to get blown up, so are you!" Said the Sgt. Major. We walked slowly and very carefully over to the sleeping grenade. The Sgt. Major ordered me to stand about a foot in from it. He knelt behind me, and using my body as a shield, carefully placed the charge next to the dud. When he was happy with the placement, he lit the fuse. "Right, leg it!" He said, and we both beat a hasty retreat towards cover. The demolition charge exploded, destroying the grenade. I explained what had happened and the Sgt. Major said. "Let this be a good lesson to you Black. NEVER trust anyone else to clean out a grenade, which you are going to use... Now, where is Broad? I want a little word with him!"

I saw my old buddy John Griffin from time to time, and we occasionally hit the NAAFI in the evening for a pint or two. Life in different Companies, within the same Battalion meant that there were always good stories to swap, which invariably got funnier, as more beer was consumed. John had been out with a mate of his called Jimmie Strickland. He and John had got pretty pissed in a local bar in Werl, and left in the early hours. While waiting at a deserted taxi rank for transport back to camp, Jimmy had been taken short, and needed a dump, pronto. Nothing was open at that time and Jimmy's need was getting more critical by the moment.

"It's no-good John; I'm pushing cloth...I've have got to have a shit!" Breathed Jimmy, unbuckling his belt. He waddled over to the nearest neatly clipped front garden, quietly opened the gate and ducked down behind the hedge.

John tried to continue his tale, but had to stop, to stem the tide of his laughter. When he got control, he continued. He said that all was quiet for a couple of moments after Jimmy disappeared behind the hedge. Then suddenly, the peace and quiet were shattered by several thunderous farts, and a load cry of "Ahhh God! That's better!" All was quiet again for several seconds, but suddenly, a bedroom light flicked on and a man's head appeared from an upstairs window. The angry householder yelled at Jimmy in German. Jimmy jumped up with a start, and buckling his trousers ran through the still open gate.

"Quick John, run!" Said Jimmy, hooting with laughter. Unfortunately, a German police car was cruising past just at that critical moment. Seeing two dodgy looking characters running up the road, it gave chase. Lights flashing, the patrol car drew ahead of the fleeing pair. The German police officer sitting in the passenger seat shouted. "Halt!" through his open window. The police car screeched to a stop, and both policemen jumped out. All German policemen carry guns, and both officers automatically put their hands on their pistol holsters.

"Halt!" shouted the driver again, and the boys stopped. The policemen walked cautiously towards the panting desperados, and one said.

"English?"

51

"Err, yes mate," said Jimmy. That was the moment when the angry householder arrived, in his pyjamas, slippers and dressing gown. He started jabbering away in German at the two policemen and pointing at Jimmy. They both looked shocked, and one said to Jimmy.

"You vill vait here." The other policeman followed the still jabbering German civilian back to the scene of the crime. It didn't take long for the officer to return. He spoke to the driver, who looked shocked again, then turned to the boys and said.

"You are both under arrest!"

John and Jimmy were handcuffed, pushed in the back of the police car, and driven to the local police station. John had to stop again several times, to control his laughter, as he described their entrance. The police driver led them in, and the other policeman brought up the rear. At arm's length, he was horizontally carrying a police issue spade, with Jimmy's turd sitting on it. This was clearly their only physical evidence, but pretty damning, nonetheless. Luckily, for both the boys, it was a standard procedure for the German authorities to contact the Royal Military Police (The Redcaps) when a British soldier was arrested by the civil police. The R.M.P.'s arrived after about an hour, and spoke to the Germans first. There was quite a heated conversation between them for several minutes. The R.M.P. Sergeant walked over to the two unhappy squaddies and asked them what happened. Jimmy told him the truth, which immediately got John out of trouble. The Redcap told Jimmy that the civilian police wanted to charge him, and if that happened, he could be facing time in a German prison.

"But I only had a dump, Sarge!" wailed Jimmy.

"Lucky for you, I'm claiming you, and arresting you, Strickland," said the Military Policeman. "You will be up in front of your O.C. (Officer Commanding - C Company) tomorrow morning. I'll let him sort you out." Jimmy got a stiff fine next morning from his O.C. and a long lecture about trying to stay friendly with our civilian German allies. John finished his tale with a quizzical look on his face.

"The only question is, if it went to trial, where would they have sent the turd to….. Forensics or Ballistics?

Competition and rivalry was fierce between Companies in the Battalion. Each Company (naturally), thinks it was better than the others, and this was used to make training more interesting and competitive. Each year a series of military events was held, and the winning Company was then presented with The Invictor Cup. It was subsequently proudly displayed in the winning Company's office for the next year. The overall competition was a mixture of physical and military tasks, and points were awarded for each event. We all had a part to play, and Mickey Collins and I were put in the Company's orienteering team. Orienteering is a cunning mix of map reading, and cross-country running. A route through the countryside is arranged by the judges, and the two-man teams must map read from one manned checkpoint to the next, as fast as possible. The checkpoints were set about three kilometres apart. Each company had five two-man teams, and pairs were set off at timed five-minute intervals. Mickey was a naturally fit bloke, so he set the pace, and I did the map reading. It was a good system, but by the end of our route, I was completely shattered. "A" Company did pretty well and amassed a good overall score. Our football team got pretty stuffed and scored badly. Our star players had all been sent on a course, and were conveniently away at the time of the all-important matches. We suspected an H.Q. Company plot, as they had arranged the course dates. I played for 'A' Company's Cricket team. I had played for Mill Hill Village III eleven before joining the regular army, and quite fancied my chances. Unfortunately, I got badly run out when Jumbo Jarvis (three platoon's Sergeant) called for a run which was never there. The last event was a drill parade, where every man in each Company had to take part.

The scores were close, but 'A' Company were just ahead on points. The whole competition hinged on this last event. 'A' Company was probably the scruffiest outfit in the Battalion, but we set to, polishing, pressing and bulling our drill uniforms and equipment, the day before the last event. Each Company was inspected by the R.S.M. before they took part in the drill parade, so it was important to look smart, as valuable points could be earned, or lost, just on the Company's overall appearance. It's a funny thing, but although we didn't really care too much who won on one level, we wanted to win on another for two reasons. The first was just to stuff the other Companies, but more importantly; we wanted to win for our Sgt. Major, Dave Ormrod. Although he was not a man to cross, with a voice like a bellowing elephant, he was a fair and reasonable man. The truth is, although none of us would have dreamt of admitting it at the time, we all liked Dave. If we won, he would get all the credit, so we tried our best really, just for him.

The NCO's and the old sweats in the Company spent the day before the drill parade fussing around all the younger blokes, checking everyone's dress uniforms (No. 2 dress), and using every trick in the book to get even the grubbiest little soldiers looking like super smart Guardsmen. When the Company fell in next morning wearing their parade uniforms, it was the smartest collection of soldiers I had ever seen. The Company looked immaculate; quite incredible! The R.S.M. inspected every man closely, and when he had finished, we had scored enough points to win the cup outright, without having to do the drill parade. We did the parade anyway, and it was mustard! The only thing that marred the drill competition was a guy from 'B' Company. The poor bastard's bayonet fell off, with a terrible 'Clang', halfway through their drill parade, and he had to march around with it clearly missing from the end of his rifle. We all had a good smirk at the time, but everyone gave their bayonet an extra wriggle when our turn came to march onto the parade square, after we received the order to 'Fix Bayonets!'

Battalion life in Germany ground on through the year, but some of us were lucky enough to go to Canada for advanced battle group training on the wide plains of Alberta, but towards the end of '73 our training switched back to internal security, in preparation for our next tour of Northern Ireland. We had drawn the short straw, and were returning to the Creggan!

Chapter 5
Northern Ireland – Round 2

The Creggan in winter is a bleak, cold and miserable place. To make matters even worse, we were going to be there over Christmas. During our final pre-deployment briefing in Germany, we were told that things had become really hot in 'Derry. The Royal Anglians, who were covering the Creggan before us, had taken a pasting from the Provisional IRA. The Anglians had lost several young soldiers, to bombs and sniper fire, during their 4-month tour. We arrived in early December '73, and it was raining hard. 'A' Company was posted to an old derelict building known as the 'Shirt Factory'. My platoon was billeted in one dark and cramped room. Bunks were three high, and laid out in three long rows. Under normal conditions, the room boasted space for maybe eight men, but these were not normal conditions. There were thirty soldiers crammed into our platoon 'room', and it was quickly christened 'The Black Hole' by its occupants.

Within he first few days, trouble started out on the streets. My platoon was on oone-our standby, when an emergency call came in from the 'Ops.Room'. Our Colour Sgt. rushed in and shouted.
"One platoon is in trouble, get your kit on, MOVE!"
So much for one hours notice. Everyone grabbed their flak vests, rifles and belt kits and ran for the vehicles. The vehicle park was almost outside our front door, and we scrambled into a convoy of Saracens and Land Rovers. Our Platoon Commander, 2nd Lt. Phil. Chapman was receiving details of the incident over the radio, as he set off in the first Land Rover, at the head of the convoy. He relayed instructions to each vehicle commander, again, by radio.
Nobby yelled at us. "One Platoon is cut off up by the Community Centre. We're going in to get them!" Our vehicles raced through the Creggan, and as we arrived Nobby shouted. "De-BUS! De-BUS!"
The rear door swung open, and we jumped out, into a real Apocalypse Now war zone. Jagged lumps of broken paving slabs and glass lay scattered everywhere. Burning tyres littered the area. Showers of stones were hitting the vehicles, and bottles smashed on the road, spraying out shards of razor-sharp glass. A petrol bomb exploded off to the right. Amidst the chaos, our section took cover in some adjacent gardens. As well as my rifle, I was carrying an FRG (Federal Riot Gun). We used them to fire 'rubber bullets' at rioters. The rubber bullet was appox. an inch and a half in diameter, and about seven inches long. It was manufactured from highly compacted rubber, and was extremely solid.

I spotted a rioter creeping up a hedge line, towards Blacky and Eaton. I brought the FRG into my shoulder and fired a rubber bullet at him, just as he was about to throw a bottle at my two mates. We were trained to fire the rubber bullet in front of the target, and bounce the round off the ground, into the targets shins. Fine in theory and practise, but this was the real world. I could only see the top half of the rioter; the hedge covered the rest of his body and legs. I aimed at his head, and pulled the trigger. With a loud bang, the rubber bullet whizzed towards the target. The baton round hit him hard; bouncing off his head just above his right ear. Not a bad shot from thirty yards. The guy dropped like a lifeless sack of spuds. I really thought for a moment that I'd killed him. Nobby shouted. "Good Shot, Dave!" A couple of seconds later, the paddy stood up, shook his head, and ran off. I hoped his bloody head hurt! The rioters dispersed quickly after a couple of our CS tear gas canisters landed in their midst, and we had followed up with a baton charge. Afterwards, the int. boys thought the Provos were just testing our reaction times.

Their message was clear - 'Welcome back to the Creggan, boyos!'

When you patrol a dangerous area, you must get to know it quickly. In a city like Londonderry, there are thousands of potential sniper positions. One of our sniper 'hot spots' was at the back of the Shirt Factory. There were two ways into our base, the main entrance, used by vehicle and foot patrols, and another, smaller, steel gated entrance at the rear. If a patrol wanted to leave or return via the back gate, it had to be unbolted by the guard first. The problem with the rear gate, was that it opened onto 'Sniper's Corner'. To get into the Creggan estate proper, we had to sprint up a steep, open grassy slope for about 100 yards, before we could get into any cover at all. This area was a death trap. Sooner or later, things would kick of. You also get to know some of the louder inhabitants, and their dogs. One old woman called Mrs. Macartney, had a huge Alsatian she'd named Rebel. She deliberately trained the dog to attack British soldiers. The old cow would let this mad beast out when our foot patrols were passing, and several of our men had been badly bitten. We decided to shoot the dog, but were stopped on the day of its 'execution'. The papers were full of a story about a soldier in Belfast being done for shooting a dog, which had just bitten one of his patrol. They wouldn't wear his defence that he thought the animal might be rabid, and he was punished severely for his actions. Our section was sitting in the cookhouse having a brew, when we were joined by a young L/Corporal from three platoon called Steve Long. The savage dog business was high on the agenda of conversation; but what could we do about it? Shooting was now out of the question, and running the bloody dog over with a Land Rover wouldn't work, as old Ma McCartney only released Rebel when foot patrols were in her street.

56

"Leave this to me," said a smiling L/Cpl Long. "I've got an idea. I'm off on leave to England at the end of the week for four days R & R (Rest and Relaxation). I'll sort it out when I come back."

We tried to find out what he had in mind, but he laughed and said we would just have to wait, and see...

Steve duly came back at the end of his short leave break, and joined us in a huddle in the 'Black Hole'; sitting amid an acrid cloud of cigarette smoke and stale farts.

"Right!" he said. "What you probably don't know is that my uncle is a chemist. When I went on leave, I looked him up, and explained our problem to him. He was a Para in the war, right, so guess whose side he's on?"

We all laughed, and leaned a little closer. Steve explained that his uncle had told him to come back in 24 hours, and he would have something nasty cooked up. Steve turned up the next day, and his uncle drew him aside, gave him a small packet and said, "This will sort that bloody dog out; I picked some Water Dropwort Hemlock down by the river, dried and powdered it for you. It's extremely lethal to animals, and humans for that matter, so be very, very careful with it."

You could have heard a pin drop in our corner of the Black Hole. Steve put his hand in his pocket, and pulled out a small white paper packet.

"This is it. This stuff will kill a bloody elephant!" He proudly declared. Someone asked how we would get the dog to take its medicine?

"I've thought of that too," said Steve. He dropped a cooked army sausage onto the table. "Right, I need a razor blade, and a needle and cotton. Oh yeah, and a pair of N.B.C. (Nuclear, Biological and Chemical protection) gloves."

The boys shot off, and moments later, the gear Steve had asked for appeared on the table, in front of him. Steve pulled on the thin black rubber gloves, picked up the razor blade, and slit the sausage open. He scooped out about half the meat, and lay the part-filled skin to one side.

"I don't now just how dangerous this stuff is, so you had better all stand well back; I don't want anyone sneezing onto the table," said Steve, picking up the white packet. We all backed off, but couldn't take our eyes off him as he continued his devilish work. Steve opened the packet, and gently tapped the deadly powder into the half-empty sausage. Finally, he was happy that it was all in. He started sowing it back together with the needle and thread. When he was finished, he dropped the sausage into a clear plastic bag, and rolled the bag up tight.

"There we are, done!" he said through a grin. "Who's going to give it to the dog?" Asked Eaton.

"Me!" said Steve, and explained that Rebel had badly bitten his Gunner, a couple of weeks earlier.

"Fair one!" Said Eaton, slowly nodding his head. Steve's platoon were out on patrol the next morning, and we had to wait until they walked through the gate at Snipers Corner, at the end of their patrol, to hear the final chapter of the Rebel saga.

"The old bag opened the door right on schedule. Out came the dog, barking its head off as usual. I chucked the sausage at its feet, when she wasn't looking. The sausage was gone in an instant, then, so was the dog. It froze for a second after it swallowed the sausage, shuddered a bit and keeled over. We just patrolled on down the street, as if nothing had happened." We didn't have to wait long for the results, as each section made a point of passing old Ma McCartney's house two or three times during their patrol period, for the next couple of days.

No further sign of Rebel........Job done!

It is a funny thing about dogs, and their bond with British squaddies. Although we had got rid of a nasty vicious animal, which had been deliberately trained to attack us, we all really liked dogs. There were always strays wandering about the camp, but one sticks in my mind. A few months before, a small mongrel called Scruffy had become part of 'A' Company. The poor little thing had taken a half brick on the nose during a riot, and had been picked up, unconscious by a soldier, and taken back to base. The medics stitched its nose back together, and nursed it back to full health. After that, Scruffy was a hard core army dog. We all slipped Scruffy the odd treat, so he was well fed. He had his private army blanket in a corner of the 'Black Hole', and slept with us in his own little bed. When we went out on foot patrol that was Scuffy's chance for walkies. The odd thing though was that Scruffy would always go for young Irishmen. He must have remembered one of them throwing the brick that hit him, because he didn't muck about. I saw him chase at least one bloke up a lamppost. Although just a wire-haired terrier, he stood there barking and snarling at the poor sod. The bloke pleaded with us to call our dog off, but we just said that he wasn't ours. When we moved off, so did Scruffy, and the bloke made his escape.

Action never came when you expected it, and always came when you didn't. We were patrolling through the top end of the Creggan one morning, when we heard several loud bangs and got a frantic 'Contact' message over the radio. 'Contact' messages always meant contact with the enemy. Shots had been fired at our mobile patrol, which was only two streets away at the time. We doubled towards the incident. The radio crackled, and Nobby yelled for us to split up. Half the patrol went down one street, and half down the other. His plan was to cut the gunman off. Vic shouted at his three men to follow him, and the rest of us legged it after Nobby. When we reached the end of one narrow street, there was a building at the far end, closing it off. If the sniper had chosen our route, he had to be in that building. We cautiously approached it, but Nobby raised his hand, and we stopped. The building was a kindergarten, and we could hear a girl's voice singing a nursery rhyme, and lots of little hands trying to clap in time.

"Shit" said Nobby "We've got to search the place, any volunteers?" Nobby was standing at the entrance.

"I'll go." I said, walking up to the door. I got level with Nobby and the door suddenly opened. There stood a very pretty, red-haired girl of about twenty-five.

"I'm sorry love, I've got to search the building." The girl frowned at me, and didn't budge. "You're not coming in here with your guns, you'll terrify the little wee children," she still stood blocking the doorway. I looked towards Nobby.

"She's right Nobby; we don't want to scare the little people inside, do we?" I said as I shrugged my shoulders, and handed him my rifle. "Right then Miss, time to take a quick look inside." The girl looked shocked, but stood aside. I really had had enough of the being treated like a hated oppressor. I had been brought up to give up my seat to a lady on the bus, and that a man's duty was to protect women and small children. Personally, I couldn't care less whether someone out there was Catholic, Protestant or a Cloud worshiping hot-and-tot. Having taken months of abuse, here was a perfect chance to prove to at least one Northern Irish citizen that the British army weren't there to oppress anyone, just keep the peace. As I walked into the main children's area, all I could see was a couple of brightly-coloured beach balls, some huge cushions and a dozen little faces looking up at me.

"Here's a nice soldier man come to see us," said the girl, sensibly playing her part.

"Hallo, children." I said happily to them and waved to the little mites. A couple of the kids waved back, but most were more interested on the T.V. and the bird on it singing Humpty Dumpty. I quickly finished my sweep; the place was empty, no gunman. As I walked out, the girl opened the door for me. I thought I had made a good impression, and built a little bridge along the way. I hoped that she was going to say something kind and meaningful as I stepped past her into the street, but alas, she did not. I smiled at her anyway. "Sorry I had to do that. Any chance of your 'phone number?" I asked. She smiled sweetly back at me and whispered.

"Fuck You," as she slammed the door in my face.

Because we patrolled a staunchly Republican, pro-IRA area, all the houses in the Creggan estate were to be considered potential Provo 'safe houses'. If they were not sheltering wanted men, they might be used to hide terrorist arms, equipment or explosives. Many of the tenants left their front door keys in the locks. Not unusual in most homes, but in the Creggan, keys were left in the outside of the lock. We were briefed that this was to make an entry easy, should a fleeing gunman need a place to hide. The doors might be closed, but they just ran up to the door, turned the key, and they were in, safe and out of sight. I was tasked once to act as an escort to a W.R.A.C. (Women Royal Army Corps.) girl, during a house search. We used our army girls, because they tended to be better with women and children, while a house was being 'sorted'. It can be tricky to deal with a very angry Irish lady, who doesn't want her house searched in the early hours. If an army girl was on hand, we let them handle that sort of problem. I was dead chuffed when I was chosen to act as the W.R.A.C. bodyguard. I strutted about the black hole, making sure to everyone, that I was the one who would have a girl to chat up. When we assembled at 01.00 hours, for our final briefing. I met her. I was horrified! The lass stood at least 6ft. 4 inches tall and probably weighed at least five stone more than I did. She wasn't exactly pretty, Steve whispered to me that she looked like her face had caught fire, and someone had beaten out the flames with a spade. She just said "Hallo," to me, in a voice deeper than mine. When the front door went in at 02.00 hours, I shouted to her to get behind me as I ran into the house. To my utter amazement, she shoulder charged me. I went one way, while she took the stairs two at a time. When I reached the top of the stairs, she had her riot baton drawn, and was leading the lady of the house out of her bedroom. My brief was not to get involved in the search, just protect the W.R.A.C. girl. I rather sheepishly followed them down into the living room, and stood guard. When the search was over, as we walked back to the Saracen, Vic whispered to me that he thought I'd pulled, and gave me a wink. I had a terrible mental flash of her scurrying away like a two-ton spider into the darkness, with me tucked under her arm! Ah well, you can't win them all. I took a considerable amount of stick from my buddies until a Land Rover arrived to take her back to her lair, wherever the Hell that was.

During another search, I was an active member of the search team, and tasked with looking around the attic. Like anywhere else in the United Kingdom, most homes in the Creggan were clean and tidy. However, unfortunately, not this one. As the children were gently herded downstairs, Blacky notice that one of the kids was covered with lice. On closer inspection, all the kids were covered in the tiny white insects. The house was heavily infested. I didn't fancy crawling around the loft, but those were my orders, so up I went. The filth and muck were almost impossible to describe. I was close to chucking up. I found used sanitary towels and soiled nappies scattered everywhere during my search, but no terrorist equipment. Why that soiled rubbish was up there, I have no idea, as I found nothing illegal, despite a very thorough search. When we got back to camp, I bumped into the Colour Sgt. In his stores; he had boxes of red tins stamped with the legend: D.D.T. I told him how awful the conditions had been in the house, and asked him for a tin. Thankfully, he obliged. When I got back to my bed space, I stripped off, and covered myself with DDT. Finally, I jumped into my sleeping bag, having covered my clothing and boots in the same white powder. I left the red can on the floor beside my bunk, and it was gone when I woke up. Someone else must have had the same idea. It wasn't just hardware we were looking for however, but information as well. I got a big pat on the head from the Company brass for finding a list of teachers from a local secondary school in a bedroom drawer, during another house search. The Battalion Int. cell had spent several months trying to find out who worked at the school, and when I spotted a long list of names typed on some A4, I took it, and passed it to the Int. rep. during the de-brief. It was a complete staffing breakdown of the school, from the headmaster, right down to the caretaker's assistant.

We were patrolling on Christmas day 1973, and what a miserable day it turned out to be. Having enjoyed many happy christmases with my family, this was the first one I had ever missed. Up until then, Christmas had always been something special. Sadly, half expecting to be shot at any moment rather spoils the Yuletide magic. As always, it was wet and cold out on the streets. At about 11. 30pm on Christmas eve, we stopped a car in the High Street. The elderly driver was full of Christmas spirit and pissed out of his tiny mind. Filled as he was with Christmas goodwill to all men, he offered me a bag of mince pies. I accepted them gratefully, and having searched his car, let him go. If the R.U.C. had been with us, they would have nicked him for drinking and driving. But we were soldiers, not policemen, and it was Christmas. As the old boy weaved off up the otherwise deserted road, I showed my spoils to the boys. "Probably full of powdered glass," said Vic.

I didn't want to find out the hard way, so I chucked the bag and its contents over a hedge. Merry Christmas from the Creggan.

After a couple of months of patrolling, guarding and searching, we were all starting to feel the strain. One Saturday night, I had just finished a long four-hour guard duty. I was stiff, cold and fed up. Having nipped into the cookhouse and grabbed a big mug of hot tea, I settled down with another mate of mine called 'Killer' to watch the television. Killer was a nickname for a real pint-sized dynamo. He had done very well during the lightweight division of the Invictor boxing contest, back in Germany. He had earnt the nickname, when he took his similarly sized opponent apart at the seams during his own bout. Although he was a pretty small and quiet bloke, he changed in the ring from Dr. Jekyll into Mr. Hyde. Anyway, there we were in an otherwise deserted room, lounging in two tatty old armchairs, having a fag, drinking tea, and watching the opening titles of Tales of the Unexpected on the television. Suddenly, there was a titanic boom outside, which shook the entire building. Killer and I fell over each other grabbing flak vests and rifles. We both tried to get through the door at the same time, and spilled out into the cold Londonderry night in a heap. Although it was dark, a huge pall of smoke was silhouetted clearly against the night sky about fifty yards from us. We ran as fast as we could towards the explosion, and found the Colour Sgt. had got there first. He was carrying Bill Simpson over his shoulder. Bill was unconscious and clearly hurt. He was bleeding profusely from a nasty head wound and our 'Colours' was getting him clear of the danger area, so that first aid could be administered. "Get up there and stand guard, you two," he ordered as he staggered past. As we turned to comply, the other former occupant of Sanger seven was also being carried out. It was Chalky Palmer, one of Eaton Gail's drinking mates. Chalky groaned as he passed us, but at least he was still alive. We climbed the wooden steps, up to what was left of the Sanger 7. The stench of burnt sandbags and detonated explosive was overpowering. Half the Sanger was blown away in the massive explosion. The roofing timber joists were six by two-inch timbers, and had been smashed like matchsticks. The blast came from the left-hand side, completely destroying that part of the Sanger. Killer sniffed. "RPG round," he said knowingly. The RPG 7 was a Russian anti-tank rocket, fired from the shoulder. The large hollow charge explosive warhead was capable of stopping a 30 ton medium sized main battle tank. We were warned that the Provos had them, but this was the first time I had seen the result of one, fired directly at us. The Provos had been supplied from Libya, where even now. R.P.G.s are two a penny. We set about trying to rebuild the left hand sandbagged wall. There were enough undamaged sandbags lying around to make a solid wall standing about waist high. The cold Atlantic wind whistled through the huge gap, and we froze. During the limited rebuild, Killer found the field telephone buried under a pile of loose sand, reconnected it, and to our utter amazement, it still worked. We heard a clipped, hollow sounding voice say

"Cpl Denny, Guardroom." We reported in, and immediately asked when someone was coming to relieve us. "No-one available at the moment, I'll tell you when," came the unwelcome and ominous reply. Killer and I had just finished a miserable, boring four-hour stag, and now; we were looking down both barrels of another four hours, freezing our nuts off. Sure enough, we didn't get relieved for almost that long, but the Sgt. Major brought us a mug of hot tea. "Well done you two," was all he said, apart from informing us that Bill and Chalky were badly concussed and cut, but both would live. Ah well, No Victoria Crosses and a double guard duty of nearly eight freezing hours. Never volunteer! I really must try to remember that.

62

One wet cold afternoon shortly afterwards, I was summoned to the Platoon Commanders room. Walking up the corridor, my mind raced with thoughts of what I'd done wrong. I hadn't dropped a clanger anywhere that I could think of, so what did he want me for? When I arrived outside his door, I squared away my beret, pulled my collar straight, and knocked. If I'd done something really wrong, I'd be up in front of the Sgt. Major. This didn't feel right at all! Mr. Chapman opened the door. I saluted.

"Ah yes, Black, come in." He smiled at me. This was getting worse by the moment. "Take your beret off, sit down and relax."......Oh Gawd!..... "How are things going, Black?"

"Emm, good Sir, very good." I stammered like a complete twat.

"I've had a long chat with your section commander Cpl. Clarke, and I've spoken to the Sgt. Major and the O.C. (Officer Commanding - Major Bullock).

Christ, this is it!...

"We are all very pleased with your work this year, and you are hereby promoted in the field to Lance Corporal."

I sat there, frozen like a statue. For once in my life, I didn't know what to say. Being promoted from private to lance corporal normally happens after passing a long, tough Non-Commissioned Officers course. Guys can serve for years without ever making the necessary grade. I'd been promoted in the field, under operational conditions, just over a year after joining the Battalion. This was a real honour!

"Wow! Um. Great, err... Terrific!" I was still gibbering. If I didn't pull myself together, he might realise he was promoting the village idiot and change his mind!

"Well done Corporal Black." Mr. Chapman shook my hand as I stood up. "I think the Sgt. Major wants a word with you, before you go back to your section." He thumped me hard on the back as I walked out. "You've done very well here, and in Germany, and deserve your promotion."

"Um. Err. (get a grip)..... Yes Sir. Thank you Sir," was the best I could manage, as he closed the door. Christ! Did that just happen? Suddenly, I was an N.C.O.! Although lance corporal is a rank below a full Corporal, both are still formally addressed as Corporal. I'd have to get used to being called Corporal Black, and taking a lot of stick from the boys. I went up to the Company office to see Dave Ormrod, our Sgt. Major. The door was open, and I walked in. Dave Ormrod was on his feet in a flash and charged up to me. "Congratulations, Cpl. Black!" he said. "Thank you, Sir." I replied, grinning like a Cheshire cat. "You have done well this year. We're moving you to three platoon, tomorrow. You're taking over as second in command of one-three-Charlie". I'd expected that, they normally moved a new N.C.O. to another platoon within the same company when a promotion took effect. I felt rather gutted at leaving two platoon, but this was the price that had to be paid for promotion. Luckily, my new patrol commander was a good bloke named Alan Biddles. He was also a L/Corporal, but had six months seniority over me, so he was in command. That night, my last with one-two-Charlie, the Sgt. Major arrived with a full case of beer. I had taken loads of good natured stick from my buddies in the section, but we had smuggled in some beers, which were nearly finished when Dave Ormrod arrived. Normally, each soldier was allowed two cans of beer, per day. He chose to turn a blind eye to the dozens of empty beer cans scattered around us.

"I thought you and your mates might like a beer to celebrate your promotion, Cpl. Black," he said. He put the case on an empty bed, and pulled out a can. When it was open, he raised it in my direction and said,
"Cheer's lads, help yourselves."

I knew all the blokes in 3 platoon, and most were good men. There were one or two I wasn't too sure about, but time would tell. My new platoon's patrolling tasks were the same as with 2 platoon, so I just got on with the job. The Provisional's were taking a break, and absolutely nothing happened for a week or so after my promotion, until one morning when my section patrolled across an open area called the Green Walk. The west side of the Creggan area looks like any other run down council estate. Loads of shabby terraced houses, with rubbish, broken prams and old tyres heaped here and there, scattered about in small, untidy front gardens. Running through the estate, from one end to the other was Green Walk. This 800 x 100 metre grass strip neatly cut the estate in two. At one end of Green Walk was the local community centre, and at the other was the heavily fortified Rosemount R.U.C. Police station. In order to patrol throughout the estate, it was necessary to cross the Green Walk via one of several roads that cut directly across it. On this particular morning, my section was crossing Green Walk somewhere in the middle of the estate. I was taking the lead half of the patrol across, and thinking of my forthcoming four-day R & R. leave, back to England. Suddenly, there was an almighty 'Crack' just above my head; followed almost instantly by a loud thump. The sounds didn't register for a split second; then they did. Jesus! I was being shot at! There was nowhere to take cover, so I zigzagged 50 metres to the other side of Green Walk. I dived down behind a heap of paving slabs, which had been piled on the pavement. It seemed that I covered that 50 metres in about 2 ½ seconds flat, but the sniper got off another four or five shots off at me, before I disappeared behind cover. At least one high-velocity bullet cracked past my nose so close that I smelt the burning tracer in its base. Keeping my head and body down, I rolled to the other side of my barricade, checked my sights, and looked back across Green Walk, along the barrel of my rifle.

The sniper was still firing, but I couldn't find him. The enormously aggravating problem was that in a built-up area, there are so many echoes, that it's almost impossible to locate a gunman by sound alone. You need to see movement, or a muzzle flash from the sniper's rifle, but I could see nothing. To add to the confusion, a stray dog, which had been sniffing inquisitively around the pile of slabs moments before, had lost the plot when I almost landed on it. The angry mutt tried to bite me, but I managed to keep it at bay with my boot, while I frantically searched for the sniper. It just wasn't like this in the movies! I managed to clip the growling dog with my toecap, and it pissed off with a yelp. The firing stopped, but I waited where I was, hoping the bastard would show himself. Two of my guys were laying prone in the gutter, in the middle of Green Walk. For a moment, I thought they were dead, but they both suddenly jumped to their feet, and ran helter-skelter back into cover. Nothing happened for several minutes, and then our mobile backup patrol arrived. The gunman had taken a powder and legged it, but thankfully hadn't hit anyone in the section. Mind you, we hadn't hit him, so when we arrived safely back at Rosemount Police Station, over a very welcome mug of hot tea, we all agreed that we would call that one a draw.

Luck plays a part in any four-month tour of Ireland, and we enjoyed another big slice a week later. We were out on foot patrol again, approaching Green Walk from the opposite direction. Alan signalled for the patrol to stop, while he checked out a parked vehicle. We all slid into whatever cover we could find. The guy ahead of me, Harry Russell, got down behind a hedge in a nearby front garden. Now Harry wasn't the brightest soldier in the platoon, but even he knew something was wrong with the small crate which lay on the ground, about two feet in front of him. It had an electrical wire running into it and had just made a noise which sounded like a loud 'Phutt'. Harry called me, and I nipped into the garden to see what he wanted. He pointed to the box and said, "I think it's a bomb!" I glanced at the smoking crate, grabbed his collar and shouted "Out!" I yelled into my radio to warn Alan, and took cover. Alan ran over to me, and I told him what had happened. "Sounds like a misfire'" he said. We both walked over to the box, saw the wire attached and came back to Harry. "I'll radio for bomb disposal; let's get the locals off the street." Apart from a woman walking past pushing a pram, arm in arm with her husband, the street was deserted. We told them to move away as quickly as possible. When the engineers arrived, they sent in Goliath, a small wheelbarrow sized tracked robot vehicle with a video camera and remotely fired shotgun. The shotgun was used to shoot into a suspect package. The blast would usually disrupt any device inside, before it could detonate. The shotgun blasted the box, and the engineer collected the pieces.

"Plenty of homemade explosive and 6" nails, but it looks like the detonator failed; you were dead lucky mate!" Poor old Harry was as white as a sheet, but at least he was alive and in one piece. This sort of stress affects people in different ways; Harry went on leave after the tour was over, did a bunk, and never came back. There was a twist to this tale, which demonstrates just how professional the terrorists we faced every day were. We later got an Intelligence report, which said that the Provo. on the other end of the firing wire had concealed himself just up the street. When he touched the electrical wire to a car battery and the bomb failed to detonate, he stood up, walked into the street and calmly put his arm around a girl pushing a pram.

"I'm IRA, don't say a word." She was too frightened to say anything. They walked through the patrol, and he disappeared off somewhere into the estate.

No sooner than I had settled in with my new section, than I was moved again. I was called into the Company office having been called on the base's tannoy system. "Come in Cpl Black, sit down," said the Sgt. Major. I did as ordered and Dave Ormrod explained there were some changes being made, because the advance party were starting work, to move the battalion in a month's time back to Germany. As a result, several key senior corporals were being taken out of the firing line, to assist with the massive job of preparing to move 600 men, their weapons and equipment halfway across Europe. Added to that, a couple of the Company's Lance Corporals were finishing their term with the army in the next week or so, we were going to come up badly short of Non-Commissioned Officers.

"You are going to be a patrol commander, Cpl. Black. Can you handle it? He said.

Yeah, I could do this, I thought. "Yes Sir!" I said, looking him straight in the eye. "No problem!" The army works on rank, and seniority. I was the youngest L/Cpl in the battalion, with only a month's seniority, but I was it, there just wasn't anyone else. He told me which section I was going to lead, added some more general bits and pieces of information then said.

"You'll do fine, Cpl Black." Leading a section wasn't a problem to me, I knew the job, had plenty of confidence, and I was working with good men. I took over the section, told them the score, and got on with it. There wasn't much action in the last few weeks; not that is, until the advance party of the Grenadier Guards arrived to learn the score on the Creggan. We had a hard core of big senior N.C.O. Guardsmen arrive one day. These guys would lead their Companies when we officially handed over to them in three weeks time. As they were all very experienced soldiers in their own right, I was tasked with taking four of them out on patrol with half of my section, so that they could learn the danger spots, and particular areas of interest. We left the base via 'snipers corner', and I started showing them the ropes in the Creggan estate. There were some areas, which were better avoided at certain times. One of the hot spots was outside a big secondary modern college, where most of the teenaged kids from the Creggan went to school. Just before nine in the morning, there were several hundred pro-IRA and very anti-Brit. teenagers loaded with testosterone outside the gates of St. Mary's, spoiling for a fight should an unwary patrol get within stone throwing range. As the school overlooked the Green Walk, it wasn't a good spot to get ambushed by hundreds of yobs. We were ordered to give the area a miss at that time in the morning under normal conditions. I thought about it, and decided these senior Guardsmen needed to see just how quickly trouble could start, in this very sensitive area. I made sure that we patrolled close to the school at 8.45 hours, and the kids kicked off with a hail of stones and bottles, right on schedule. We were taking some serious flak, when I used my FRG. I'd been carrying a CS (tear gas) round for three months, and I was itching to fire it at the little bastards. They had spent the last few months chucking half bricks at us whenever they thought they could get away with it. Enough hearts and minds already, now was my chance for a bit of payback. I broke the large bore single barrelled gun open, and slid the shiny CS round into the breach. It went home with a satisfying 'Clung'.... I snapped the piece shut.

"Firing CS" I yelled, to warn the patrol, they might need their respirators. BOOM! The tear gas cartridge arced through the air towards the angry crowd, leaving a thin wispy trail of white smoke behind. It landed and burst in the middle of them, and the effect was instant. The teenagers ran coughing into the school in a matter of seconds, and the 'riot' was instantly quelled and over. What I didn't know, however, was that a Brigade H.Q. order had been issued to our Battalion that morning, forbidding the use of CS gas without specific permission from the Brigadier. I hadn't been told, and acted to defend our 'guests' from the Grenadiers, by firing the minimum gas to quell what had the makings of a nasty riot. Well, that's what I innocently told my Commanding Officer when he roared, moments later, around a corner in a two Land Rover patrol.

"I see." he said frowning. He knew I was pulling a fast one, but there was nothing he could do about it. "I'll have to sort this out with Brigade," he said absently, shaking his head as he climbed back into his Rover. As the Colonel's convoy moved off, the R.S.M. was standing up, looking through the top hatch of the second Land Rover. In fact, he was staring straight at me. His eyes were slits, but there was nothing he could do about the stunt I had just pulled either, and he didn't like it one little bit. I could feel his laser eyes burning through my flak vest, until his vehicle turned a corner, and disappeared. My Sgt. Major knew all about the incident when we returned, and he loved it! So did the Guards Sgt. Majors. To a man, they all volunteered to go out on patrol with me again next day!

My second tour was nearly over; when we got word that my old patrol had scored a huge success. Acting on information received, they smashed their way into a house at about eight o'clock one morning. The house overlooked our base, and enjoyed a commanding view of Sniper's Corner. Two IRA terrorists entered the building during the night, and locked up the elderly occupants in a cupboard, at gunpoint. They were preparing to shoot the next patrol that left camp via our base's back gate. The bastards gave up without a fight. A WW2 American Garrand semi-automatic rifle was recovered from the scene. It was fitted with telescopic sights, and loaded with armour piercing bullets. If my old crew hadn't arrested them, it would have been a slaughter, when the terrorists had opened fire. Nice one, one-two-Charlie!

Chapter 6
The End of the Beginning

The next phase of my life went wrong, seriously wrong. It was the third and most crucial stage of my military life so far, which inevitably steered me towards the SAS.

The Battalion move back to Germany went well, and we had ten days to sort ourselves out, before we went on leave. I finally sowed on my Lance Corporals stripe. On an emergency tour to Northern Ireland, no-one wears rank insignia. Officers and N.C.O.'s are always the first target for snipers, so it isn't a good idea to advertise rank status. First names were always used when out on patrol, irrespective of rank. Anyway, I spent the ten days poncing about wearing my new L/Cpl's stripe, sampling the delights of the Corporal's Mess for the first time. As my mates couldn't use the Corporal's Mess, I still wanted to drink with them in the NAAFI. I got a shock one evening when I had a pace stick shoved in my ear. Apart from the fact that it bloody hurt, the R.S.M. was on the other end of it!

"If you want to keep that stripe, I suggest you get off to the Corporals Mess, where you belong!" He growled. I jumped up, and shifted locations damned quick!

We packed our kit, and went home on leave. Three weeks rest. My dear old mum cooked a special late Christmas dinner for me, and I got my presents then. On Easter Sunday, I was invited to an unofficial air rifle shoot, with some old mates from the T.A. John Griffin only lived a mile from me, so we both went along. This is where things went badly wrong. Through a million to one chance, I took a .22 Cal. airgun slug in my right eye. It wasn't anyone's fault, just a bloody silly accident.

The boys rushed me down to Edgware hospital's Accident and Emergency Dept. The Doctor admitted me, and I was quickly taken down to theatre for an operation to save the eye. The slug had shattered the sunglasses I was wearing, and my right eye was full of bits of slug and glass. The surgeon spent several hours rooting around, picking out various sized shards of razor-sharp glass. After 187 micro-stitches, and several pints of blood the operation was over. I had to wait for nearly two weeks, before the dressings came off. Had they saved my sight? The long wait was terrible. In fact, it was two weeks of real hell. Finally, the big day arrived. I wanted to know, but I was dreading the outcome. When the last bandage came off, the surgeon told me to open the eye. I slowly complied, and was rewarded with a bright fuzzy image. The eye still worked! The surgeon had removed my eye's lens during the operation, because it was so badly smashed by the glass and slug. I was assured that could be sorted out with a contact lens in due course.

There was still a lot of pain, and the surgeon suspected there was still some glass embedded somewhere at the back of the eyeball. I had a second operation a month or so later, and they found two more big shards of glass. The surgeon told me after the second operationthat that there were still a couple of tiny bits of glass embedded in the back of my right eye, but they were both insignificant, and too difficult to remove, so the plan was to leave them where they were. He also gave me some more bad news. With traumatic eye injuries, he said, there was a remote chance that sympathetic ophthalmitis could set in. He explained that sometimes, the sight in both eyes could suddenly shut down permanently after an accident such as mine. He assured me that it was highly unlikely, but still a possibility. If it didn't happen in the first two years after the injury, I'd be in the clear. On the bright side however, the intense pain had stopped. To add to the pot, I now had a cataract forming on the damaged eye. It takes months before a cataract is 'ripe' and can be removed surgically. The nearest I can describe it, is that it's like looking through a frosted glass window. The worse the cataract gets, the thicker the frosting. The army were brilliant during this period. They checked the details of my injury, and placed me on temporary UK sick leave. I got the message from the Battalion to get my arse back to Germany, as soon as I was fit and well. The injuries to my eye were healing, but as the eye is so delicate, I was forbidden to do any physical training. After six drab months, I was climbing the walls with boredom. I was cut off from all my mates in Germany, and was starting to feel really sorry for myself. The doctors fixed the cataract, but I made the mistake of opting for a local anaesthetic. I didn't want to take up a bed space while recovering from a general anaesthetic; I thought some little old lady might need it. It wasn't very nice having a numbing injection straight into the eyeball, or having someone rooting about with a bloody great needle in the damaged eye while I was fully conscious. Still, the operation was completely successful, and I got over it.

While walking home from the hospital, I made up my mind; to sort things out. I contacted the army and requested to be returned to duty. After making a thorough nuisance of myself, I was finally sent back to the depot where I had done my basic training. I helped out in the stores for a couple of weeks, and was then attached to 'Tiger Company', 4th Royal Anglian Regiment at Windmill barracks in Canterbury, Kent. 4th Royal Anglian was only at Company strength, and acted as a demonstration unit for the army's officer Training Academy at Sandhurst. It only happens maybe once in a lifetime, but I immediately fell foul of the Administration officer of 'Tiger Company'. His name was Captain Bass, an ex-R.S.M. who had been commissioned, and now acted in a purely administration role. It started when he ordered me to change my cap badge. I was proud of my Regiment, and wore the badge in my beret with pride. It represented the focal point of my identity, which now of all times I desperately needed to hang on to. I had nothing against the Royal Anglians, but I was attached to them, not transferred. I refused point blank to change, and it kicked off. Capt. Bass still had the voice of an R.S.M., and he blasted me with both barrels of it. As I was standing to attention in front of his desk at the time, I felt that his roaring was going to blow my eyebrows off. R.S.M.'s usually get their own way because they know Queen's regulations backwards and keep within the framework of rules and regulations that govern army life. I dug my heals in, and requested a court martial, as I would not re-badge. This made him even angrier, but I can only assume that he was trying to operate outside his authority as he finally gave in and yelled.

"GET OUT"

I didn't hang around, but beat a hasty retreat. I spent the next month avoiding Capt. Bass, acting as Guard Commander, on permanent night time guard duty. This wasn't a punishment; it was all I could do, as I was still medically downgraded, and not yet fit for full active duty. I requested permission for a medical board to re-establish my fitness. If the Board of army doctors were happy, they could order me back to my own Battalion in Germany. For some reason, which I've never fathomed, Captain Bass rejected my request for a Medical Board. I was trapped. If I wanted to get away from this grumpy old bastard, and get back to Germany with all my mates, I needed a plan...

From time to time; my progress was monitored by the Military Eye Hospital at Millbank, London. The army's top eye surgeon was Brigadier K.P.Milne. He was a charming old gentleman, and had always been very kind and sympathetic to my situation. I telephoned the Hospital at Millbank, and organised a change to my next appointment with Brigadier Milne. I had a days leave due, so jumped on a train for London when it came. I hopped a tube, and walked the final part to the hospital. When I was called in to see the Brigadier, I explained the problem to him.

"I think I can help, young man," he said with a wink. "I can do your Medical Board examination now!" I passed the examination with flying colours, and he told me not to worry, he would see to the paperwork. I thanked him profusely, and left, clutching a medical 'Chit', which showed my new, higher medical grading: Fit for active service. I was going back to Germany, or so I thought. I marched into Captain Bass the next morning and presented him with my 'chit'. He put on his reading glasses and looked at it....I've never seen a volcano erupt in real life, but Bass gave an amazingly lifelike impression. He grasped the arms of his chair, and his knuckles went white. His whole body shook, moments before he started bellowing at me. He was clearly very, very pissed off at what I'd done. He was bellowing about the chain of command, and that I'd sidestepped his authority, and gone over his head. All quite true, but he wasn't finished yet. He ended with a statement of fact. He couldn't care less if I was fit for duty or not. He would not permit my return to Germany. As I sat in my room later, pushing my eyebrows back into place, I decided there was only one thing for it. I wrote a letter to my Commanding Officer in Germany, and explained the whole story, and said I had passed my medical board and done my duty etc. etc. and simply couldn't get any orders cut to return. I posted the letter, crossed my fingers, and waited...

I left the guardroom a couple of days later after finishing my usual night time Guard Commander duties. The sun was shining in a cloudless blue sky. The air smelt clean and fresh; it was a gloriously beautiful Kent morning. The birds in the trees were singing their little hearts out as I approached the administration block. I heard Capt. Bass in full flow, bellowing, I assumed, at one of the clerks. I couldn't make out exactly what he was saying, but he clearly wasn't too happy with something, and was giving vent in true ex-R.S.M. style. I pitied the poor sod on the receiving end of his ravings, and wondered what had started him off this early? As I opened the door to my room, a clerk rushed up to me.
       "Capt. Bass wants you in his office, NOW Corporal!" The penny dropped; he must have heard from my Commanding Officer! That's what all the noise was about. Full of antisipation, and some forboding I doubled around to the Admin. Block and arrived at his door. I was really for it this time. I squared my beret, said sorry to my eyebrows, swallowed hard and knocked.
       "Come in!".....I opened the door, and saluted. "Right, you're going back to Germany, get your kit packed." He was looking down at a signal sitting silently on his desk. That was that, the interview was over, best not to say too much.
       "Yes Sir" Trying not to smirk, I saluted again and beat it. The clerk gave me a travel warrant, and my movement instructions, which ordered me to RAF Lynham the next day. I was to catch a Royal Air Force flight to Germany. I'd done it; I was going back!

I caught the flight on time next day, and arrived in Germany at RAF Guttersloe an hour and a half later. When I had collected my kit from the baggage reclaim hall I made my way to the Arrivals desk. I checked in with the duty RAF clerk and was sent outside, to a waiting military bus, which would drop me at my base in Werl. There were several drop off points before mine, so I had to wait for my turn. Eventually, after a long tour of North-western Germany, we arrived outside the main gate of my Battalion. When I got off, and my kit was unloaded, the coach roared away, heading for its next stop. No brass bands, flags or cheering crowds, in fact, nothing. I picked up my suitcase and kitbag, and walked up to the guard, who was standing by the gate. I didn't know him, must be a new boy. Having shown him my I.D. card, I wandered up to the 'A' Company's office, to report in. I saw Moggy Moore, the 'A' Company Clerk. After shaking hands and a bit of idle chit-chat, he gave me the good news. I was on guard that night. So nice to be back.

I found that most of my kit had been pinched while I was away. Nothing personal, the boys didn't know if I was coming back, and it was quite usual to share out a missing man's gear. I spent the first few days tracking down some bits and pieces, and scrounging what couldn't be recovered. It was strange, but something more than just my kit was missing. It was wonderful to be back with all my buddies, but it just didn't feel the same. I suppose that the last nine months had changed me, and I needed something more out of soldiering. The routine was really much the same, but I didn't feel that I was 'growing' as a soldier any more. Infantry soldiering is great fun, but when you know it, there isn't really anything new to learn. Promotion is fine, as leading men is always a challenge, but even that ends up as the same-old thing. Although I had left the Battalion as its youngest and most junior lance corporal, I had returned with nine months seniority! There was a big exercise brewing in Saltou Training area, and I was given the rank of acting Corporal, with a section of my own. Like my internal security job in Northern Ireland, I knew the armoured warfare role, although I had never controlled a full, mechanised infantry section before. The Sgt. Major once again voiced his confidence in me, and that was that. I had been away for nine months, and was suddenly a full section commander! I was potentially in the shit, and had pulled the deep end. Saltou Training area is situated on a vast, flat heathland plain in central West Germany. It is ideal for mobile armoured warfare training, and the entire Battalion, including its tracked armoured vehicles, faced a long slow train ride, to get there. On the morning of the start of the exercise, the vehicles were driven about twenty kilometres to the civilian railway marshalling yards at Hamm. Each 432 was carefully driven onto a long series of flatbed railway wagons, and firmly chained into position. I hadn't been a 432 commander before, and had never been responsible for loading a fifteen-ton armoured vehicle onto a train either. It wasn't difficult though; I simply guided the driver, using standard hand signals, as he slowly edged the 432 forwards along the train. When all the vehicles had been secured, and the connecting ramps stowed, we boarded the railway coaches at the front of the train. My section was comprised of mainly new boys, but my second in command, L/Cpl Ricky Brass was a good man. The journey took seventeen hours. The German railway network uses a priority system, and military trains in peace-time rank pretty much at the bottom of their pecking list of important trains. We were shunted into sidings more often that I can remember, while higher priority civilian express trains thundered past. Our train was being pulled by a big old steam engine, which managed the journey slowly, coughing out clouds of thick black acrid smoke. When we arrived, the engine was uncoupled, and the train was shunted up to an unloading ramp. The flatbed connecting ramps were re-attached, and the vehicles were driven off.

Saltou was a hot dry dust bowl; it hadn't rained for weeks. The sandy soil threw up clouds of thick choking dust, and it was a relief in our second week, when my patrol was ordered to stop, dig in and guard an important crossroad. When the trenches were correctly sited and prepared, we sat in our camouflaged foxholes and waited. Although armoured battles are fought on the run, we now formed part of the 'front line'. A small group of our 'blue forces' battle group was going to withdraw through the crossroads, then regroup, ready for a massive armoured counter attack. The 'red forces' (enemy) would then punch through our strategic position, and drive straight into a blue forces trap. We had been safely dug in for a few hours, and nothing was happening when I absently started to scratch. We were all hot and dirty, but we were used to that. When I noticed the itch, it felt rather strange. I itched all over my stomach. I undid my jacket and shirt, and spotted something white and very small scampering into the darkness of my waistband. "Christ, I've got crabs!" I yelled, jumping out of the trench. I dropped my trousers and spotted more of the tiny spider like insects scurrying about my body. It was at that moment when the radio crackled, and I heard my call sign. I quickly pulled up my strides and answered. Company H.Q. reported that contact with the enemy was imminent. I yelled to the section to stand to, and jumped back into my fire trench. Within a couple of minutes, we heard the sound of vehicles coming towards us. I scanned the area to our front through my binoculars. Driving towards us at great speed were three fox armoured cars, flying blue flags.

This must be our rear guard, beating a hasty retreat. The foxes flew past us, and the last vehicle commander gave me a wave, and pointed back in the direction they had just come from. He finished his signal with a thumbs' down. This was the standard army hand sign for 'enemy'. As the sound of their engines receded, we picked up a new sound coming towards us. It sounded like a deep rumbling, a rolling thunder, and was getting louder by the second. There is only one thing that makes that dreadful sound....Tanks! After what seemed like moments, the first huge tank turret breasted the ridge, four hundred metres away. I called in a 'contact' over the radio. The ground was beginning to shake, as more of the monsters appeared. Five, no six, of the 60-ton giants rumbled towards the crossroads. These were 'red forces' Chieftain main battle tanks. If this had been the real thing, we wouldn't have stood a chance. The sections anti-tank weapon was a single 84mm Carl Gustav rocket launcher (or Charlie Gee, as it was often known). It looked like a fat stubby bazooka. It packed a fair wallop, but wouldn't have scratched these beasts. On my order, the Charlie Gee Gunner chucked a couple of thunder flashes to simulate firing his anti-tank gun, and we immediately received a salvo of red very cartridges from the tanks. This meant they had simulated firing their huge 120mm main guns at us, and we were now history. The ground shook like an earthquake as the tanks rolled past us, and the noise of their mighty engines was deafening. One of the tank commanders gave us a cheery wave as he roared past. We returned the wave with a hand sign which only means one thing...Wanker! He grinned, and waved again, then disappeared into the bowels of his steel monster.

When the tanks had gone, and the dust started to settle, I received orders over the radio to re-deploy the section to another location. Abandoning our slit trenches, we quickly boarded our 432 and set off. Using my map, I found the best route to our next point. It was necessary to leave the road, and follow a long and winding track across the vast training area. Unfortunately, as we crossed a dry, sandy river bed, the 432 decided to throw a track. My driver hit the brakes hard, to avoid further damage. The vehicle shuddered to a halt. I ordered the section out of the vehicle, and we surveyed the problem. Sure enough, the steel track had parted company with the 432, and lay like a huge twisted snake, just behind our vehicle. The complete track is made up of heavy 'links' held together by thick steel rods. There is a fixed drill for putting a track back on. We had all seen the SKC army training film, and I'd helped replace one once before. It looked so easy in the film; all the soldiers were wearing smart, clean uniforms, and carried out the operation in near perfect conditions. The 'Corporal' issued clear, crisp instructions and after a couple of shouts of "Hup, Hup and Heave, Heave" the track was on, and the job was finished. Yeah, Right! Here we were, miles from anywhere, with only two of us who had done it before. And to cap it all, I'd got crabs. I collared the 432's driver, and told the boys to get a brew on. I talked through the entire routine with my driver and sorted out who was going to do what. Over a mug of tea, I briefed the section on how we were going, to get things sorted. I reported our situation to our Company H.Q. via the radio, and we got down to it. It's a long, slow business putting a track back on. Each track weighs in at around a ton, and it takes a lot of serious effort to split the track, and then position it, ready for re-attachment. It's all down to a good plan, and plenty of brawn at the end of the day. H.Q. had informed us that they would send a recovery vehicle at some stage, but it was tasked elsewhere at the moment. We were to proceed with repairs ourselves. After several hours of heaving, pushing, pulling (and in my case scratching), we had the upper hand. The track was in the right position to be re-attached, and it only remained to hammer in the last retaining steel pin. We were all pretty shattered, and it was getting dark. When the pin was in, and the job was finished, the recovery vehicle arrived.... Bloody Typical! When the R.E.M.E. (Royal Electrical and Mechanical Engineers) Staff Sgt. had checked our repair and made sure we were in good mechanical shape, he called me over and opened the back of his specialised 432 recovery vehicle.

"OK" he said to me, out of earshot of the others. "Do you want a case of beer? 15 marks!" The R.E.M.E was famous for two things....They were excellent mechanics, and they could always be relied upon to have plenty of Beer on exercise! I gladly fished out the money, and unloaded a case of decent German ale. I asked the R.E.M.E. staff Sgt. to radio in that we needed another hour to finish our repairs, which. with a smirk, he did. When he had gone, I walked back to the section, and passed each of them a couple of beers. I told them they deserved some decent refreshment, for a job well done. Lots of little faces lit up, and suddenly, life wasn't so bad, after all. We all felt a bit better, when we arrived at 'A' Company's concentration point. When the vehicle was camouflaged, the section put up their poncho tents. I had given them their arcs of fire and briefed them on that night's password. I handed over to Ricky and went to see the Colour Sgt. I told him about the 'crabs' and he asked me what they looked like.

"No, Crabs are black. I know, 'cos I've had them," he laughed while I scratched my crutch. "Sand lice," he said, and fished out my old friend, a cure-all red tin of D.D.T. When I returned to my section and started splashing the powder all over myself, the boys asked for some; they all had the same problem, but didn't like to say....

After three weeks living in the cuds in Saltou was over, and we had returned to Werl, I needed to make some very serious decisions. My three-year hitch with the regular army was coming to an end. I had been offered a second stripe on a permanent basis, if I extended my regular service and signed on again. I loved soldiering but felt that the infantry didn't have anything else to offer me. I knew I could do well if I stayed on, but there just wasn't anything new to do, within the confines of the infantry. I also still had a problem with my eye injury. Not a physical problem, the injuries had long since healed. I was approaching my 21st birthday, and didn't quite feel a complete man. The truth was that the trauma of the entire incident had left me feeling less than 100%. To my mind, there was only really one solution. I needed to take on a challenge and beat something so overwhelming, so ludicrously difficult, that if I could crack it, the whole history of my injury would mean nothing, and I could move on. Over and over during my regular service, I'd heard references to the shadowy SAS Regiment. 22nd SAS, the regular Regiment, was based in Hereford. There were also two Territorial (part-time) Regiments. 21 SAS, which covered the south of England, and 23rd SAS, which covered the Midlands and Scotland. Having made some enquiries, I now knew that these three regiments made up the Special Air Service 'Brigade' (or 'Group'). I would have to re-enlist in the regular army to have a crack at regular SAS selection, and if I failed, it would be soldier on back in the infantry for another three years, minimum. I wasn't sure that was the right path to follow. No, I had a better idea. The army has its own telephone system, and I picked out the number of 21 SAS (T.A.), at the Duke of York's barracks, in London's fashionable suburb of Chelsea. I chewed it over. Should I give them a call? I thought about it hard for several days. If I wanted to learn new soldiering skills and find more adventure, then this seemed the path I must follow. I had nothing to lose, so to hell with it, what harm would a phone call do? I waited until I was battalion Guard Commander, and had access to the military phone system. I dialled the number, and it rang several times.

"Orderly room, 21 SAS Regiment," said a voice from distant Chelsea. I explained who I was, and that I was coming out shortly, and was thinking about having a crack at selection. The voice said. "One moment, please," and the line went silent. There was a hollow click, and I heard the line ringing again.

"21 SAS Training Wing, Sgt. Smith speaking Sir!" Said a gruff voice. I introduced myself, and explained again what I was thinking of doing. "Best you come in and see us laddie, when you're back in England," said Sgt. Smith. I thanked him, and hung up. I sat looking at the 'phone for several moments. Blimey, I'd done it; I'd made first contact with the famous Special Air Service.

PHASE TWO

Chapter 7
Selection, SAS Style.

Within the British military, there are several elite Regiments. The Royal Navy has the Royal Marine Commandos and the Special Boat Section, and the army has the Parachute Regiment and the Special Air Service. All these units use their own tough selection courses to weed out the unworthy, and their pass standards are extremely high. The ultimate goal of any candidate is to pass the selection course, and earn their chosen Regiment's coveted beret and cap badge. The Royal Marines have a green beret, and the Parachute Regiments is maroon (red). The SAS wears a sandy coloured beret, with the now famous winged dagger cap badge. The Green, Red and Sandy berets are only presented to successful candidates, after they have passed their full selection. It is their ultimate prize, earnt only after months of hard gruelling work!

I chose the SAS, because, with all due respect to them, the Parachute Regiment are airborne infantry. Their main reason for being is to be able to parachute large numbers of men into a specific area, to carry out a specific infantry job. The Paras are renowned for their ferocity in battle, and have earned their reputation through courage, determination and true grit. But I needed more than an infantry role; I wanted to learn all the military skills I could, and get away from the same old basic training. I had set the ball rolling, now was the time to stand up, and be counted.

My first face to face contact came shortly after I had left Germany. When I was back in England on four-week pre-release leave, I decided to visit 21 SAS Training Wing in Chelsea, and have the 'chat' with the training staff. Having reached the nearest tube station at Sloane Square, I walked up the King's road to the Duke of York's barracks. When I reached the main gate, I enquired where the Regiment's Training Wing block was. The guy in the Gatehouse directed me towards 'B' Block. "Training Wing is opposite mate," he said, pointing me in the right direction. I followed his line across the car park and walked past 'A' Block, where 10th Battalion the Parachute Regiment (T.A.) was based. 'B' Block was dead ahead, and I could see a small winged dagger sign on the building opposite, with the legend 'Training Wing - 21 SAS' emblazoned on it. The car park outside Training Wing had several military Land Rovers, and a four ton lorry parked outside. I went to the door beside the sign. It was open, so I entered, and walked up the stairs. At the top, I hit a short corridor. To my right was a door marked 'Training Wing Staff Only', and to my left were doors marked 'Training Wing Office' and 'Classroom'. I knocked on the office door and waited for a moment before the door opened. In front of me stood a short, stocky guy wearing a normal army green fatigue uniform, and German para boots. On his head was a sandy beret complete with winged dagger cap badge. On his right arm was a set of black SAS parachute wings.

"Yes mate, what can I do for you? He enquired. I explained why I was there, and he simply said, "Come in." I sat down in the office, and he explained the outline of selection. SAS selection is broken down into two very different phases. The first part is the famous 'mountain phase', and the second is the less well known 'Continuation Training'. The course kicks off with a series of weekend hikes across the Black Mountains, in South Wales. These are really just conditioning weekends where each candidate carries increasingly heavy loads in their bergan, and starts practical map reading. The bergan is a large green military rucksack, which holds its shape with the aid of a tubular 'H' frame. Large pockets are attached to either side of the main 'sack' to increase the bergans load carrying capacity. The whole bergan is held close to the body with the aid of broad shoulder straps. When the work up phase of selection is complete, he told me, the course moves onto the Brecon Beacons. After several weekends marching individually on the Beacons, Test Weekend arrives. Passing this gets the candidate to a week on Selection Camp. At the end of the Selection camp phase, the dreaded forty-five kilometre 'Long Drag' march must be completed, within a set time limit of 24 hours. Only when Selection Camp has been successfully passed, can a recruit move on to the Continuation training phase. Special tactics, Weapons, Escape and Evasion, Survival and Resistance to Interrogation were just some of the skills to be learnt during this period.

"You can get binned anytime on the mountain phase," warned my S.A.S. instructor. "But don't think it's easy, because we normally lose about 80%+ of recruits during the mountains. We lose another 10% during Continuation!"

Sweet Jesus, this guy was quoting an over 90% failure rate. What on earth was I letting myself in for? I was used to military selection, after tough regular basic infantry training, but this was going to be something else! The instructor finished his introduction to selection with something, which has always stuck in my mind. "You don't have to be Superman to pass, if it was impossible, no-one would make it. But you do have to be very fit, and want to pass more than anything else in your life!" These words were still ringing in my ears, as I sat on the tube rumbling up the Northern line, on my journey home. More than 90% wouldn't make it...Christ! What sort of bloke would get through I wondered? Did I stand even the slightest chance. Had my daft plan to re-invent myself, made me bite off more than I could possibly chew? Well, I'd just signed the papers at the Dukes, so whatever happen in the coming months, I was certainly going to find out the hard way!

I received orders through the post, instructing me to report to Training Wing at the Duke's on a Tuesday evening at 19.00hrs, in three weeks time. The orders didn't say much else. I was still trying to decide what I wanted to do as a civilian job. I didn't fancy working in an office, and I was eventhinking about it when I went for a Sunday lunchtime drink with dad and my uncle Ernie. My Uncle had just qualified as a London black cab driver, and he was full of it. His mate Vic was with him. Vic was a real character, and was also a London cabbie. They suggested I thought about doing the 'knowledge' and becoming a cabbie, like them. There was a Royal British Legion school for London Taxi Drivers based in Brixton, and with my military background, they were sure I'd get a place. It sounded like a pretty good job, good money, working for myself, with hours to suit. It could fit in nicely with selection...but there were two main drawbacks a.) I couldn't drive, and B.) I didn't know London at all. OK these problems could be overcome. Pass my driving test, and do the 'knowledge' and learn London's streets. I was already, in ' I can do anything mode' so what the hell, why not? I applied to start learning to be a cabbie at the Metropolitan Police's Carriage Office in Penton Street, Islington, and was duly enrolled on the knowledge. They issued me with a Blue Book; which listed seven hundred 'runs' through central London. Each run had a formal start and finish point, and I had to work out the shortest route between them, and memorise every road and turning between the two. The Blue Book was actually pink, but it used to be blue, so the name stuck. I already had a small 50cc Honda motorbike, so I fitted it with a millboard. Each route was written on a sheet of paper, and attached to the millboard. The idea was to follow the route on the motorbike and memorise which roads lay between the pick-up and drop-off points. By the time all seven hundred routes had been committed to memory, I'd know London's streets backwards; literally. After a bit of dodging and diving I managed to get into the British Legion's taxi school, and began my training to be a London cabbie.

The first Tuesday parade date arrived, and I presented myself outside Training Wing. There were several fit looking instructors standing by the door chatting, and around a hundred new recruits, all dressed in their own civilian clothes. One of the senior SAS instructors organised us into three ranks, and began to call the role. We were told to answer "Yes Staff" when our name was called. When he had finished, we turned to our right and were led off in single file. The first man was guided through the

Training Wing door, and up the stairs. At the top, we turned left and entered the classroom.

"Find yourself a seat, and sit down...and keep it quiet!" Said a short, mean looking member of the Training Wing staff. When the last man was seated, the instructor said. "Right, this is how we do it. The Colonel will come in and will give you a few well-chosen words. After that, it's down to the stores and draw your kit. When you have all your gear, I want you to come straight back here for a further briefing by the Sgt. Major."

We all sat silently, and let that sink in. "When the Colonel enters the room, I'll give you the order to 'Sit Up'. Sit to attention until the Boss tells you to relax, and No Smoking!" He fixed us with a baleful stare. A couple of coughs from the back, but no-one said anything. The classroom door opened, and the instructor bellowed "SIT UP!" In strode a lean, fit looking Lt. Colonel wearing a sandy beret.

"Thank you Gentlemen, please sit easy" said the officer. Everyone resumed a relaxed sitting position, some slouching more than others. The Colonel looked thoughtfully around the room. He cleared his throat and began speaking to us. He went through a brief history of the Regiment, telling us that the SAS was formed in North Africa in 1941, by David Sterling. At that time, the British 8th Army was locked in battle with the German Africa Corps in the Libyan Desert. The Regiment was dedicated to unorthodox small team operations, which were carried out deep behind the enemy's lines. After formation and initial training, the Regiment scored some huge successes, destroying much of the German's desert air force (and pilots), and causing havoc with the Africa Corp's supply lines. When he had finished his briefing of the origins of the Special Air Service, he got down to us. He told us that we were starting with ninety-three recruits on the course. He invited us to look around, and be aware that most of us would not make it. He warned us that injuries were common, and to avoid them like the plague. Many good men would damage themselves, and be unable to complete the course. Others would fail to meet the strict fitness pass marks. A few would find that family problems would develop, and fall by the wayside. Then there were those who would just give in. They would fail themselves. He advised us that we would not receive much encouragement from his training staff. It was an individual effort. In simple terms, he told us we would get ourselves through the course, or fail. When he felt he had given us enough stick, we got the carrot.

"If you pass, Gentlemen, this course will change you forever. You will start to realise just what you as individuals are really capable of...you will be amazed, truly amazed of what physical punishment your bodies can take, and exactly what you can achieve where lesser men would fail. If you pass selection Gentlemen, and make it into the Regiment, you will have adventures which other people simply couldn't imagine, or even dream of. This is a wonderful Regiment, and absolutely worth the effort. Thank you for your attention, and good luck." With that, he gave a curt nod to the instructor.

The N.C.O. bellowed "SIT UP!" For a second time and the Colonel left the room.

We arrived at the main stores, in the bowels of 'B' block, and were fed down a line of store-men who issued kit to each man, as we shuffled along the counter. We were asked our shoe size, and a pair of brand new black DMS (Directly Moulded Sole) boots was issued. Army shirts, trousers, socks, pants, the list went on. Each man was issued with a surplus WW2 Denison Para. smock and a woollen hat. When we reached the end of the counter, a green army woollen pullover finished off the kit issue.

"Straight back to the classroom," yelled someone wearing a sandy beret. "Come on, MOVE YOURSELVES!"

When we were all seated once again in Training Wing's classroom a tall, dark-haired Sgt. Major walked in.

"Right, shut up and listen. My name is Sgt. Major Swainson. I am the senior N.C.O. in charge of Training Wing 21 SAS" He went through some general administration details, and reminded us that the instructor's word - was Law! "We operate normal military discipline in this Regiment. Backchat an instructor on this course, and you will find yourself binned. You will address all members of Training Wing as 'Staff', and stand to attention when you speak to them . You only have to say that you don't want to continue, and we will take you off the course, and that's you finished. How many of you have been allocated a Squadron yet?" All the hands went up.

"OK hands down. You will use only the clothing and equipment we have provided you with while on selection. If you pass selection, and make it to your Squadron you will see that Squadron members wear plenty of their own gear. You however, will use and wear standard kit while under Training Wing's direction. You'll draw your webbing and bergan from your own Squadron stores, and weapons will be issued by Training Wing before you start each weekend. I'll hand you over to Sgt. Day, who will brief you about your first weekend. Sgt. Day stood up and addressed the assembly. He explained that our first weekend coming up was a 'doddle'. All they were going to do was run us through some basics, which we needed to know, and give us some practical map reading and basic weapon handling. Because it was only an introduction, we would be going to an army training area in Surrey, by lorry in two weeks time. "Move out Saturday and return on Sunday."

After that, it would be every other weekend in the mountains in Wales until Selection camp. Mountain weekends required a Friday night parade, and a collective move up to Paddington Station, where we would get the train to Swansea. From there, it was coaches up into the mountains. 'A' and 'B' Squadron recruits would spend every Tuesday evening in the classroom at Training Wing, at the Dukes. Outlying squadrons would handle their own Tuesday 'drill nights', at their respective drill halls. Basic map reading, mountain survival and weapon handling would be taught during lessons each Tuesday evening. We would need the map reading and survival training when we started working in the Welsh mountains. Having finished his introduction, he told us to parade next Tuesday, in uniform at our respective drill halls, to begin our training.

The next two Tuesday evenings were spent being introduced to the mysteries of the Ordnance Survey map and the Prismatic compass. Time and practice were necessary to master these vital navigation tools. These were the days before G.P.S. satellite navigation systems, we had to do it all the hard way. Our instructors also started teaching the recruits how to strip and assemble their assault rifles. This was all basic stuff to me, but we needed to complete all the drill nights and weekends to pass, so I didn't dare miss anything. Because recruits don't need prior military experience with the Territorial Regiments of the SAS, training starts from scratch. The Territorial Regiment's attitude is that with the proper training, they can mould a man into exactly what they want, and given the intensity of the training, the selection system pumps out men in very small numbers who will do just fine. The course was made up of men from a host of different occupations and backgrounds. Barristers, postmen, bank clerks, even an ex-Hells Angel. Accents ranged from Public School to East End Cockney. There were Commissioned Officers from other Territorial Regiments, ex-regulars N.C.O.s (like myself), policemen, bricklayers, dustmen, a Doctor and a professional stunt man. Our cross-section of society was very varied indeed. It was all the same to the Training Wing staff though. They treated us all as raw recruits. No concessions were made to anyone on the course, irrespective of prior rank or status; we were all just 'recruits', and were treated accordingly.

The first weekend was an easy introduction, and the staff had unofficially nicknamed it 'Exercise - Robin Hood'. I arrived at the Dukes early on the Saturday morning. When the roll had been called, we climbed into the lorries at 07.00 hours, and drove down to the military training area just outside London, in darkest Surrey. We spent the first part of the morning learning how to put up a 'basher' with our green ponchos and elastic bungee cords. Our instructor Cpl. Dean then went through the contents of a 24-hour army ration 'compo.' pack. The ration pack was filled with small tins. Baked beans, bacon grill, rich fruitcake, all sorts of goodies. Salt, matches and a tiny can opener are also included. The briefing was detailed, and even included an explanation of the army toilet paper, which was also in the pack.

"One up, one down, one for the Queen and one to polish." These guys didn't miss a thing. He demonstrated the Hexi stove, and made a brew with one mess tin, while he heated a small tin of chicken curry with the other. He suggested that we stocked up with Mars bars and boiled sweets, because calorie consumption in the mountains over a 24-hours period always exceeded the total calorific value of a 'compo' pack. The pack contained approximately 2,500 calories, but we would burn in excess of 7,000 calories on an average day and night in the Welsh mountains. He went on to say that one of the tricks to passing, was to keep sugar levels high in the bloodstream, because it would be exhausting work when we started selection proper. He guaranteed that we would all lose weight, but would quickly replace it with hard muscle. He laughed, shook his head, and ominously told us we didn't have a clue what we were in for. With hindsight, he was dead right! We had a good practical lesson on using the British army's famous prismatic compass. Then it was time to grab a snack from our 'compo' packs. I fell in with several other ex-regulars, and we chatted and compared notes on the course so far, as we munched on plain biscuits and cheese processed. When 'lunch' was over, we packed everything away in our bergans, and followed the instructor for several miles across the training area. Our next lesson was how to properly pack, balance and waterproof our kit in the bergan. It was looking pretty cloudy, and the wind was getting up. When our lesson was finished, we were told to make camp, and put up our own basher. The army poncho may start life as a waterproof item, but it soon loses that quality. When stretched between some trees in a tent shape, the trick is to get the angle of the sloping side's just right. The tent must be low anyway, but if the side angles are too shallow, the poncho will leak like a sieve. If the angle is too steep however, the poncho leaks when the occupant's body touches it from within; the water leaches through and soaks him. It isn't a barrel of laughs to wake up in the middle of a black night and find one side of you is ringing wet and freezing cold! Our Corporal checked each basher, re-adjusting most. When he was satisfied, he briefed us for our practical map reading exercise. We were put into groups of three, and set off on a cross country map reading course. We were to navigate around a circuit of instructors, each spaced out by a couple of kilometres. We were given a six-figure grid reference, and then took it in turns to show Cpl. Dean where we were going. He set the first trio off on the course going clockwise and the next anti-clockwise several minutes later. He alternated us like this until all his groups were gone. Before each group left 'base camp', we had to set our bearing to the next checkpoint (or RV) on our compasses. We followed the course, going point to point, receiving a new checkpoint from the resident instructor each time we found an RV. It was dark and raining hard when we finally finished the course.

We ended up back at our 'base'. Cpl. Dean simply said to get our heads down and be prepared to move at 05.30 hours the next morning. Someone asked who would wake us, and Cpl Dean told us that it was entirely up to us to make sure we were ready to move at 05.30. By now, we were all soaked to the skin. Some of us stripped off our wet gear and dressed in dry clothing before wriggling into our newly issued sleeping bags. Some couldn't be bothered, and got into their bags wearing their soaking uniforms. Those of us that were dry slept well, but those who were wet must have had a miserable night. It's a hard lesson, but you retain plenty of body heat in dry clothing and sleeping bag. Wet kit means you are going to get very cold, very quickly. We had been told this on mountain survival - lesson one, but some guys thought they knew better, and spent a cramped, cold and dejected night learning they were wrong. The next morning, those of us who were dry, had to strip off and re-dress in our old wet kit. It was freezing cold, and felt grim for several minutes. Once moving about though, the clammy coldness wears off a little. When all my dry clothing and sleeping bag were stowed in my bergan, I lifted it onto my back, and wandered over to the point where Cpl. Dean had told us to muster. Most of the guys were there, and with a minute to go to the deadline, we were still three men short. Cpl. Dean sucked his teeth and walked over to the 'basher' area. There, in one corner were three bashers, still up. Their three occupants were all fast asleep. I'd woken up several guys when I got up, and had wrongly assumed that they would do the same to the others. Cpl. Dean was not impressed.

"What the bloody hell are you doing?" He roared as he hit each basher in turn with a large stick. The poor sods inside woke up with a start, and rolled about; desperately trying to unzip their sleeping bags, and stand up. When they were all finally vertical Cpl. Dean wrote their names in his little black note book. "Get your kit packed, and fall in with the rest" he growled. Three sheepish looking recruits joined us shortly afterwards. "Not too impressed Gentlemen, all of you drop and give me twenty push-ups with your bergans on. Always remember to help each other, always! One, two, three," he counted as we did our punishment. When we were finished, he lined us up for inspection. "And where is your hat?" he said to the first man. "Err, in my pocket Staff," said the recruit. "Well it's not doing any good in there, is it? Put it on and give me 20, and keep your bergan on." The recruit dropped into the prone position and started his second set of 20. Cpl Dean went from man to man, finding fault with everyone. I was one of the last to be checked. I didn't have any pockets undone, and had my hat on. "Smart arse eh? I don't like smart arses, give me 20!" I was nailed, like everyone else. No one escaped; we all did an extra 20. "On your feet and stand still, the lot of you." Cpl Dean walked back to the basher area. He returned a minute later with a handful of litter. "We never leave sign that we're in the area. The hunter force will call in the dog teams, and they will catch you!" he spluttered. "Always clear your basher area, check for any rubbish, and take it with you!" All of you give me 20, NOW!" We quickly assumed the position and pumped out yet another set of push-ups.

"Stuff this," said someone close to me.

"Shhh; or we'll get some more," whispered someone else in a very upper-class accent. When the last man was finished Cpl. Dean doubled us all the way back to the lorries. As we caught our breath, he said,

"You had better buck your ideas up lads, and switch on." He shook his head. "Some of you are in for a big shock when you get to Wales!"

We continued with our Tuesday evening drill nights, still concentrating on the three key subjects at this early phase of our training. They were survival, weapon handling and navigation. During one survival lecture, our instructor had hammered us with the warning that exposure lurked everywhere in the mountains, like a deadly, invisible predator. It would constantly stalk us, and kill us, if we let it. The human body will only work properly within fairly tight temperature parameters.

"Too hot and you die from heat stroke, too cold and you die from hyperthermia." He went on to tell us that we would begin working in the mountains in small groups with an instructor, but as training continued over the coming months, eventually we would be walking in pairs, then alone. He continued his lecture with another warning; the weather on the mountains in South Wales could be savage. It changed incredibly quickly, and unless properly prepared and trained, we might face death on selection. We were taught how to recognise the symptoms of hyperthermia (exposure) in others, and how to avoid it in ourselves. If a member of the patrol we were working with developed any of the symptoms while on the mountains, we would have to stop, and give the necessary treatment fast, or the patient would die. Heat stroke was less likely, but had to be treated with the same caution and respect.

Our first mountain weekend arrived. We paraded on the Friday evening at the Dukes, but noticed several faces missing already. The mood among the remaining recruits was one of apprehension, as none of us really knew what was going to happen over the next couple of days. When we boarded the train at Paddington Station, everyone was lost in their own thoughts. The train journey took several hours, but was uneventful. We arrived at Swansea Station at about 22.45 hours. The rain was lashing down as we paraded outside in the dark windswept station car park. We were split into two groups, and directed onto a couple of large civilian coaches, which were parked close by. When everyone was seated, the drivers started their engines, and pulled out, onto the wet main road. After fifteen minutes, the engines started to strain slightly as we began to gain height. There were increasingly steep banks on either side of us, as our coaches continued to climb through the wooded foothills of the Black Mountains. We passed fewer and fewer houses and vehicles, until eventually we passed none at all for the last ten minutes of our journey. The coaches slowed, turned into a lay-by and stopped. One of the instructors stood up and said.

"Right lads, grab your kit and fall in outside." The rain was still falling heavily as we formed three ranks beside the road. An instructor spoke quietly to the driver in the lead vehicle and stepped off the coach. The door closed with a loud pneumatic hiss, and the civilian drivers started their engines. The coaches turned sharply and disappeared back towards the warmth and glow of civilisation. "Put your bashers up in the plantation over the road, and be on parade at 06.30 hours. Get a good hot breakfast inside you before you come on parade; you're going to need it!" And that was that. We picked up our bergans, crossed the road and carefully climbed over a low barbed-wire fence, which protected the plantation, presumably from sheep. I found a sheltered spot, and quickly put up my basher. It was a relief to sit under it, out of the rain. I pulled out my sleeping bag, and unrolled it. I took off my wet Denison smock and wriggled into the bag. It had been a long day, and I was ready for some sleep. I woke up several times during the night; a mixture of cold, damp and thunder. At 05. 30 hours I gave up trying to get back to sleep. I stretched my back, leg muscles, and unzipped my sleeping bag. The air was heavy with moisture, and I could hear the cold drizzle still hitting my poncho. I climbed out of the end of my basher and stood up. The morning was dull and heavily overcast. After another good stretch I put my damp smock back on. The instructor had said we should have a hot breakfast, and I had plenty of time. I fished out my Hexi stove, and a 24-hour ration pack. When my little cooker was alight, I filled a mess tin with water from a nearby stream and carefully placed it on top of the cooker. While I waited for it to boil, I wandered around waking the others. When I had found as many as I could, I moved back to my basher site. Having made a brew with half the boiling water, I dropped a couple of small, pierced tins of bacon grill and baked beans into the remainder, to warm through. While breakfast was heating I took down my basher and stowed it with my sleeping bag inside my waterproofed bergan. There was plenty of movement around me, as the others stirred and start to get up, and sort themselves out. When breakfast was over, I stowed the empty tins in my backpack, along with the Hexi stove. It was nearly time to be on parade. I climbed back over the fence, and dropped my bergan beside several other guys. The lay-by turned out to be beside a large flat civilian picnic area, which was deserted, apart from us. We were surrounded on three sides by steep valley sides. The road was a dead end, and stopped as it entered the picnic area. As we stood comparing notes on the previous night, two military long-wheelbase Land Rovers arrived, and our instructors climbed out. They stood in a huddle chatting, as the rest of the course assembled beside us. A few of the lads looked fresh and rested, while most looked tired and haggard. At exactly 06.30 hours, Sgt. Major Swainson opened the passenger door in one of the Land Rovers, and climbed out. He cast an eye over us and nodded to a pint-sized instructor.

"Get fell in lads, quickly now!" When we were in three ranks, he called the role. We were then broken down into groups of nine, and given an instructor. We got Cpl. Davies. He explained that the group was large, but would get smaller as the course progressed because of dropouts. "Right lads, pick up your bergans, its time to warm up a bit. Follow me". Cpl. Davies led us up onto a path in single file, leading away from the picnic area towards the cold, grey misty mountains. Cpl. Davies forced the pace, and we gained height quickly. After 20 minutes, we were approaching the end of the tree line. Above this height in the mountains, trees cannot grow. It is too cold, wet and windy. What was left of the highest plantation was shrouded in damp tendrils of clinging mist, as we continued to march upwards, along the track. We were all feeling the results of our fast, 500-foot climb. To those of us uninitiated in mountain walking, calf muscles quickly started to burn, and thigh muscle began to ache. Cpl. Davies eventually called a halt. This gave us all a quick and very welcome breather. Several lads needed to catch up. When we were all together again, Cpl. Davies pointed to a mountain peak, a long way off to our right. It rose nearly 300 feet above us.

"That's our first RV point lads. Now you are all nicely warmed up, take off any pullovers you have on. You'll cook if you wear too much when we climb."

We quickly obeyed his instructions.

"OK lads, keep your bergans as high on your shoulders as possible. Nice and steady now, follow me."

The slope leading to the peak began gently, but quickly became much steeper. It was possible to remain upright, but it felt like trying to climb a very long, steep flight of stairs. Before we were half way, each man had found his own pace, and had begun his private and very personal fight with the mountain. My legs were burning. Every muscle was screaming. The pace slowed, as each man struggled upwards. Cpl. Davies had reached the top, with several super fit recruits, but the rest of us struggled on. He didn't shout a word of encouragement to any of us, just sat and watched as each of us, sweating profusely, finally reached the summit. As we arrived, we were instructed to put our green woollen pullovers back on, under our Denison smocks. When the last man had finally joined us, we were sitting on our bergans in a tight group. Cpl. Davies instructed us to take out our maps and compasses, and began a practical map reading lesson. We had to give six-figure map references on points he indicated from our panoramic view of the other mountain peaks. This session had two purposes. It gained our aching bodies some valuable recovery time, and got our minds switched on to the tasks in hand. If anyone screwed up, they were given the standard punishment of twenty press-ups. After thirty minutes the lesson was over. We stood up and pulled on our bergans. Cpl. Davies pointed to a misty peak about three kilometres distant.

"That's our next RV lads, let's go."

The ground looked fairly flat, with a long slow dip, then a sharp rise to the summit. Silently, we all came to the same conclusion. This one was going to really hurt. Cpl. Davies led off, and we followed. The ground was covered with short, tough grass. It wasn't grass that you see in a lawn, but patchy, brown and half-dead looking. Clearly, hanging on to life up,here wasn't just a problem for us recruits. We covered the first two kilometres at a steady pace, but some guys (including myself) were starting to feel blisters forming on various parts of our feet. When DMS boots got wet, they held the moisture, and doubled in weight. When the moisture had been squeezed through the leather, the socks quickly became wet. Friction results, which can, and normally did cause blisters. I could never understand, with an army as professional as ours, why on earth were we were issued with such dreadful boots? Probably nothing more than penny pinching, by our good friends in the Ministry of Defence? When we reached the base of our next target peak, Cpl. Davies told us to look at it carefully. It looked much the same as the others at first glance, but not so. He told us that straight up was one option, but if we looked closely, there was a sheep track, running diagonally up the slope. Sure enough, after looking carefully, there it was.

"These tracks were rarer than rocking horse shit, but if you spot one, it makes the climb a wee bit easier, and you'll use less energy making the top."

We set off in single file, carefully following the 'track', which was probably no more than nine inches wide. Sheep are normally left to fend for themselves on the mountains, and graze wherever they can find fresh grass. Over countless generations, the tough mountain sheep have worn these narrow paths, which they use to move from one grazing area to another. The climb was still incredibly hard work, but the going was a bit easier. We branched off the sheep track near the summit and stopped. We were all sweating again, but put on more clothing without being told. Cpl Davies told us to get a brew on, which we gladly did. When our Hexi stoves were alight, and mess tins filled from our canteens, Cpl. Davies ordered us to take out our compasses. We had ten minutes to kill before the water boiled, so we had a quick practical lesson on taking back bearings. They are a big help to find exactly where you are, by cross triangulation of your current location. The downside is that visibility must be good, and you can only take back accurate bearings in daylight. When our very welcome brew was over, we packed up and set off towards the next peak. This routine continued throughout the day, as the weather got worse. The wind steadily grew in strength, and the sky was becoming more and more overcast. Cpl. Davies eventually told us it was time to head back to our original basher area.

"We're going to do it in one long hit, so drink as much water as you need. We'll go in two minutes."

He set off at a cracking pace, and we followed, as it began to rain again. The weather was changing fast. The wind had nothing to slow it down on the mountains. It sped up, and heavy with rain lashed into us. By the time we reached our destination, down in the valley where our trek had begun, we were soaking wet, and exhausted. Every muscle in my body was shot, and I felt totally shattered. As we arrived back at the picnic area, Cpl. Davies told us to get a brew and hot meal inside us. Then he gave us the bad news. "I want you ready in one hour, so I can brief you for your night march" Jesus, we were going out again! I sat on my bergan for five minutes, trying to find the energy to start cooking. When I had a hot compo curry and rice inside me, I did start to feel better. It was still raining, but at least we were sheltered from the gusting wind. I lay on the ground, chatting to some of my group. I took off my boots, and inspected my blisters. We had been told not to pop them, as this could lead to infection. Best to put on clean dry socks, and put up with the blisters. After lacing up my soaking boots, I grabbed my empty canteen and limped over to the steam to fill it. Mountain water isn't naturally clean and must be sterilised. We used the issued army Steritabs to kill the bugs. Drop a small white tablet into a full canteen, shake it well and wait five minutes, then add a blue tablet to kill the taste of the chlorine. Boiling water is fine for brews, but if you need a drink during a march, it comes straight from your canteen. There is no guarantee that there isn't a dead sheep floating in the stream higher up the mountain, so sterilisation is vital. The mountains are no place to develop stomach trouble and a severe case of vomiting or the explosive shits. As I walked back to my bergan, I noticed one of the super fit blokes in our group talking to Cpl. Davies. I couldn't hear what was being said, but Cpl. Davies nodded, shrugged his shoulders and pointed over to the plantation. I guessed what the conversation was about; the guy had jacked it in! Before our briefing, I noticed several men from other groups heading for the shelter of the plantation. It had been a tough day, and I wasn't looking forward to the night march, but they had warned us often enough that selection wasn't designed to be easy! When our night march briefing was over, we were broken down into three-man patrols. We had been given our first RV, and warned that we were finished tonight when we were finished. No final RV was mentioned, and Cpl. Davies wouldn't be coming with us. Like our initial weekend, each patrol was quietly set off into the dark at staggered three-minute intervals. The first RV was a point about three kilometres away. It was very dark, and we followed a luminous compass bearing towards our destination. To make it a little easier, the RV was at the corner of a plantation, over a ridge, somewhere in the next valley. Keeping upright is difficult in the dark. As you can't see the ground beneath your feet, it's easy to stumble and overbalance. The weight of the bergan could easily turn the stumble into a heavy fall. We were supposed to move quietly but our tactical move was regularly interrupted, with a scuff, thud and curse, as one of us fell over and hit the ground. After an hour or so of struggling and cursing our way towards the RV, we arrived at our destination. The instructor was sitting under a tree, exactly where he should be. He didn't give us a word of encouragement. Using a shielded torch, he shone a small red light onto his map, and asked each one of us in turn, to show him where we were. Having written our names down, he gave us our next RV. It was almost at the top of the valley, beside a stream junction. He told us to get moving, as another patrol had just arrived behind us. We set off through the rain, and stopped to re-set our compass bearings after fifty metres. It was another three kilometre hike up to the stream junction, but the going was a little easier. Following the same routine as the last RV we were bounced from one RV to the next. After another four hours of marching, and finding another three RVs we were heading back towards the picnic area. I couldn't remember ever being so totally, utterly exhausted in all my life. Because we had been briefed that our times were always recorded, we had done our best to keep up a good pace. My blisters had gone from bad to disaster zone during the night march and I was suffering badly. It was a huge relief to limp back to one of the Land Rovers at the picnic area, and report in.

"Your next RV is ... only joking, go and get your heads down. On parade at 06.30 hours sharp. Coaches at 7.00 hours," said the Sgt. Major. The relief was incredible as I slowly climbed over the fence and allowed my bergan to slide off my aching shoulders. I took my poncho out of a side pocket in my bergan, and strung it on some handy trees. New aches and pains jumped out at me all over my body, as I took off my sodden boots and soaking wet clothes. When I was dressed in dry kit I carefully wriggled into my bag. I needed a brew, but was just too tired to make one. Not much went through my mind, as I fell into a deep, exhausted sleep.

One of the boys banged on my poncho, and I woke up with a start.
"Morning campers," he said cheerfully. I felt as though I had been pulled out of a train wreck. I got some relief after some serious stretching and bending exercises. I felt much better as I started getting breakfast on. My feet were still killing me; each step felt like walking on broken glass, but I just had to lump that. I noticed that most of the boys were limping as they got on with their own admin.

"How do you feel?" I asked one of my fellow recruits.

"Bloody terrible," came the reply from the ex-Paratrooper. That made me feel a little better, it wasn't just me then. Several recruits had returned the previous night with strains and twisted ankles, and a medic instructor had checked over their injuries. The coaches arrived just after 07.00hrs and we sank into the large comfortable seats. The hills looked dark and overcast, and the mountain peaks were shrouded in low cloud. The rain had held off so far that morning, but there was a real chill in the air. Winter was coming, and conditions on future weekends were going to be much worse. When we boarded the train going back to Paddington, that's when the feeling of real relief set in.I made it through the first mountain weekend. It had been a tough and stark introduction, but it was one under my belt, and it was a start.

Chapter 8
Onwards and Upwards

My first mountain weekend away on SAS selection taught me several important lessons. The first was that I needed to work up my fitness level, quickly. Although the weekends would doubtless make me fitter, I clearly had a lot of work to do on personal fitness between each of them. Someone gave me an old style 'A' frame bergan, which I loaded with a fifty-pound block of concrete. Having wrapped the block in an old blanket to protect my back and spine, I secured it into the bergan and tried it for size. The fit wasn't too bad, but I'd try it out on a five-mile run, and see how I got on. Another thing I'd learnt on the first mountain weekend was that the instructors really didn't give encouragement. They had a rather strange air of detachment, bordering on indifference towards the recruits. There was no 'beasting'. They didn't shout and bawl at us, like the corporals at my old regular infantry depot had. During basic infantry training, if a recruit fell behind on a training march or run, the corporals would grab the failing recruit and double him up to the head of the column. They would then yell a mixture of threats and encouragement at the exhausted recruit, and force him to continue. The training was geared to break down the individual, and rebuild him into a team player. It was totally different with Special Air Service selection. A task was set, and it was completely up to the individual whether he successfully finished it or not. If a recruit gave up, or was injured and gave in to the pain, he was finished. The motivation had to come from deep within each candidate. It wouldn't, and couldn't come from anywhere else. Either you completed the set task, or you didn't. It was up to the individual; simple as that.

I finished my first fitness run, a few days after the end of the initial Wales weekend. I'd had to allow several days for the blisters to heal, before hitting the streets. Various suggestions were made on how we might avoid blisters. One recruit suggested wearing two pairs of socks, another recommended pickling our feet in brine. One of the instructors had suggested taping our feet up, prior to marching over the mountains next time. This would reduce friction, and help prevent blistering. It seemed the best option, so I laid in a stock of surgical tape from a local chemist's shop. The initial run had gone well, but the pack was difficult to balance, loaded as it was with the heavy concrete block. I found that the pack slowed me down considerably, but I felt that it was strengthening my legs. It was really hard to go out every evening, and pound the pavements in all weathers, but I had no choice; it had to be done.

After finishing our lectures at the Dukes on one particular Tuesday evening,I was chatting with the boys over a beer. Two of them were fitness training together and had come up with a novel way of building up their stamina. They both lived close to the same block of high rise flats. Wearing track suits and trainers, and carrying their loaded bergans, they climbed to the top of the building using the stair well. Climbing fifteen flights of stairs two or three times per session worked wonders until the caretaker chased them out of the building and told them to bugger off! The number of recruits had fallen after mountain weekend one. We had lost several fit looking blokes, who had decided that it just wasn't for them. Another had been removed because his mother was Polish, and still living in Communist Poland. Security vetting was tight, given that the Warsaw Pact was our greatest threat.

Weekdays were filled with riding around the streets of London on my little motorbike, and gradually, the city's chaotic layout began to fall into place, and make some sort of sense. It was a tough lonely job driving in the traffic clogged roads, but like selection, I needed the challenge.

The next mountain weekend was looming large, and we were briefed about it on the preceding Tuesday evening. We were going to have our bergans weighed during the next weekend, and Heaven help anyone who was caught underweight. We would still be marching in patrols, but as predicted, numbers on the course had diminished, so they would be smaller in size, this time around. I hoped that my extra ten-day fitness training would help, as we were told that distances would increase, and the routes would become more arduous and physically demanding and difficult.

The beginning of the second mountain weekend followed the same format as the first. We arrived at the same picnic area in the Black Mountains, at about 23.00 hours, and set up our bashers. Early the following morning, having had a good breakfast to fuel the start of our day, we paraded as normal. We had a different instructor this time. There was no comfort in getting to know a regular instructor, as they changed each weekend. The course was jumbled up, and I was put into a new six-man patrol. The latest instructor, L/Cpl White ordered us over to one of the Land Rovers. There stood our Sgt. Major, with the Regiment's Adjutant, Captain 'Spike' Fielding. Both men were scowling at the recruits. Sgt. Major Swainson pulled out a large circular set of weighing scales. The scales were hand held, and sported a big steel hook which hung suspended beneath it.

"Right, first man, bring your bergan here, now". The bogey weight was 35lbs for this weekend, and we had all tried to guess, by hefting our bergans earlier that morning. The first recruit came up well short, and was sent over to a nearby scree slope to gather 10lbs of rock. When he had arranged them in his bergan, it was re-weighed.

"Smack on!" said Capt. Fielding with a grin. "Next!" We were all under weight, and each one of us had to make a visit to the scree slope. When our patrol was ready, L/Cpl White led us a short distance away and gave us our first RV of the day, while the next group arrived at the weigh-in point. My bergan certainly felt heavier; I could feel the straps' digging deeper into my shoulders. We set off, initially following the same track, which would lead us up into the mountains. We took a left turn shortly after leaving however, and began following a broad logging track, which led us up into a new area of the mountain range. Clearly, this area was used commercially as a source of harvesting timber, as either side of the track had neat piles of long straight logs stacked along it. The loggers must have only worked during weekdays, as there was no sign of any civilian activity as we trekked along the deserted path. The trees were grown in tidy rows and disappeared up towards the top of the tree line, which was shrouded in the low damp cloud, somewhere high above us. As we continued to climb and finally neared the end of the tree line, visibility closed in around us. The fog grew thicker, until at best; we could only see ten metres in any direction. There was no wind blowing and our cold, white world became enveloped in eerily silence. We marched on, and it became steadily colder. Visibility was still closing in when Cpl White called a halt. He asked us to show him where we thought we were using our maps. We all tried to estimate our location on a time and distance basis. We had been marching for about an hour, and had climbed about five hundred feet, give or take. The track had long since run out, and we seemed to be walking close to a sheer drop on our left. We had crossed a large stream just before we stopped. That should give us the key. We all studied our maps and eventually found where we thought we were. We agreed the spot and showed him our estimated location.

"Hmmm, OK, close enough, let's go" was all the praise we got from him. "While you have your maps out, check how far we have to walk to the cairn."

To mark some points in the mountains, large piles of stone, called Cairns had been built up over the years. We estimated about another two kilometres. We set off once again and reached the cairn after a steep climb. The silence had followed us, there wasn't a sound as we stood beside the ten-foot pile of rock. L/Cpl White gave us our next RV and having set our compasses with the correct bearing; we marched on through the wet clinging fog. Because visibility was by now down to less than ten feet, we were all told to count the number of paces we took. That way, we could tell almost exactly how far we had marched, from our last check point. Given that we knew the distance from our maps between start and finish we should be able to calculate when we were close to our destination. As visibility was down to almost nil, it was vital to check our bearings regularly with our compasses. The RV was a stream junction somewhere ahead of us. I had nearly reached counting up to a thousand paces when we heard running water. We continued for another thirty metres, and there it was. The stream was where it should be, but where was the junction? At L\Cpl White's suggestion we send two men left, and two men right, following the edge of the stream. We had orders not to go more than three hundred paces. My buddy and I counted off three hundred paces, but found nothing. The stream just continued, and vanished into the swirling fog. We marched back in silence.

"Nothing, Staff" was all we could offer. The other pair found the junction one hundred metres to our left. That was a big margin of error, given that we had only marched a thousand metres.

"You must check your compasses all the time when you can't see dick all around you." Our patrol practiced one way of saving energy and making up time. We reached the edge of a long downhill slope, which had a sheep track running down and off to our right. It lay in the direction we wanted to go and L\Cpl. White told us what to do. "We're going to run down this slope, lads. The trick is to keep your backs as straight as you can, and only move your legs from the knees down. It's a sort of flip-flop run, but once you hit the rhythm you will make up for time you lost climbing up to the top, and as a bonus, you will save a lot of energy. One word of caution though, keep it steady, and don't fall. Chances are that you will break something if you do."

We ran down the slope, and it worked! We lost seven hundred feet in no time. When we reached the bottom, we were all panting hard, but carried on without needing to stop for a break. That was a trick worth remembering, as it was bound to come in handy in the future. The rest of the day entailed the usual point to point, but as we had been warned, there were more of RVs than last time. The extra weight was starting to tell, and I was feeling hollow and burnt out again by the time we got back to Cefn Lwyd. It was dark; I was soaked in sweat, and we only had three-quarters of an hour to get our evening meal and hot brew. Before we were allowed to take a break, we were called over to the Land Rover, and our bergans were weighed again. Most of the bergans were fine, except one poor sod who had made up his weight that morning with a couple of extra full canteens of water. He had drunk the water during the day, but hadn't bothered to refill them when he had the chance. He got an almighty bollocking from a senior member of staff, and was sent with his tail firmly between his legs to the scree slope again. He had been ordered to bring at least a twenty-pound rock back, which put him way over the 35lb required weight.

"Do that again my son, and you will be failed on the spot. Understand?"

"Yes Staff …. Sorry Staff," came the sheepish reply.

I wandered off to the fence and pulled another layer of clothing on, and got cooking. When I had a hot meal inside me, I sat down and lent on my bergan. I rested for the fifteen precious minutes I had left. My feet were blistered again. The skin which I had taped up was fine, but new areas were red, raw and burning. All too soon, it was time for our briefing. We were split into pairs, and I got rock man. When we had received our first RV my new partner, and I checked our maps, and set off. The pace was slow, as I was suffering badly with my blistered feet, and my partner was carrying plenty of extra weight. We plodded along and reached the first RV. The corporal sent us off to the next RV, which involved a long climb, up a steep rocky slope. The pain in my blistered feet had eased off a bit. Jump starting them after a short break at the RV was always murder, but they numbed out a little once I had been walking for a while. We found the second RV, after wandering around in the dark for a short while, and checked in. This went on until the early hours when we were finally directed back to our base. As I limped in, the Sgt. Major was waiting with his scales. He grinned wolfishly at me.

"Feet bad, Black? Want to jack?"

"No Staff, I'm fine thanks," was the best I could manage with a weak smile, as he checked my bergan.

"Get your head down, coaches at 07.30 hours." He called to my companion "Right Rocky, get your began off, and bring it here."

There was no question that things were getting tougher. Comparing our first and second mountain weekends in the bar, after training on the following Tuesday evening, we could see that everything was becoming more demanding. The Staff were less friendly and more remote than ever, and we were all starting to feel a bit hunted. We had one more weekend left in the Black mountains, before we moved over to the Brecon Beacons. We were told that if we felt the Black mountains were bad; we were in for a real shock when we hit the big time on the Beacons. More guys had disappeared off the course, but I just couldn't understand it. They appeared miles fitter than I was, and always finished ahead of me, but suddenly, they just weren't there anymore. I felt sure I could make the distances, and carry the weight, but the constant fear was could I make the times demanded by the Wing? We all carried the same worry, but in the end, we just had to get on with it. Comradeship is a powerful factor during adversity, but it was difficult to make any really close friends at this stage. We all shared the same worries (and blisters), but how can you establish firm friendships, when they might not be there next week? My fitness training was hampered again by waiting for the blisters to heal, but I cracked on as soon as I could. I could now easily run the five miles carrying my 50lb. Bergan, but decided that I must try to improve my times, and started running against the clock. If I could reduce my overall time by a minute or so each time I went out, it stood to reason that I had to be improving my stamina and fitness. Not being a natural athlete, I had to work very hard indeed at my general fitness levels. I had lost what little body fat I had been carrying and my thigh muscles were like iron when I tensed them. My calf muscles were much bigger. OK, things were not perfect, but I think I was still ahead on points, just!

Our third Black Mountains weekend was different. The format to get there was much the same, but when we fell in on parade early on the Saturday morning, there was a strange air of urgency among the instructors. We queued up to have our bergans weighed with a few extra rocks added here and there for those who had just guessed wrong. Some of us had borrowed the scales before the weigh-in, and had opted to go up to forty pounds. Ultimately, we would need to train up to 45lbs on the Beacons, and we wanted to try and get a bit of extra benefit beforehand. The Sgt. Major fixed us all with his most baleful stare.

"We're looking to bin some of you this weekend lads. The course is still too big. It's our last weekend, before we go to the Beacons. If you struggle on the marches today or tonight, there isn't much point in going on with the course. It gets much, much harder on the second half of this phase of your selection!"

There were a lot of glum faces when we started that morning. We were already down to half the number we started with and were now in five-man patrols. We had Cpl. Connor. He looked like a lean greyhound on two legs. To our great surprise, he started us off at a reasonable pace, as we marched off in single file up into the mountains. It passed off as a nice day for a change, with no rain, a bit of wind, and good visibility. As we reached the high ground, he picked up the pace. After following him for about half an hour, he gave us some bad news.

"We're going to cross some long stretches of moon grass, and believe me; it's a bitch to walk on, but you must get used to it!" He pointed to a peak about four kilometres away. "That's our first RV today."

We checked our maps and set our bearings. Without this preparation if the weather suddenly clamped in and visibility worsened, without reference points to guide us, we would be lost, before we knew it. Shortly after we set off, the patrol reached the moon grass. Thick dustbin lid sized clumps of coarse grass stretched out in our direction of march, as far as we could see. The clumps were tightly packed, fighting for every available inch of space. Because each clump was humped in the middle, it was simply impossible to put a foot down on level ground any more. Every step invited a twisted ankle, and our pace slowed as a result.

"You must keep up with me" yelled Cpl. Connor, who didn't seem to notice the grass at all. As we increased our speed, we were using more energy staying upright. He was right; this grass was an absolute bitch to march on! When we finally struggled to the peak's summit, we were all showing early signs of exhaustion. All except Cpl. Connor, that is. He looked as if he had hardly broken into a sweat. Bastard! We stopped for a brew, as we sheltered from the growing wind just below the peak's summit.

"It's almost all moon grass country on the Beacons lads; anyone want to jack?" Laughed the lithe corporal as he took a long swig from his water canteen.

Our next RV was closer than the last, but once again, we had to cross an ocean of moon grass to get there. Brew over, we set our compasses and moved off. The combination of the extra weight and slippery wet grassland was starting to take its toll. We all tried our best to keep pace with our instructor, but inevitably, we started to slow. Falls were frequent, and consumed even more precious energy with the added effort of standing upright again. To make matters worse the wind picked up and was driving cold squally rain into our faces. This was proving to be our toughest test so far. Unfortunately, we were not yet really being tested; this phase was still just classed as 'conditioning'. We had climbed several hundred feet crossing this area of moon grass, but so far, I had not started feeling any more blisters. My feet were wet, but heavily plastered. So far, so good; it seemed fine in that department. When we reached our next rendezvous several of the lads were limping from falls they had taken over the last few kilometres. Two of them looked done in. We had been walking for three hours and needed a break.

"Right, lunch time lads, we'll take a short break." Said our instructor.

Someone whispered. "Thank Christ for that." Cpl Connor must have heard, but with a wry smile chose to ignore it. We started cooking, and Cpl. Connor checked the two lad's injuries.

"Nothing broken, but they need strapping," he said. We all carried elastic bandages, for just such injuries. When the ankles were firmly strapped, and their boots replaced, Cpl. Connor offered them a way out. "There's shed loads more moon grass ahead of us lads, if you want to jack it in, there's no disgrace." They both protested, and insisted it was nothing serious. "OK, it's your call at this stage, but if it's too bad when we get back to base later, I'll call in the medic, and he will decide if you carry on, or not!" It was cold as we ate in silence, reflecting on the fact that anyone of us could be terminally stuffed by nothing more than a badly ricked ankle. We had made it this far, and it would be awful to get binned over something as stupid as a pulled or twisted muscle.

We cleared the ground of any trace of our short stay and set off on the next leg of the days march. Cpl Connor had warned us that there were boggy stretches ahead. We had all heard the stories about these deadly mires. The rumour was that some were bottomless, and behaved like quicksand. If you blundered into one, it would hold you tight, as your own weight made you slowly sink ever deeper into the morass. One recruit had a lucky escape on selection several years earlier. He had reached the stage of marching across the mountains alone when he had become trapped in a bog, and had slowly sunk up to his waist. He didn't panic, and had the sense to drop his bergan and use it as a floatation aid. He hung on for several hours, until, purely by luck; a local sheep farmer had found him. The farmer managed to pull the recruit out. Although he was very late making his next RV, he explained what had happened. After contacting the farmer and checking his story, the Regiment decided to let the guy continue. He eventually was successful and passed the selection course. We hit the first bog after half an hour. Looking lush and green, it sat silently waiting for anyone foolish enough to try to cross it. Cpl. Connor stopped at the bog's edge and showed us how to recognise this natural booby trap.

"The colour is your first clue; its rich green colour comes from all the water underneath it. Look at the ground. See the slight depression it's in? If you're on your own, and you fall in, this bastard will kill you! Always walk around it, never ever try to save time by going through it." The bog looked about two hundred metres across. We walked around its edge until we were back on our original line of march. As the hours ticked by, we struggled through more moon grass and managed to reach our next RV. After a short break Cpl Connor gave us a new grid reference. To our surprise, it was down in one of the valleys, on a road junction. We continued until we started to lose height. The mountain side was steep, but at least there was no moon grass. It only seemed to grow on fairly flat ground. We half-walked and half-slid down the mountain until we reach a green pasture full of bleating sheep. The ground was quite flat. According to our maps, the road junction was only a kilometre away. High hedges surrounded the fields we were crossing. They were too thick to push through, so we had to make our way to each field's gate. We reached the RV, where a Land Rover was parked. Two fit looking instructors climbed out as we approached.

"Alright Tom? Enquired one of them to Cpl. Connor.

The Corporal grinned. "Yeah, fine. I've got two ankles for you to look at Charlie; one of them might be bad!" The instructor Cpl. Connor had spoken to looked past us towards the two limping recruits, who had fallen way behind. When they arrived, the instructor called them over.

"I'm Staff Sgt. Bannister, and I'm the duty medic this weekend."

SAS medics are taught to an incredibly high standard. They are trained to stitch cuts, patch up gunshot wounds and administer drugs and antibiotics. They can diagnose and treat a huge number of ailments. They need this high level of skill, as when a four-man patrol is out in enemy territory on operations; the patrol medic is doctor, nurse and medical orderly to the rest of his patrol. However shot, mangled or burnt they are; he has to treat and hopefully save them, using his medical skills and training. When the two recruits had their boots off, S/Sgt. Bannister checked the first man. He gently pushed, pulled and rotated the damaged ankle, and asked various questions about the injury.

"It doesn't look too bad; I'll strap it up again, and we'll see how you get on tonight. If the pain gets worse though, tell the instructor on the next RV you come to. I'll pass it on beforehand that you are carrying an injury. Now get away, get a hot scoff inside you and rest the ankle as much as you can."

Muttering his thanks, the recruit hobbled away, and joined the rest of us. S/Sgt. Bannister looked at the next man's ankle. He carried out the same examination and thoughtfully shook his head.

"It doesn't look good, son. I'm not 100% sure that it's broken, but the swelling and colour indicate that you could have a hairline crack here" he said, pointing to the centre of the very swollen ankle. "I think we had better get you x-rayed. No more walking today, sorry son!"

The recruit, from 'C' Squadron, tried to protest, but to no avail.

"No, no arguments, I can't allow you to continue in that state. You could do permanent damage to yourself." With that, the medical examination was over. S/Sgt. Bannister stood up and walked back to the Land Rover. He talked into a radio mike, and fifteen minutes later, another army Land Rover bearing large red crosses on its sides arrived. The injured recruit was helped aboard; his kit was loaded and the Land Rover sped off, in the direction of the nearest civilian hospital.

Darkness was beginning to fall as we were called for our night briefing. Things were going to be done very differently from now on. We were to be sent out alone. The night march was fairly straightforward. Leave our current location individually at three-minute intervals and go from RV to RV until we were told we were finished. Times would be recorded, and anyone failing to arrive at the final RV within the timescale was out, binned and finished. The only drawback was that we weren't told how much time, or how many RVs there were. Once again, as a result, we also didn't know where the last RV was going to be.

The recruits lined up ready to go. Bergans were weighed by shielded torchlight, and the first RV's grid reference was given before each recruit was released into the moonlit night. I was somewhere in the middle of the pack. I set off, having studied the map and set my bearing. I began at a moderate pace, to allow my stiff muscles time to warm up. The first RV was higher up on the other side of the next valley. The going was steep, but I managed to find it without mishap. Having received my next RV, I set off at a faster pace. As I marched through the darkness, I bumped into another recruit.

"Where's the RV mate?" Whispered the mystery voice. It was one of my Squadron's recruits who had started before me and had overshot the first checkpoint. "Its back down the hill about 100 metres. Hit the stream and turn left. The stream junctions about fifty metres further on"

"Cheers mate" and he was gone. I plodded on, heading towards my next location. This was the first time I'd walked the mountains alone, and it was quite eerie. There was no noise from anywhere save the occasional bleat of a sheep, in the distance, or the sound of water rushing down a stream. When there was nothing else, all I could hear was the wind; and that was almost non-existent. By one o'clock the next morning, I had climbed and descended several mountain ridges. My bergan straps were digging into my shoulders, and I was really feeling the effects of the day's exertions. I had just arrived at the top of another ridge and stopped to check my location. I shone my small pencil torch onto the map and looked at my compass. Strangely, the compass needle wouldn't stay still. Instead of pointing north, it slowly spun around the compass face in a circle. There are large, rich underground deposits of iron ore in the general area, and I appeared to be standing directly on top of one. I knew roughly where I was, and was making my way down towards a corner of a big timber plantation, with a tarmac road running down the South-East side of it. I didn't dare waste any time, so I had to get a move on.

I checked the map again, and worked out my next direction of travel. I set off at a good pace and soon started to descend towards my next RV. In the moonlight, I could just make out the black shape of the plantation. It was way off, but straight ahead of me. The ground started to level off, and I had no warning, as my left leg hit the bog. I knew instantly that I had stepped into one, as I heard a loud squelch, and felt myself tipping forward as my leg plunged into the sticky, clinging morass. In near panic I frantically threw my body backwards, and the weight of my bergan saved me. The bloody thing was so heavy; it acted as a counter balance, and ripped me free of the mire's deadly suction. I lay on the edge of the bog for several moments, breathing hard and fast. The rotten eggs' stench of marsh gas was overpowering, where my leg had released it from the bog. Shit! That was too close. Another pace forward and I would have been straight in. Not much chance of a shepherd finding me up here; in the dark. As I stood up, I felt a savage sting in my groin. I'd pulled something when I fell backwards out of the bog. Well, there was no one else about and nothing I could do, but push on. I could still see the plantation in the moonlight, so carefully skirting the bog; I set off for it. The pain in my groin was uncomfortable but bearable. I could still walk, but I couldn't maintain the pace. I limped into the RV an hour later feeling like death warmed up. The instructor took my name and asked me if I wanted to jack the course in. When I told him, I didn't he gave me by next RV. When I checked the map, it was about a hundred metres away. "That's right Black, get down to the road, and find yourself a basher spot inside the tree line. Coaches at 07.30 hrs."

It was welcome news. I'd finished for the night!

"Thanks Staff, how's my time?"

He flicked on his torch back on and shone it on his millboard. "Hmmm, not brilliant, but it looks OK, just about. I thought you would be a bit faster?"

I explained about the bog, and he shone his pencil torch onto my legs. My left leg was still black, covered with thick mud from mid-thigh down.

The instructor sniffed. "You were dead lucky mate. Get the duty medic to check your groin before you get your head down. He's parked on the side of the road."

I thanked him, and hobbled a little further down the hill. When the medic had finished his examination he just said.

"No sign of a hernia, but go and see your own G.P. if it flairs up during the week." I climbed into the plantation and found a good spot, close to the road. After putting up my basher, I took off my boots. The left one was full of foul smelling black bog water, which I poured onto the ground. I pulled off the other boot, and put some clean dry kit on. My groin hurt like hell, as I wriggled into my sleeping bag. I felt really sore and shattered. I couldn't get comfortable, and slept badly during what was left of the night. When I got up the next morning, I felt very stiff, and my groin still hurt like the blazes. As I moved around the pain subsided a little, but the injury was still there. I chatted to the boys as we waited for the coaches. There had been several more twists and sprains during the night, and we were all glad the weekend was over. Most of us spent the journey back on the train sleeping. Next stop would be the Brecon Beacons, but now...I was carrying an injury!

The Taxi knowledge continued, adding runs across London every day. I went for my first test at the carriage office, and scored a big fat zero. The examiners could ask me to recall any route at the beginning of the Blue Book. I didn't know at the time that they could also begin the run from anywhere within a quarter of a mile of the listed start point and finish anywhere within a quarter of a mile of the listed finish. Alternatively, if they felt like it, they could reverse the run. It could be tricky with some of the one-way systems. I just didn't know enough yet, but I stuck to the training, regardless. It would take a minimum of two years to crack the knowledge, and I'd only started two months earlier. There was plenty of time for that.

The groin injury had subsided, but I ran for a week without the concrete. I figured that the extra weight might hamper my recovery, so I just ran without it. We were off to the Brecon Beacons soon but I heard a good story in the bar at the Dukes, which impressed me. A recruit had slipped and fallen badly on a previous course at the end of 'Test week'. He was nearing the end of the infamous final test march called 'Long Drag'. His left collar bone was broken in the fall. He strapped up his left arm, slung his bergan over his right shoulder and pushed on. Finishing the march within the time limit he passed selection. Nice!

We paraded as usual on the Friday evening at the Dukes, before leaving for South Wales. A quick head count showed we had lost even more 'faces'. The next phase of selection was all going to happen on the Brecon Beacons. Two more gruelling training weekends in moon grass country, then Test Weekend. If we passed that, we qualified for almost a solid week of continuous selection marches culminating in one final and ultimate endurance test exercise - 'Long Drag'. Pass all of that and we were done with the mountain phase. As always, we got the train to Swansea, and were met by our coaches. The drivers took a different route, and followed the road signs for Brecon. The coach journey took longer, and the terrain seemed even more foreboding. One minute we were driving through gently rolling hills, and the next we seemed to be surrounded by the dark silhouettes of the towering Brecon Beacon Mountains. It was impossible to make out any detail at night, but the outline of these huge mountains shouldered their way into the starry night sky.

I have got to admit, even with all the mental and physical conditioning to a tight knot in my stomach. The whole course had led us to this point, and things were about to get much worse. The coaches drove slowly along the winding mountain road until they pulled into a gravel car park. We were told to get off and paraded nearby. It was cold, freezing cold. As before, the Regiment had picked a drop-off point with a handy plantation close at by. The sound of a rushing stream could clearly be heard nearby. We were instructed to be ready at 06.00, and told to get our heads down in the new plantation. Under the weight of our bergans, it was a difficult scramble to get up a steep bank, over the ever present barbed-wire fence, and into the trees. When our bashers were up, we all got our heads down, glad to be out of the biting cold. Drifting in and out of sleep, the freezing night ticked slowly by. When we woke next morning, everything was covered with a thick layer of glistening frost. The ground was as hard as iron, and the trees in the plantation looked like a stalled production line of shimmering white Christmas trees. Shivering, I climbed out of my sleeping bag, and started preparing for the coming day. When we were ready and on parade at 06.00 hrs., the Sgt. Major addressed us. He told us that we had finished the easy first half of the mountain phase, and from this day forwards, things were going to really test us both physically and mentally. He added that we were going to walk over some serious buckets (mountains) today, starting with a leg stretching climb over Pen y Fan (pronounced penny fan).

We all knew the mountain by reputation. It was the highest, most dangerous peak in South Wales, and lay in the heart of the bleak Brecon Beacons mountain range. Its reputation had been drummed into us over the last couple of months by our instructors. Numerous military and civilian people had died on the mountain through falls and exposure over the years. There were no easy approach marches to get to its base, and the climb was long, difficult and exhausting. We would be walking alone from now on, and it was up to us as individuals to pick the routes between each RV. Times would be carefully recorded from this point onwards; we had to give maximum effort on every march. Sgt. Major Swainson handed us over to one of the corporals who gave us two grid references. The first was our present location. We were standing on the site of a long since dismantled mountain railway station. The second grid reference was the summit of Pen y Fan. On closer inspection of my map, it showed that the mountain soared to a massive height of two and a half thousand feet above sea level (886 metres). The first half of our approach could be made using, surprisingly enough, an old Roman road.

Two thousand years earlier, the ancient Romans crisscrossed England and Wales with a brilliant road system, following their invasion and settlement. Using their road network, they could move troops and supplies quickly to anywhere they were required, whenever the need arose. As in many places, which had been touched by the Roman Empire, the brilliance of their engineering meant that the remains of their construction still exist to the present day. After turning off the remains of the Roman road, the second part of the approach to Pen y Fan's base entailed climbing and crossing several high ridges. The training staff marshaled us into a straight line, and we were released at two-minute intervals. We had been warned not to walk in pairs, as this was to be a strictly individual effort. As I moved out of the old station area, a fantastically rugged panorama unfolded in front of me. The Roman road was now no more than a broad, well worn track. Cut into and running along a slope, it snaked off into the distance. The track slowly gained height, eventually vanishing between two small peaks on the misty horizon. The slope to my right cut off any chance of seeing what lay beyond, but ahead and to my left, the view was simply incredible. On the other side of the huge valley, opposite the ancient Roman highway, was a sheer granite wall. It rose majestically, towering above, hundreds of feet above us. Huge rocky outcrops and evidence of massive rock falls were to be seen all along its forbidding length. At its end, shrouded in clouds, was Pen y Fan. It stood above everything, and lay brooding and silent, in the distance. The scale of the landscape was quite overwhelming. The feeling of being in true wilderness was overpowering. There was no sign of civilisation anywhere. No houses, no roads, power pylons... Nothing! Just vast, barren open spaces, guarded on all sides by the ever present, and unforgiving mountains. The Roman road was in poor shape. The muddy, rock strewn surface was regularly eroded by fast flowing streams, cutting across it at right angles. One particularly broad stream cut deeply across the track. I had to climb fifteen feet down, jump from rock to rock across the foaming torrent, then climb up the other side. None of it was easy, with a heavy 40lb bergan, belt kit and rifle. I was forced to walk around several huge boulders, which had come to rest on the track, having become detached over the years from the rocky face, higher up the slope. I passed one guy after twenty minutes, but it meant nothing; I, in turn was passed by two others. The first part of this march felt more like a walking steeplechase. A long jagged line of sweating recruits making their collective way towards a distant brooding horizon. Each man marching alone, focused on his own private thoughts.

The muddy ground remained wet and treacherous. A moment's lack of concentration and a stumble and subsequent fall became inevitable. Every step took me closer to the point where the Roman road vanished. After nearly an hour of hard marching, I reached that point. The Roman road crossed over a ridge and dipped down into the next valley. That explained why it seemed, from a distance, to disappear suddenly. My route for Pen y Fan took me off the Roman road, to another well-worn track. It led past Cribyn, another peaked ridge close by. The going became much steeper, and sweat flowed freely. It is vitally important not to become dehydrated through sweat loss, so drinking small amounts of water regularly was recommended during a lecture, earlier on the course. Cramp was another enemy, as heavy sweating washes vital traces of salt out of tired muscles. If left unattended for too long, cramping muscles simply stop working, and it is impossible to continue. Adding an extra good pinch of salt with meals can make all the difference, and keep agonising cramps away. We kept passing each other as we toiled up the slippery path around the summit of Cribyn. Guys who had slipped and fallen already were, in some cases, slowed down to a painful limp.

Probably the most depressing thing that happened during our baptism on the Beacons was when two instructors doubled past me as I was close to reaching the top of the ridge. If they had run past me going down the slope, fair enough. But these guys were running up it. However, both carried what appeared to be heavy bergans, but didn't change their pace, as they disappeared over the ridge. As I broke the ridge line and started to descend, I got my first close look at Pen y Fan. enough, it didn't look too bad, but as I was shortly to find out, looks can be very deceptive. There was another long approach march, which would take at least half an hour. The beginning of the slope, which eventually led to the top, looked steep, but manageable. The last part before the summit appeared craggy and very difficult. As I surveyed the mountain from afar, Pen y Fan looked as if its right side had been ripped away. Almost sheer cliffs fell hundreds of feet from the summit to the bottom of the valley, far below. Gritting my teeth I carried on with the march. The long approach took nearly an hour, much longer than I had first estimated. There was a large patch of dead ground which I hadn't spotted or bargained for. The going was difficult; this was now, real hard core moon grass country. The clumps of grass were much bigger than I had recently experienced on the Black Mountains. The central tufts were higher, making it absolutely impossible to put a foot flat on the ground. My ankles took the brunt of each footfall, and were starting to get sorer by the minute. When I reached the mountain's base, I needed a serious energy fix. I had a pocket full of Mars bars, and I was ready for an almost instant sugary boost. I munched as I started the assent. I could feel some of the tiredness starting to ease a little, but looking up...Jesus, it was going to be a long hard climb. I could see some of the boys who had been released long before me already approaching the summit. They looked no more than tiny black dots above me, high up against the backdrop of the forbidding grey mountainside. They had an hour's head start, and they were just reaching the top! It didn't take a rocket scientist to work out that I had a tough, gruelling hours' climb (at least) before I made the first RV. There is no easy way or trick to marching up the side of a big mountain, it's just a case of putting one foot in front of the other. On the way up, those who convinced themselves they couldn't take the next step failed at that moment. It was no disgrace, bearing in mind the extra weight; a bergan which weighed in at about three and a half stone and rifle which weighed over half a stone. Add to that wet boots and clothes, plus spare water carried in canteens hanging off each man's web belt. The average recruit was carrying at least an extra five stone up the mountain. An important lesson was learnt that day by those that made it; a human being can overcome incredible physical tasks, providing they ignore pain and believe they can make it. By the time I had battled my way up three quarters of the mountain, I admit I was feeling pretty shattered. The effort of lifting each leg higher than the last was becoming more and more difficult. I had seen one man turn round above me, and begin his descent. He passed me in silence, looking utterly exhausted and totally defeated. I wasn't going to face the shame of saying that I couldn't make it, so I pushed on. The last fifty feet were probably the hardest, and the steepest. Not a climb in the true sense but it came in very close. Handholds helped, as the angle was now precariously steep and the rocks loose and very slippery. The relief I felt when my eyes came level with the nearly flat top of the mountain, was overwhelming. I couldn't suppress a broad grin as I climbed the last few feet. I did not stop when I had made it though; I had to push on as soon as I could safely stand up. There, about fifty yards in front of me was the trig. point. These were short four sided concrete pillars, which exactly mark the highest point on the mountain. Sitting on their bergans at its base were two Training Wing instructors. I straightened up, and did my best to look as fresh and switched on as I could. As I approached, to check in, one of the eagle-eyed instructors said.

"Your button is undone, down and give me 20!"

Bugger it, I'd forgotten to do up my mars bar pocket. Cursing myself for being so stupid, I complied, as best I could. When I'd finished, I stood up and gave my name. I was told to get my map out, and show them exactly where we were. When the Corporals were satisfied that I correctly knew my current location, they gave me my next RV. It was a car park, beside the base of the Fan. It lay close to the main road running through the bottom of a valley, on the far side of the trig. point I currently stood beside. When I left the RV I had about half a kilometre of fairly flat, rocky ridge line to traverse. It was easy going. I followed a well-worn path, until it disappeared down to my right. As I began my descent, the track looked ideal for the flip-flop running technique I learned a few weeks earlier in the Black Mountains. I had to keep a tight control of my speed, one slip and I'd lose it and break something; quite possibly my neck. Running from the knees down worked very well. I was using minimal energy, but covering the steep downhill route quickly.

I was panting hard, but arrived at the bottom of the mountain in fairly good shape. Checking my pockets, I went to the Land Rover parked in the car park. The next RV was over the road and straight up the next mountain: Fan Fawr. It was another beast of a climb, which entailed marching diagonally up to another wet, slippery path, which eventually led to the Fan Fawr's summit. I was running very low on energy again. I hit another Mars bar, as I left the RV at the top of this latest mountain. The next leg was due west. It entailed a long, slow downhill march, through some very nasty moon grass country. The checkpoint was a stream junction, maybe six kilometres distant. The going was hellish. The grassland was very wet, and I was soon soaked from the knees down. I could feel the bog water squelching in my boots, and they began to rub. New blisters were starting to form, despite my feet being almost covered with surgical tape. When I reached the stream junction, I was told to fall out and get some hot food inside me. I joined the other recruits who still had some down time left. It was a huge relief as I eased my bergan off my aching shoulders. It felt almost like moon walking when I moved around, without the dragging weight of my heavy backpack. I had felt exhausted during previous selection marches, and this was worse, much worse. It seemed like no more than a blink of an eye; my meal was finished, and it was time to jump start some very tired muscles and get ready for the next leg of the course. When I was given my next RV, I set off at a pretty slow pace. Every muscle in my body wanted to be on the train going home, and I had to dig really deep to force myself to keep moving. As I marched alone, over the dreaded moon grass, I finally realised that pain is all in the mind. If you force yourself to ignore it, it goes away. Well, maybe it doesn't go completely, but it lives somewhere in the back of your mind, where with sufficient practice, you can manage it. If I wanted to pass selection, I needed to become adept at overcoming these constant aches and pains. If you are constantly close to a state of exhaustion, your feet are killing you, and your shoulders feel that they are being cut in two by your bergan, the Americans have a saying, which covers it. 'When the going gets tough, the tough get going', An annoying phrase, but absolutely 100% accurate. At any moment on selection, the easy option to stop the pain was simply to tell a Staff member.

"I've had enough. I give up."

Getting into the SAS has to be difficult, so if you really want in, there's only one option, just grit your teeth and lump it! By the time I reached the final daytime RV, I felt way past shattered. My body was living in a land somewhere between utterly exhausted and dead. Luckily, because of my position in the daytime running order, I had about an hour and a half before the night marches started. I found a fairly dry spot, and slowly eased my bergan off my aching shoulders. I thankfully sat down on the ground, using my bergan as a backrest. I lit a fag, and watched the smoke drift slowly away from its glowing tip. Selection was getting harder, but I wasn't giving in. I would now rather die than admit to the world (and myself) that I couldn't hack it. They would have to bin me, if they wanted me gone. This had become a deeply personal issue now. I knew what was required of me. I had set myself a near impossible task to wipe the past, but now I was in too deep; failure was simply not an option.

Initially, the night march went OK, but the temperature had dropped like a stone. By midnight, everywhere was dusted with a thick coating of sparkling frost. The icy ground crunched under my boots as I marched towards my next destination. Feeling exhausted, I wasn't thinking straight. I made the nearly fatal mistake of stopping between RVs and taking my bergan off. I sat down on my heavy pack, and pulled the map out of my pocket, to check my position. The next thing I remember was being fiercely shaken awake. By pure chance, another recruit had literally stumbled across me in the dark. I was covered from head to toe in a thick layer of glistening frost, and felt mind numbingly cold. I slowly stood up and shook myself. It scared the living shit out of me. Another half-hour and I would certainly have frozen to death. I shivered violently as I slowly lifted my bergan onto my back. I should have checked my compass, but instead, I just followed my rescuer. He already suggested that we stay together for a while, in case I started showing signs of exposure. It was a good idea, because I couldn't concentrate, I was simply too cold. He set a fast pace, and slowly I started to revive and warm up. I had been teetering on the absolute edge of hypothermia, but through good luck had caught it just in time. There is an old saying, which says - 'Those who don't learn from their mistakes are doomed to repeat them'. SAS selection was a long, serious and dangerous adventure. I had learnt a damn good lesson that night, and never made the same mistake, ever again.

The second Brecon weekend followed the same muscle tearing exhaustion as the first, but the weather took a distinct turn for the worse. The weekend involved long gruelling marches over the mountains, where I did not see another living soul for hours at a time. It's a funny thing, but an overwhelming feeling of loneliness crept in, as I struggled on, hour after hour, beaten by roaring winds and torrential, freezing rain. Without the warm and cheerful banter of friends, it is all too easy to begin feeling sorry for yourself. I was constantly on the edge of mental and physical exhaustion, soaking wet, and having to march on blisters the size of golf balls. I did not have anyone to ease my pain and suffering; not a gentle soul to offer me the milk of human kindness, sympathy or any form of comfort. It was all too easy to sink into a sea of self-pity. Who really cared if I made it or not? With a start, I forced away such pathetic mental weakness; I shrugged my heavily laden shoulders and cursing myself for being such a whimp. With a growl, I pushed myself on. Perhaps the intense feeling of isolation got to some recruits; and helped to explain why they continued to fail themselves and disappear off the course. The ground was murder to march on, and the weather continued to be unrelenting and awful. The wind blew hard, much harder than I had ever experienced before. I reached the top of one ridge, and couldn't stand upright. Even with the extra weight of my bergan, I had to crawl on my hands and knees as I traversed the exposed top twenty metres of the ridge. The howling wind was so savage; it was simply impossible to cross the featureless crest in any other way than on all fours. I felt some relief when it became a little easier on the lee side of the ridge, but trying to balance against the roaring wind made the going painfully slow. As I fought my way up the next steep slope, I noticed something very unusual. There was a stream running down the hill beside me, but the wind was so powerful that it was actually blowing the water back up the slope! There were frequent, very heavy hailstorms, which badly stung my hands and face. The ice particles shot-blasted my exposed face until it became numb. The Regiment's policy was strict. Hoods were never worn, even in the worst weather, as they impair hearing.

I think that everyone's times were on the crap side that weekend, as recruits were scattered far and wide by the ferocious storm. Would they cancel the darkness marches because of the terrible weather? NO! Dream on...Not a chance. When the exercise was concluded and the Staff finally called a halt at the end of the night navigation exercise, we had all been pushed to our absolute limit. As I lay in my sleeping bag, I listened to the latest downpour lashing the outside skin of my basher. It felt wonderful to have stopped and be at last out of the driving rain. Something was tickling the back of my mind though, and worrying me. During the initial Saturday morning briefing, the senior instructor made a point about us always keeping something in reserve. I'd heard that before, which made the omens bad. The Sgt. Major had grinned wolfishly when he said it. Nothing unusual had happened during the day to explain his warning, and that just wasn't right. The Staff never said anything, which did not have a reason behind it, so surely, they must still have something unpleasant up their sleeve? Knowing them, it would be something bloody awful, another way of forcing wavering recruits to crack. When I woke the next morning, the storm had blown it's-self out. The skies were grey and overcast, but at least it had stopped raining. When we fell in for the coaches at 07. 00hrs, I began to find out what the Sgt. Major had in mind. Strangely, the car park was empty of vehicles. With his feet planted firmly on the ground, the Sgt. Major gave us the good news.

"Right lads, you are going on a nice little early-morning road run. The coaches won't be here for a while yet, so you will have time to run ten kilometres down the valley, and then ten kilometres back." He paused for a moment to let the news sink in. There were a few muffled groans. "One of the Staff will be at the halfway mark, and he will take your name, note your time and turn you round. You won't be wearing bergans, but you will take your rifles and belt kits. It's an individual effort, and of course, times will be recorded." As he was about to hand over to his Corporals, he stopped and turned back to us.

" Oh yes, there is one other thing. Don't forget. Always keep something in reserve."

Damn it! He had said it again. We looked quizzically at each other...Christ! Now what? We were lined up and set off at thirty second intervals. There were many blisters bursting and the air was thick with curses, when we were safely out of earshot of the Training Wing staff. The downhill section of the run was relatively easy, as we had been allowed the luxury of jogging down the long winding mountain road. The sky was clearing, and the sun was beginning to shine. When I reached the half way mark, there was one of the Staff, faithfully sitting under a tree, by the side of the road. I gave him my name, and the instructor pointed back up the road. I didn't say anything, just about turned, and started jogging. About halfway back to base, I overtook the guy, who had woken me up on the mountain, the previous weekend. He was puffing hard, and I slowed down and started jogging along with him. We chatted as we went. Our nice little conversation was rather rudely interrupted when a member of the Training staff suddenly jumped out from behind a tree and stopped us.

"This is supposed to be an individual effort, drop and give me twenty, both of you!"

We sheepishly did as we told. When we stood up he warned us both that we would be failed outright if we were caught running or walking together again. I took him at his word, winked at my mate and ran off. I was still wondering about the 'keep something in reserve' comment when I finally rounded the last corner and reached our base camp. There were the coaches, neatly parked, silently waiting with their engines switched off. They had passed me earlier in a cloud of acrid diesel exhaust as I jogged back up the long, valley road. I doubled over to the Sgt. Major and halted smartly in front of him, glad to be finished. As I opened my mouth to give him my name, he held up his hand.

"No son, I'm not taking names today...He is." He turned away from me, and pointed up towards the top of a mountain, which rose majestically into the sky nearby. I could just see someone standing on the skyline at the top of its misty summit. On closer inspection, there was a long, well spaced-out line of recruits climbing towards the top. "Give your name to Cpl. White when you get to the top. Double away now laddie!" He had that same wolfish grin on his face. This twist caught me on the hop, but this was their lesson about keeping something back, just in case. With a deep sigh, I started upwards. It was a steep climb, and took me at least half an hour. The only good thing about it was that I wasn't carrying my bergan. Without the extra forty pounds strapped to my back, it was sort of fun....well, almost. Just before I reached the top I checked for undone buttons, and squared off my hat. I was stuffed if I was going to get a bunch of press-ups for being switched off and slack. When I reached the summit, I got them anyway, for not running up the mountain. It was Cpl. White's idea of a joke, as he gave everyone some for luck. I was told to run downhill or else, and readily complied. When I arrived panting heavily at the Land Rover, the Sgt. Major told to me grab my bergan and get on the coach. This was good news, as personally, I was heavily overdrawn at the energy bank, now had absolutely dick all left in reserve.

One of the best parts of each weekend was getting home, having a long hot shower and changing into clean, comfortable civilian clothes. My dear old mum always had kittens when I peeled off the tape and exposed my raw, blistered, and sometimes bleeding feet. She would cluck around, tut-tutting, and offered to give me a note for those nasty army men. Mums are wonderful things, bless them. When the local pub opened, I'd slowly hobble round each Sunday evening with my dad, and take on board numerous pints of pain killing anesthetic, in the form of the Brewery's cheapest and nastiest lager. Good company, good conversation and excellent beer. It was the stuff of life. Ah, they were happy days!

Chapter 9
Pass or fail, black and white

We now faced the Brecon Test Weekend. It was a simple concept. Get round the entire route within a fixed time limit, or fail selection. Pass or fail - no grey areas. As always, we wouldn't be told the number of RVs, the distances involved or the time limit. We were to carry the full 45lb bergan, plus rifle, belt kit etc. There would be snap weigh-ins during the course, with instant failure and removal for anyone unlucky enough to be caught even slightly underweight. This Test Weekend decided whether we were mentally and physically fit to go onto Selection camp. One of the Training Wing staff had explained that if we couldn't pass Test Weekend, there wasn't any point in going back to Brecon for a full week of endurance marches across the mountains. We had to be good enough to crack this test, or we were out! Over the last arduous months, the course had shrunk from its original 93, down to a hard core of just 29. I may have been a bit dim on the subject, but I still couldn't really understand why blokes continued to fail themselves. It always seemed to happen at the top of a windswept mountain. Having struggled all the way to the summit of one of the high peaks, a guy would just run out of steam and give up. He still had to walk all the way back down the mountain after he had jacked it in. Exactly, what did any of the failures expect? The Staff wouldn't call in a helicopter to evacuate them. I just couldn't get my head around it. It made no sense at all to me. I felt no scorn to any one of them though; at least, they tried. Adding to the decline in numbers had been injuries, personal problems and security issues, just as the Colonel had warned us, which had all helped to thin out the ranks over the past few months.

When Test Weekend arrived, we moved onto the Brecon Beacons in the usual fashion, by train and coach. We were to be tested in an area unfamiliar to us, in a new region of the mountain range. The mood of the remaining recruits was now very sombre. We had all worked so very hard to get this far. No one wanted to be summarily removed from the course at this late stage. When the remaining recruits assembled at the start line early on Saturday morning, we were all pretty quiet. We were told once again that it was pass or fail time, and that we must go for it, balls to the wall. This exercise was ominously called 'Mountain Express'.

The low skies were grey, and hung dark and sinister above us. With our bergans weighed, we were given the grid reference of our first RV. We set off one by one, at three-minute intervals. Route selection and planning had always been up to the individual during the latter part of the course, but would prove critical today. Pick a bad route, which took too long, and what little reserve time there may be in the bank would soon start to decay. I stopped just beyond the release point and looked hard at my map. There wasn't much of a choice, a difficult steep climb to the top of the initial ridge, then motor as fast as possible along it to the first checkpoint, about four kilometres into the mountain range. It was not too far, but the initial climb would be a real bastard. Having set the bearing on my compass, I pushed my map into my thigh trouser pocket, buttoned it and set off. The climb was even worse than I feared; the ground was very wet and slippery. It was too easy to lose my balance, slip and fall. Nothing for it though, I had to maintain a good steady pace. I pushed hard and made it to the top after about thirty hot, sweating minutes. The map showed me that I must turn right and follow the ridge line. The going was flat and to my great surprise, pretty easy. Now I was here; I had another choice to make. Should I plod along and conserve my energy for later, or should I double forward at a steady jog and put some extra minutes into the bank. I decided that the extra minutes might be vital, so I set off on a four kilometre speed march. It was a technique which I had learnt long ago in the regular army. Double forward two hundred metres then march quickly for one hundred metres. Then double forward for two hundred metres and so on. It gained ground quickly, but helped to conserve a little energy. When the pace was too much, swap the distances and double one hundred metres and march two hundred. The change in pace and rhythm help ease stiff sore leg muscles too. Battle marching only worked on reasonable, flat ground, so I must make the most of it, as I correctly guessed that the chances of having this sort of terrain again during the rest of 'Mountain Express' were probably zero. I reached the RV, reported in and received the next. It would take me over some very rugged country to a stream junction many kilometres away. The weather was starting to close in. The rain had held off so far, but it was starting to get very misty. During the leg, I tried to maintain as much height as possible, as it cost precious minutes and energy to regain it, if it were lost. I had decided that in-flight refuelling was important today, as I couldn't afford the time to stop and brew up or eat. I stocked up with cold cooked sausages, and a fearsome supply of parkin biscuits. My dear old mum had cooked the sausages and parkin for me the day before. The parkin was a delicious mixture of oatmeal and treacle cooked into fat chunky squares. Packed with sugar and energy, it was mum's way of helping her little boy. We had had a lecture during our Tuesday evening training at the Dukes about nutrition, and learnt all about the urgent necessity for carbohydrates and sugar when under enormous physical stress. I munched away as I marched. Mars bars are excellent for a quick, short-lived energy burst, but under mountain conditions, the body burns up its sugar reserve very quickly. The parkin biscuits released energy into the body more slowly, and helped to avoid energy spikes at the wrong moment. I hit the second RV., and asked the

Instructor how my time was doing. I was told to just keep moving and concentrate on my route and pace. Once again, not a sign of any encouragement, support or extra information from the instructor. When I looked at my map, I had to climb about six hundred feet to a summit ahead of me. The mountain top was shrouded in mist, and sat patiently waiting for me. It turned out that there were a series of false ridges to climb. Each promised to be the top, but each one lied to me. I'd seen this sort of feature before; it reminded me of Tan Hill, four years previously. Beyond the ridge lines lurked sections of bog, which had to be crossed or circumnavigated. I chose to go round each one; to get stuck in one of these mires could be fatal, or at least would be a time disaster. As I marched higher towards the next RV I gradually entered the mist, which silently and eerily closed around me like the womb. As I continued to climb, and reached the next flat section, I came across a sheep standing in a large puddle. It looked at me, decided I wasn't a threat and took a drink from the pool of rainwater it was standing in. To my surprise, it was busy having a dump into the same pool, while it drank. What would David Attenborough make of that one?

I pushed on. Visibility was closing in fast as I continued to gain height. The next ridge line levelled off and suddenly there was the instructor, sitting on his bergan. Having checked in and received my next RV I saw that the next leg was almost as far as I had already walked, about eight kilometres. The going would be difficult (again) and would probably be mostly moon grass. I wasn't wrong, as I hit the bloody stuff almost immediately when I arrived at the base of the mountain. I had run down most of the way, but had a bad feeling that I had wandered off my bearing during my very rapid, undulating descent through the fog. I wasn't sure if I was left or right of the correct line of march. The white blanket of dense, clinging fog made it impossible to be sure. I stopped for a moment and took a long swig of water, as I tried to make out exactly where I was. According to my map, the ground ahead of me consisted of two parallel ridge lines stretching away into the distance. One led in the direction I wanted, the other gradually curved down towards the old Welsh mining town of Merthyr Tydfil. I couldn't apply any of the lessons I had learnt. I was not able to take a back bearing on a distant point, because of the fog. I couldn't retrace my steps as the climb would waste an hour at least, and there were no reference points, which would give me a clue as to my exact location. My compass needle wouldn't settle. There must be more iron ore deposits beneath my feet. Without its help, it was down to the best guess, so I went for it. I marched on for maybe twenty precious minutes, but things just didn't feel right. A knot was growing in my stomach; I was losing far too much height. The ridge's height should have stayed fairly constant, but I was continuing downwards. Damn this bloody fog, visibility still remained no more than just a few metres. I stopped and looked at my map again.

Come on boy, THINK! I had an awful feeling that I had dropped an almighty clanger in the last half hour. I had no choice but to push on and find a reference point of some sort. Luckily, it didn't take long. The fog swirled and lifted momentarily. Instantly, I knew I was in trouble and was facing disaster.

I saw a red telephone box, beside a road in front of me. Desperately, I whipped out my map and scanned it. Christ! I was on the wrong side of the wrong ridge, several bloody miles from where I should have been. I frantically set a fresh bearing on my now stable compass and started to run back up the side of the mountain. If I was to stand even a chance of making it, I had to move faster than I had ever gone before. I had to assume the arse up, head down position and really go for it. I frantically pounded my way up the ridge, until I reached the top. I sucked one desperate chest full of frigid damp air after another into my burning lungs, as I forced myself forward. The bearing had taken me back onto the correct ridge line, and I was sure that I was now in the right place. I couldn't afford to ease off and finally reached the RV at the run. The instructor asked me why I was late. Panting hard, I told him the truth; that I had screwed up in the fog. I desperately asked him if I had a hope in hell's chance of completing the course in time. He scratched his chin, and told me I would have to really motor, but there was a slim chance, if I didn't make any more mistakes. I thanked him and ran off into the mist. I found a track, which I felt sure would save me some vital time. Thank heavens I had used the battle march technique to gain precious minutes at the start of the course.

As I charged over a ridgeline, I scattered a small group of elderly civilian ramblers, who were also using the path. "Hallo!" I shouted as I zoomed through them. Their startled faces disappeared into the fog behind me, as I ran up the fairly gentle slope ahead of me. Absently, I noticed that the skin on my forearms had turned white. This could not be due to the cold air, as I was sweating profusely. I guessed what it was, and licked the back of my wrist to see if my theory was correct. Salt! I had been running so hard and fast that the salt was leaching straight out of my body through my sweat. It was then that the cramps hit me. My thigh muscles locked up, making it agony to move them. My muscles desperately needed salt to function, and I was all out! I had to act fast. I dropped my bergan and pulled out a little tub of salt from my emergency ration pack. I poured out enough to cover a twenty pence piece and swallowed it. I took a long hard swig of water and waited a couple of minutes. The effect was magic. The cramps quickly disappeared, and I gratefully shouldered my bergan, picked up my rifle and pushed on.

117

The next RV was at the end of a long curved path running just below the crest of a ridge line. When I arrived, the instructor warned me that I was running well behind schedule. It was late afternoon, and would be getting dark soon. He gave me the next RV. When I quickly showed him on the map where it was, he let me go. I took some more salt and water and moved on. The effects of the day were really kicking in now, as I hungrily finished the last parkin biscuit and mars bar. I really needed a quick energy boost. The RV was on a stream junction, and I reached it after about an hour's hard march. To my surprise and delight, there were recruits cooking and chatting to each other on the far side of the stream. In front of me was Major Brook, the boss of Training Wing and Sgt. Major Swainson. I doubled up to them and stopped. "Where on earth have you been Black?" I explained what I had done. "You just made it with four minutes to spare; you passed Test Weekend by the skin of your teeth. Go and get a brew on." That was that, no 'Well done' or slap on the back. Pass or fail, black or white.

I grinned broadly and crossed the stream to my buddies. I did a quick head count; about twenty, more than half a dozen missing. I compared notes with the boys about the route as I waited for my brew to boil. We had all found it bloody awful, and agreed that every leg of the route had traps, which would cause the unfocused to lose time. I showed them where I had gone wrong and landed up by the phone box and was rewarded with a collective groan and various well deserved comments of 'tosser' and 'wanker.' Over the next two hours, the missing recruits slowly drifted in. Some were limping badly, and others just looked physically and mentally shattered. One guy came in helping another. He was carrying both bergans and supporting the injured man. It turned out that he had found the poor bloke, sitting on his bergan with a badly twisted knee. He decided not to leave the injured man alone as it was getting dark. He had opted to help the injured man instead of worrying about the test. Major Brook gave him the benefit of the doubt and passed him anyway, as his times were good before he had found the casualty. We had lost another eight men on Mountain Express, and were now down to 21. We lost one of those when it was later found out during a random blood test that he had taken the drug known as 'speed' before starting the Test Weekend march. As the drug's name suggests, anyone taking it will go like a train. The boss had no option but to bin him on the spot. Personally, I had no sympathy for him whatsoever, cheating bastard!

Those of us who had successfully completed 'Mountain Express' now faced the final stage of passing the mountain phase of selection. Test week was different from what we had experienced so far. It involved marching over the mountains for three consecutive days, and then, on the fourth day, facing the terrible 'Long Drag' endurance march, which could run on for up to twenty-four cruel and punishing hours. Having faced the numerous hardships of the course so far, I just wanted to get it over with. All the stories I had heard in the Duke's bar about the marches, and Long Drag were starting to fill me with enormous apprehension. This was going to be the worse part of it, but I was almost there. Could I crack it? To be honest, I didn't know, but one thing I knew for certain was that I was going to have a bloody good try!

All too quickly, Test Week arrived. What was left of the course arrived at a small army camp close to the Brecon Beacons, late one Sunday afternoon. The skies were grey, and it was very cold. We were given our own barrack block, which resembled a large old wooded shed. Inside the basher was one big room, with a dozen standard iron framed army bunk beds. In the centre of the room was a large metal stove, which had a black iron pipe which disappeared up through the roof to the chimney outside. A large sign had been fixed to the stove, which read: 'OUT Of BOUNDS, DO NOT LIGHT!' It was signed officer Commanding – Training Wing 21SAS Regt. There were radiators attached to the walls, but the controls were locked in the 'off' position. At one end of the room, an interior door led to the toilets. A table and four chairs near the stove were the only other items of furniture. We all claimed a bed space, and then went over to the bedding store to collect a mattress and pillow. When our bed spaces were set up and ready, we were fallen in outside and marched as a squad to the Admin. block for a final selection briefing. When we were all seated, an SAS Regimental Sergeant Major whom none of us had seen before stepped up to the podium. He was a middle-aged Irishman, and stood no more than 5ft 5" tall. He looked fit, hard and wizened. He introduced himself as W.O.1. O'Leary, R.S.M. of 23 SAS, our sister Territorial Regiment in the North. He would be senior N.C.O. in command of our Test Week. His face showed no emotion as he outlined the coming week. He told us that we were to be tested under the most arduous and severe conditions, to finally decide if we were good enough to pass selection. We would then move on to Continuation training, and again, if successful, into the Regiment. Our final selection marches would begin tomorrow morning (Monday) and continue each day until Friday morning. Each selection day would entail longer and more difficult marches. We were to carry 45lb bergans during each day's marches, which would be weighed before and after each, and would be subject to spot checks at any time between. We would be individually scored on each days march times. At the end of every test day, we would receive an A, B, C or F grade. We must achieve at least two Bs and one C by Wednesday evening to qualify for the final hurdle of Long Drag. If we were successful and made the start line of Long Drag, we would have a maximum of 24 hours to complete the forty kilometre course. While we were on camp, we were subject to Queen's Regulations (military law) and were expected to act accordingly. We were confined to camp during the evenings, and the NAAFI bar was strictly forbidden to all. There would be classroom lectures during each evening, after each day's march. When he had finished his briefing, he asked for questions. One bright spark asked if we would now be given any information about times or distances, which received a curt "No!"

In closing, 'Spud' O'Leary fixed us with a steely eyed stare.

"Gentlemen, the SAS is invincible. We can be run over by a tank and continue with our mission, if we choose to do so."

With that, he stepped off the podium and left the room. That was the nearest to any form of encouragement we had heard on the course so far. We were issued with one 24-hour ration pack, which was to be carried, but not to be opened, except in the case of an emergency on the mountains. We were also given a couple of refresher lessons on exposure and map reading and the rest of the evening (or what was left of it) was our own. This was a good time to visit the camp shop, and stock up with plenty of Mars bars and other edible goodies.

MONDAY: Day One.

Our first full day began at 05.00hrs when the day's duty N.C.O. crashed into the room yelling that it was time to get started. The block was bitterly cold. Out of our sleeping bags, wash and shave and into uniform. Double away to the cookhouse for a quick breakfast. The meal was small, one fried egg, sausage, a rasher of bacon, a thin slice of fried bread and a few baked beans. All washed down with a mug of hot tea. No frills, just an absolute minimum to sustain us. When we had finished breakfast (which didn't take very long) we were issued with a packed lunch in a paper bag. Not much in there either. One round of cheese sandwiches, a small chocolate biscuit bar, and an apple. We were permitted to fill our thermos flasks with tea, which was a real bonus. Carrying a thermos was an excellent idea, as it gave us the opportunity to snatch a hot sweet refreshing cuppa, without having to stop and waste valuable time waiting for it to brew. The only thing to remember was that it was vital to take it out of our pack before a bergan weigh-in, so that the bergan didn't go underweight when the thermos was empty. Dawn hadn't broken, and it was still dark when what was left of our initial intake of ninety-three runners fell in on the camp's parade square at 6.25hrs, after drawing our rifles from the armoury. We had our bergan's contents checked and weighted by torchlight. Then it was all aboard the four ton lorries and out of the camp, and away towards our start point.

The lorry ride only lasted about 15 minutes, and we pulled off the main road into a lay-by and stopped. When the lorry's engines were switched off, we were ordered out and fell in beside the road. The nearest mountain's base was only a few hundred metres from us, just the other side of a field full of weather-beaten sheep, which were partly visible in the now breaking dawn. We moved, one at a time, over to a nearby Land Rover, and were given the co-ordinates of our first RV. With a warning about marching with anyone else, we were set off at the usual three-minute intervals. Exact start times was recorded against each recruits name, by an instructor, as they departed on the first leg. When my turn came, I set off at a good steady pace, after climbing over the style and entering the sheep field. There were about a dozen blokes ahead of me, all following the same route up the side of the mountain. Navigation wasn't an issue at this early stage; the guys in front were all heading in the right direction. The important part was to make ground, and not get injured. I was breathing hard and sweating profusely by the time I reached the summit, and annoyingly, had to wait for several precious minutes while the guys ahead of me checked in at the RV. This was very frustrating for all of us as every second counted.

When the bloke in front of me cleared the RV, I doubled in and pulled out my map. The instructor wanted me to show him where we were now before he gave me the next RV, which just added to the tension and frustration. I doubled away from the RV, stopped, and checked my map. The route was simple enough, but looked suspiciously like solid moon grass country all the way to my next RV point. My analysis proved correct, as I was soon stumbling across an unending sea of the filthy stuff. The ground was saturated: my boots were sodden in minutes. Stinking bog water squelched from my boots eyelets with every pace. I pushed on as fast as the uneven ground would permit, with the constant stress of knowing I must try to achieve a B grade at the very least. The next few hours were as tough as any I'd encountered so far. As a result, the running order was pretty jumbled up, by lunchtime.

I had passed several guys, but had been passed by several others. I ate my lunch without stopping; I didn't dare waste a single moment. The contents of the thermos went the same way. The ground conditions got steadily worse, and to my dismay, it started to rain. In the first minute or two, the downpour was refreshing. But slowly and surely the rain saturated everything, and I was soaked to the skin. I wasn't wearing too much, just a shirt and my Denison smock, lightweight trousers and DMS boots, plus my woolly cap comforter, of course. By mid-afternoon, the faster pace was really starting to tell. Every muscle was aching as I had been walking hard over the mountains for about eight hours without a break, save for short pauses at each RV. The next RV was down in a valley, close to a road. Could this be the last one? I offered up a silent prayer that it was, and pushed on. My route down the side of the mountain was steep. I slid part of the way down on my backside. The ground was covered with ordinary thick, wet coarse grass. The angle of the slope was so steep that it was impossible to walk, so slide down on my arse it was! I'd hit one or two rocks on my rather swift descent, but a few bruises on my butt were a fair trade for the extra few minutes I'd gained. I quickly crossed a couple of fields and made it into the RV. There was a small group of tired looking recruits to one side, lying on the ground resting against their bergans. They all looked done in, and I knew exactly how they felt. My name and time were recorded, and I asked how I'd done. The instructor shrugged.

"Sorry matey, I haven't got your start time or the grade scale. You'll have to wait for 'Spud's' debriefing later. Dump your bergan over there with the others, and take a breather."

I complied and eased off my bergan. Oh! What bliss! I lay down and chatted to the other boys, while we waited for the rest of the runners to arrive. I had several blisters, which throbbed away as I made the most of this very welcome break. I had long since drained the thermos, so made do with a long deep swig of cold water from my canteen. When the last guys checked in, we were ordered onto the four tonners. As I learnt long ago, standing on fresh blisters is a bitch, and I limped around to the back of the lorry and swung my bergan aboard, with a little help from the blokes already inside. When I had climbed in, I stowed my pack, and helped the next man in with his.

When we got back to camp after about twenty minutes, it was straight off the wagons and into the basher. Clean our rifles before a weapon inspection and then sign them back into the armoury. We then headed straight into the cookhouse for our meagre evening meal. Time always seemed against us, so we had only about thirty minutes spare, which was just enough time to peel off our wet clothes, grab a quick shower and try to find somewhere in the basher to hang our damp clothing. There was absolutely no heat, anywhere in the building, so the chances of drying our uniforms was nil. Clean dry kit on, and into the lecture room to get our scores and then some more lessons. We all sat quietly as the staff filed into the room. 'Spud' O'Leary led them in. He carried a millboard which he dropped onto a lectern; which stood on the podium in front of us.

"Right Gentlemen, your scores!"

There wasn't a sound as he called out the first day's grading. He read out each recruits name and the grade letter they had achieved. I closed my eyes and breathed deeply.

When my turn came, he said, "Black; B grade."... Thank God for that, I'd got the 'B' grade that I wanted. There was one A grade, mostly Bs and a couple of Cs. 'Spud' warned us not to be too pleased with ourselves. He said that we must all work harder tomorrow, as the ground was worse, and the distances greater. He warned those with C grades that they must hit a B, or they would be failed tomorrow night. There were plenty of glum faces dotted around, as 'Spud' handed us over to one of the other instructors, and left the room. We sat through two hours of lectures, and were finally released at about 22.00hrs. We headed straight back to the basher. Everyone's kit remained stubbornly wet. Someone had asked an instructor during a lecture if there was any chance of some heating in the basher. He was told that the Camp Commandant had ordered the heating system to be switched on next Sunday. Perfect, the day after we returned to London. We were all stiff from the day's march, and then having had to sit through several hours of lectures. I opened my bergan and pulled out my sleeping bag. Because it was in a waterproof plastic bag, at least it was dry. I laid it out on the bed. I couldn't jump into it yet; I needed to re-tape my feet, and try to get my boots dry. I removed the old dirty tape and covered the blisters with compression bandages, which should help cushion them tomorrow. When I had finished both feet, I turned to my boots. They were wet through so I stuffed some old newspaper into each one and hoped for the best. When I had finished everything, I sank into my sleeping bag. OK, Day 1 was over, and I hadn't done too badly. Like everyone else in the basher, I had not done another mountain march the following day, so it was going to be tough tomorrow. I tossed and turned for a while worrying about the coming day, before falling into a deep sleep.

TUESDAY: Day Two.

CRASH, BANG "Wakey, wakey, rise and shine!"
Christ! Morning already. It couldn't be, I'd only been asleep ten minutes. Well, it felt like ten minutes. The lights went on, and Sgt. Day was pacing up and down shaking beds.
"Tea please Sergeant," said one idiot.
"Yeah, very funny, get out of bed!"
I stretched, still lying in my bag. God! My entire body felt so stiff. I stretched again and reluctantly unzipped myself out of warmth of my cosy green cocoon. The atmosphere in our room was bloody freezing. Shivering, I looked around the room at my fellow candidates. Everyone looked bleary eyed and dog tired.
Satisfied that his charges were all awake, Sgt Day bawled at us over his shoulder as he left the room.
"Come on lads, you know the drill. Shit, shower and shave, then off to breakfast. Get moving. You only have twenty minutes."
I shuffled into the loos and sorted myself out. Back into the main barrack room. The clothes I had laid out so carefully the night before were still damp from their previous days soaking; and had taken on the room's

temperature, which remained bloody freezing! To maintain a reserve of dry clothing, there was nothing for it; we had to use the same uniform we'd used yesterday. The room quickly filled up with collective groans as the cold, damp clothing touched our bare skin. Boots were still wet, and we all felt frozen to the bone until we reached the cookhouse. It was blissfully warm, compared to the rest of our frigid world. Breakfast was the same as the day before, but very welcome, nevertheless. Packed lunches were issued, which were also meagre and identical to the previous day. When our thermos flasks were full, we reluctantly left the comfort of the warm cookhouse and headed for the armoury to collect our weapons. After signing for our rifles, we picked up our re-packed bergans from the basher, and headed over to the parade square.

We all shivered as we waited for our appointment with the weighing scales. It was still dark and ice glittered across the parade square. The sooner we got cracking, the better. Finally, everyone had been checked, and we climbed aboard our transport. No one said much on the journey to our day's start point. We were all wrapped up in our own reflections on what the coming march might entail. The format for beginning the march was the same, but our start point was in a completely different location, which none of us recognised from previous marches. I had looked at my map the night before, and reckoned that we had covered about eighteen kilometres on our first days march. The distance had not been too far, but there had been several heavy climbs and the ground was very difficult to traverse. Already warned that today would be further and harder, we had the extra disadvantage of marching on fresh blisters.

Oh, Deep joy, what fun! Released from the base camp, I followed my usual routine, and shivered as I stopped to look closely at my map. One of the instructors had told us months before that two minutes map study could save us a lot of extra time and walking. I checked the route. There were really only two viable options. The first was a long straight climb, which would involve a lot of fighting across numerous streams and moon grass. The second was a stiff climb, and then follow the contour along the side of the valley. Which one should I take? The ground looked bloody awful if I crossed all the streams. It would be an easier climb but murder to traverse. The other option would mean half an hour's hard march and climb up the side of the valley, but once I reached the top; I could motor along at the same height almost to the first RV. OK, I decided. It's make your mind up time. I plumped for the second option and started to climb. It was hard going, much harder than I had expected. The ground was slippery, and it was difficult to balance. When I reached the correct height, my legs were already feeling spent. It did not matter though; I should have some easy walking ahead of me if my plan worked. I set off in the direction of the RV. Because I was walking high up at right angles to the slope, I was clear of the moon grass. I covered ground quickly and was soon half way around the side of the valley.

I looked down into the valley, and could see a line of guys slowly struggling up through the stream infested middle. Some were almost at the top, but most had a long tough walk ahead of them. I pushed on towards my goal, my legs felt better, and the blisters weren't too bad. As I reached the check point, I reckoned I had saved about fifteen minutes. It had been a very good start. The next leg was a long one, across the solid moon grass country. No alternatives now just head down and go for it. Three hours; that was my best guess. It didn't really matter, there were no short cuts or tricks I could pull out of the bag. This one was just going to be a pure hard slog. There were plenty of boggy sections, which I had to walk around. It was difficult to tell if some of the bogs were big or small? Should I go left or right? Just look at the ground and take my best guess. I got it really wrong on one section of bog, and ended up having to jump from one clump to the next, to avoid the thick clinging mud beneath. I got out eventually, but had used up a lot of reserve energy and precious minutes. I could see one or two other guys around me. Where were the rest? God knows. It did take three hours across that leg. I reached the RV and got my next one. It was at almost right angles to my last line of march. More moon grass, and several deep, fast flowing streams to wade through. When the first was crossed, I was soaked from the waist down, and could feel the cold water squelching in my boots. No point in stopping to empty them; it would just happen again at the next stream. The RV was only a couple of kilometres from the last and I finally reached it, only to be sent back towards our original start point. Yet another long hard slog, through three more long hours of punishing moon grass. I was approaching the RV from a different angle, so I didn't have a route which I already knew. It was just harder marching, hour after hour. I didn't see a living being on that leg, and was getting more than a little bit concerned. Were they all ahead of me, around me, or behind me? For that matter, had I screwed up on my navigation and wandered off course? I had to trust my map reading and stick to my planned route. I reached the head of the original valley. I stopped for a moment and dug out my last Mars bar I had brought with me for today's march. Although the last part (I hoped) of the march was fairly easy compared to the last seven hours, I felt just about done in. Maintaining my rhythm I marched as quickly as I could along the contour but began losing height gradually to avoid a steep descent at the end. When I reached the original start point there was only one lorry. Had the other one already left, were they waiting just for me? I checked in and was told to stretch out on the grass and wait. I dropped my bergan where I had been told and nipped around to the back of the four tonner. Empty, Great! I must be in the middle of the field. Should be another B grade? I certainly hoped so. I walked back to my bergan, and removed my boots. It was a tremendous relief to get them off, and felt great to peel off my soaking socks. I turned my boots upside down, and poured out some filthy black bog water. I wrung my socks out and put them back on. It was still around sub-zero, and they would quickly freeze up as stiff as a board if I left them out. I replaced my boots, as the next recruit arrived.

"You look like I feel" I said to him as he dumped his bergan. His face looked ashen and drawn with fatigue.

"Yeah," was all he could manage.

I told him that the lorry was empty. He nodded, but didn't even manage a smile. Another recruit arrived several minutes later, followed slowly by the rest of them, over the next frigid hour. The last guy was limping heavily. It turned out that he had slipped and fallen heavily earlier in the day, and badly twisted his leg. Judging by the sharp intake of breath from him as we helped him into the lorry, the poor bastard was going to be hard pushed to continue tomorrow. When we arrived back at camp, the first lorry load of recruits were already showered and changed. I set to with my rifle, and handed it into the armoury as soon as it had been inspected. The shower was only tepid at best, but I was still very glad of it. It seemed to be colder in the basher than when we got up that morning. I was glad to put on my dry reserve clothes. I felt pretty done in, and sat on my bed with my map to see how far I had marched today. It looked about twenty four kilometres, give or take. They had been right about the country too. It was bloody awful. Someone mentioned it was time for tea, so we all limped and hobbled down to the cookhouse. I've always wondered if army cooks go on some special flavour removal course as part of their basic training. Our dinner of warm, brown lumpy stuff didn't taste of anything, in particular, but despite this we were all starving hungry, and soon, nothing was left on anyone's plate. A big tin mug of hot sweet tea was just great to wash down whatever it was we had just eaten. Even our cooks couldn't screw that up.

When we were ready, we left for the lecture room. 'Spud' arrived, followed by his hit squad of instructors.

"Scores, Gentleman." He said without looking up from his clipboard.

I got another B. Fantastic news. No one got an A, mostly Bs and a couple of Cs. He gave out three Fs. One was on medical grounds. The guy with the twisted leg was taken off the course. Poor sod. The other two just weren't fast enough. I didn't look at them; they must have been so totally pissed off. Failed outright; without the benefit of a Court of Appeal. Not good for either of them. Nevertheless, for the rest of us though, and tomorrow was another day.

Wednesday: Day three.

I was already awake when Cpl. Dean slammed on the lights at 05.00hrs. I had slept badly during the night, a mixture of the cold, and the numerous aches and pains in my battered body. Two days hard marching in the mountains were beginning to take their toll. It was easy to tell that everyone was suffering as they slowly climbed out of their sleeping bags. The air was blue with sulphurous curses aimed at Brecon, the army and selection, in particular. Unfortunately, several of the lads were starting to show signs of real physical distress. One guy's back was rubbed raw by his bergan. Most of the top layers of the skin on his lower back had gone, leaving a red, raw, weeping mass of damaged tissue. We helped him tape a large flat wound dressing over the damaged area. The poor devil was in a really sorry state, but he shrugged off his injury, and his face remained a grim mask of determination. Several other guys were nursing twisted ankles and knees. There was a strong smell of liniment in the room, and elastic bandages were out in force. After the usual breakfast and preparation, we fell in by the pre-dawn light, beside our lorries, which were parked at their usual spot on the parade square. The only change to the routine that morning was that the Sgt. Major made a point of asking each man in turn if he had any serious injuries, he wished to report. He was met with a wall of silence; lips were sealed, and no one admitted anything. We had all seen what had happened to the injured bloke at the end of day one.

We started the third day with a long tough march along the ancient Roman road leading towards Pen y Fan (the Fan). There was a heavy powdering of snow up on the peaks, and a bitingly cold wind blew into my face, as I struggled to maintain a decent pace. The rock strewn track was covered in glistening ice, which made the going dangerously treacherous. Carrying a heavy 45lb back pack changes the body's centre of gravity, making it much higher than normal. This makes staying upright considerably more difficult on a wet, slippery angled surface. When the pace must be forced, it's just too easy to slip on the ice and fall heavily. Although an individual effort, we were all collectively under the cosh, and had to keep going as fast as possible. Thoughts of personal injury just had to be pushed to one side. After more than an hour of hard and difficult marching, it was time to turn off the Roman road and head towards the misty summit of the distant Fan. As once or twice before, I could see a well spread out crocodile of runners ahead of me, all grimly heading towards the base of the biggest mountain in South Wales.

I had traversed about a kilometre around the approach track, which skirted another mountain called Cribyn when it happened. Without warning, my boot caught a patch of ice, and I slipped and pitched forward. All my weight landed on my left knee, which made hard contact with the corner of a rock, half-buried in the ground. The edge of the rock hit me just under my left knee cap. The pain was indescribable. It felt like someone had slammed a chain saw into the middle of my leg. I couldn't speak for a moment, and lay on the ground like a beached turtle clutching my leg. I felt hot tears of pain running down my cheeks as I gasped for breath. I think I must have lain there for several minutes on the cold wet track, holding my injured leg and groaning with agony. I heard someone coming up fast behind me. It must be the next recruit, or so I thought. I opened my eyes. It wasn't another course member. It was Major Dave Roberts, the boss of 'B' Squadron, based in Dulwich. He stopped beside me, and gave me a cold, disdainful look.

"Do you want to pass selection?" I groaned that I did. "Then fucking well get off your arse, and get on with it!"

He stared at me angrily for a moment longer and then just strode off, towards the Fan. I lay there once again alone in the mud, in a state of shock. No, I wasn't shocked; I was staggered. I had just received a severe bollocking for not getting my finger out, without the slightest help or sympathy. I rolled onto my front, gritted my teeth and slowly stood up. Despite the burning pain, I could still move the knee joint. It was stiff and painful, but I carefully put my full weight on it. The knee hurt like hell, but I could cope with that. I took a few steps. Nothing seemed broken. I picked up my rifle and started making slow limping tracks towards the Fan. My injured knee throbbed, but I wasn't going to call in sick. No way, not a chance. I'd show that bastard that I wanted to pass. Still hobbling, I finished the route around Cribyn and reached the base of the Fan. Digging deep, I began the climb. Another recruit passed me after a minute or two. He didn't say anything, totally focused and saving his breath for the climb. I slowly fought my way up towards the top, and thankfully, the pain didn't get any worse as I gained height. It was a punishing climb at the best of times, and took me nearly an hour. When I made the trig point RV, Dave Roberts was sitting on his bergan drinking tea, casually chatting with the two instructors, who were staffing the checkpoint. He looked at me hard and simply said.

"How's the leg?"

"Yeah, it's OK Sir."

"Do you want to jack it in?"

"No Sir!"

His face impassive, he nodded and stood up. After shouldering his bergan, Dave Roberts said good-bye to the instructors and took off towards the next RV, without saying another word to me. I asked one of the instructors why he was there.

"He's just come down for a couple of days to see how his recruits are doing, and to stretch his legs," replied one of the Corporals. "You quite sure you want to carry on?"

"Yes Staff, I'm fine thanks." I mumbled.

Of course, I didn't feel fine, but I wasn't going to admit it, or they might pull me off. The next RV was on the other side of the mountain, way down at its base, in a car park. The main road beside the parking area eventually ran out of the mountains, away down to the ancient town of Brecon. I got going quickly, as I didn't want my injured knee to get too cold and lock up. As I dropped over the ridge, I had to decide urgently what to do about this next stage. If I wanted to make up the time on my slower than usual ascent of the Fan, I would have to run quickly down the long steep track in front of me. Running down the slippery track would constantly throw all my weight onto the damaged knee, every time I flicked my left leg forward during my planned descent. It might do more damage and stop me altogether; this was a serious shit or bust moment. If I didn't run down the mountain I'd lose too much time, arrive late, and get an F. There was only one decision to make, no question about it. I started the flip-flop run down towards the car park. If I maintained a steady pace, I should be there in about fifteen minutes. After five minutes of pounding down the muddy, rock strewn path, I knew I had made the right decision. My knee still throbbed painfully, but it was withstanding the constant heavy impacts. I reached the RV at the bottom of the mountain safely, thankfully without any more slips or falls.

When I gave my name, one of the instructors asked how my leg was. Either Dave Roberts had mentioned it on his way through, or the Staff at the top of the Fan had radioed down during my rapid descent. When I grinned and lied to them that my leg was feeling fine, I got my next RV, way up at the top of Fan Fawr. The mountain's base was on the other side of the road, several hundred metres away. This next mountain is the little sister of Pen y Fan. It stands some four hundred feet lower, but the route to the top is very steep and difficult. After a lot of hard work climbing up the treacherous track, I made it safely to the summit, but I knew I was slowing down. I checked in and received the next RV. I inspected the map closely. It lay several kilometres westward; at a big stream junction. The route was all gently downhill, but involved crossing solid moon grass country. It's impossible to run on moon grass, so I'd be really pushed to recover lost time. With my compass set and ready, I limped off as fast as I could. I managed to maintain a pace which was steady, but still worryingly slow. We had been told something early on in the course; which kept ringing in my ears, as I plodded on through the moon grass. One of the Training Wing Sergeants had said during a lecture.

"We are looking for character and attitude, as well as fitness and determination. If you fail yourself by withdrawingduring a march you are finished,no second chances.If you keep putting one footin front oftheother, you are alwaysin witha chance. Don't give in, just keep going!" the road, several hundred metres away. This next mountain is the little sister of Pen y Fan. It stands some four hundred feet lower, but the route to the top is very steep and difficult. After a lot of hard work climbing up the treacherous track, I made it safely to the summit, but I knew I was slowing down. I checked in and received the next RV. I inspected the map closely. It lay several kilometres westward; at a big stream junction. The route was all gently downhill, but involved crossing solid moon grass country. It's impossible to run on moon grass, so I'd be really pushed to recover lost time. With my compass set and ready, I limped off as fast as I could. I managed to maintain a pace which was steady, but still worryingly slow. We were told something early in the course; which kept ringing in my ears, as I plodded on through the moon grass. One of the Training Wing Sergeants said during a lecture.

It was the last part which kept echoing over and over in my mind. 'Don't give in, just keep going'. 'Don't give in, just keep going'

It was sound, solid advice. He was absolutely right, of course. I was very tired, sore and slow, but I must keep driving myself forward. I'd set an enormous task by going on selection in the first place, but I was now close to the end. I had to find the grit, if I wanted to pass. No one would help me; it would happen because I had it in me; and only I could make it happen.

I reached the RV, and was sent immediately on to the next. The staff didn't say anything to me, so I must still be in with a chance of making it to the final test of Long Drag. When I finally reached the last RV, I had a huge rush of relief. I had completed day three, and it just remained to find out my score. When our journey back to camp was over, my injured knee was feeling very stiff. I eased myself down from the back of the lorry very carefully, as I didn't want to aggravate the injury. After cleaning my rifle, and myself, I headed to the armoury, then on to the cookhouse. There were several long faces among the recruits. They had sat on their beds with their heads down. They knew they had done badly during the day, and must have already scored a C on one of the previous days.

I didn't feel too confident; it all hinged on whether I'd screwed up too much on today's march. I might be looking down both barrels of a big, fat F grade, and out. When it was time to get our days grading, the tension in the lecture room was unbearable. We had all given it our best over the last incredibly tough, exhausting three days, but not knowing the times put a huge knot in my stomach. R.S.M. 'Spud' arrived as usual bang on time with his posse.

"Right Gentlemen, before we start I should warn you that a few of you are due for the chop, and are going home."

My mouth was as dry as a bone, and the knot in my gut felt as big as a house. He started in the usual order, which meant about ten people before me, would get their marks first. He handed out a couple of Bs then a C. He stopped and looked up.

"That's your second C Harris, so you've failed." He went on and handed the next guy an F. "You're off as well Osbourne." Another head dropped miserably among us.

The next three guys each received a B grade, the next a C. It was getting close now, so I braced myself. A couple more Bs, then he said.

"Black.......C".....

I'd done it!! I let out a huge sigh of relief. I looked at the floor for a moment and let it sink in... 'Just keep going.' I'd paid for my ticket and was on Long Drag in the morning! No shit, absolutely brilliant! I didn't hear the other blokes grades; I was lost for a moment in my own little private world, filled with pure unadulterated joy. After so much effort, I was so very close now. One more enormous push and I was through selection and onto Continuation. We still had our two hours of lectures that evening. I don't think there was one recruit who didn't fall asleep at least once. The room was warm and full of very tired, nodding heads. I dozed off and was soundly reprimanded by the lecturer. I was so tired when we got back to the basher, I shoved my dry kit into a bag, stuffed it into my began and zipped myself up in my sleeping bag. I was asleep before my head hit the pillow.

Thursday: Long Drag

I was still sound asleep when the instructor bounded in and switched on the lights. I half opened one bleary eye. Christ, morning already.

"Come on lads, big day today, rise and shine!"

I stayed where I was, hiding from his bright and happy demeanour. I stretched. My knee felt ominously sore, as I tried to get out of my bag. Christ! The bloody thing had locked solid overnight. I struggled, but couldn't get out of my sleeping bag. I called a couple of the boys over. They helped me to ease myself out of the bag and lowered my leg onto the floor. It felt as if I had an invisible plaster cast fitted, from thigh to ankle. After massaging the joint for a minute or so, I managed to move it slightly. I sat back down on the bed, and pulled on my cold damp shirt. The trousers took a bit longer, but I finally managed to pull them up. I don't think I had ever felt more dejected and miserable in my life before. I was still very tired, freezing cold and covered in damp clothing. I could hardly move my leg, and I was off soon to start the toughest 24 hours of my life. A little voice in my head said.

'Welcome to selection, if you can't take a joke, you shouldn't have joined!' Despite the pain, I couldn't help smiling to myself. I must be completely round the bend, putting myself through all this. I stood up, this time without help. I slowly flexed my knee joint. It was starting to move, little by little. After another ten minutes, I was walking. Socks and boots on. Smock, hat and off to breakfast. The boys asked me if I was OK when I sat down in front of my little breakfast. I nodded in silence and ate quickly.

We were on the start line just before 06.45hrs. The lorry (we were down to needing just one now) had taken longer today to reach our drop-off point. We had skirted way around to the east of the mountain range, and had followed a narrow country road as it slowly twisted its way up to our ultimate destination. I got off the wagon slowly, trying to hide my injury as best I could. None of the assembled staff seemed to take any notice of me. So far, so good. I wasn't alone; about half of us were carrying an injury of one sort or another. Burgan burns, twisted ankles and strained knees, and countless blisters. Nothing serious, all the injuries were just bloody irritating and painful. I had taken a couple of mild painkillers before I got on the truck. My knee still felt sore, but good to go. We all looked around at the terrain. There wasn't much to see. A long, long grass covered slope ahead of us, which seemed to go onwards and upwards for miles. An army ambulance accompanied the usual Land Rover today, sporting big red crosses on its sides and back. We had a quick briefing by the Training Wing Sgt. Major. He reminded us that this was the Regiment's ultimate endurance march, and we had enough time to complete the course, provided we didn't slow down too much or get injured. We were set off in the usual fashion, one by one. The first RV was way ahead of us, out of sight, hidden somewhere up the slope. Dawn was just breaking as I was released, at exactly 07.00hrs. I felt in better shape now, and made ground well as my body and muscles warmed up. The sky was clear, but it was bitterly cold. Walking conditions were fine, in fact, the best I had experienced in the Brecon's so far. The slope seemed to be endless and took good forty-five minutes to climb. There was the usual wait before checking into the opening RV, and several guys growled at each other to get moving when it was their turn. The next checkpoint was way up on top of Pen y Fan. There were several different route options available to us. I chose what I thought would be the quickest, and was eventually rewarded with the welcome sight of the other recruits ahead of me using the same path. I say path, it wasn't a path as such, just a narrow, well worn sheep track, just a few inches wide. It wound off in the right direction, towards the distant mountain peak. The march was a long one, and part of it took me right to the edge of several sheer cliffs, which dropped hundreds of feet, down to jagged scree slopes far, far below. The track became even narrower, and I was putting my right foot just inches from the edge. Small rocks were embedded everywhere in the track, and every one glistened with a thick covering of ice. One slip now and my trip would be a whole lot worse than yesterday. The danger of falling aside though, I was making ground well. The view from the cliff's edge was fantastic. The entire magnificent panorama of the east side of the Beacons could be seen through the freezing, crystal clear air. Not much chance to enjoy it; I was too busy looking where I put my bloody feet. When the track finally led away from the top of the cliffs, I dropped down onto the Roman road and pounded my way along it. The streams, which crossed the ancient route, seemed to have cut even deeper. Impeded by my heavy bergan and rifle, one of the deepest streams involved a careful hand over hand descent to its muddy bottom. Cross the torrent which roared and foamed angrily around my legs, and climb out again, hand over hand. As I marched alone along the old Roman road, I couldn't help thinking of the Roman soldiers who had used the same route, two millennia before me. They were weighed down with body armour and heavy primitive shields and weapons. The Roman troops would have been wearing nothing but togas and sandals. They must have been a pretty tough bunch of blokes. Little wonder they conquered the known world of the time. Here I was, two thousand years later, a young soldier carrying plenty of heavy gear, and a weapon, travelling exactly the same route. Nothing changes.

I reached the base of the Fan without any mishaps this time. The pain from my knee and the blisters on my feet was always there but manageable. Climbing up the fan was just as arduous and gruelling as the day before. Although the air around me was freezing, I was sweating profusely when I reached the top. Two Training Wing instructors were camped by the trig point. They had set up a small two man orange tent bearing the logo 'Storm Force 10'. A long aerial poked out of one end of the tent, and I could hear the background hiss of static on the military radio net somewhere within. The car park I had visited the day before was next on the list of RVs. I took off at the double, with my back to the trig point. The ground beneath my feet was solid granite, scoured by the ferocious winds, which regularly lashed the summit of Pen y Fan. I followed the same route as the previous day, and dropped over the ridge off to my right. I moved down the mountain as fast as I could go, until I reached the car park. As usual, there was no-one for company, apart from the occasional scraggy looking sheep. When I arrived at the RV, one of the instructors weighed my bergan. It remained slightly overweight, so no problem. Fan Fawr was next. Yet another long hot and difficult climb. It was getting close to lunchtime when I cleared the top of Fan Fawr. I hadn't eaten anything since breakfast. We had been told to use our 24-hour ration pack during Long Drag, and hadn't been issued with a packed lunch. Should I stop and cook, or keep going? I decided to stay with it, and keep going. I wanted to make the most of every available moment of daylight. I didn't feel too knackered, and also wanted to make the most of the rhythm my body was in. The next leg was gently downhill, and almost due south to a big stream junction about five kilometres away. It was hard going, thick treacherous moon grass all the way. My boots were still full of gritty muddy water, and my ever-present blisters were starting to really kick in again, but I just had to grit my teeth, and accept the constant stinging pain of each step. I reached the RV limping slightly. I had by then, been marching for about nine hours. The instructors who were staffing the checkpoint had set up the same type of orange tent, and were clearly expecting a long stay. I got a set of press-ups for not having my hat on when I entered the RV. It was a fair cop; I forgot to put the bloody thing on. We were always supposed to be correctly dressed on entering an RV, but all of us stuffed our woollen cap comforters into our smocks, as soon as we were clear. Marching fast, carrying a heavy pack generates a tremendous amount of body heat. It helps to dump that heat, when your head is bare. I should have gone through the usual routine on approaching the RV and checked hat, pockets and kit. I must be getting tired; certainly, no argument there. The next RV was bloody miles away, across more difficult moon grass country. I struggled on, across the barren, desolate landscape. This particular leg was a real bastard and took three or four hours of solid, hard slog. It sapped the strength out of my legs, faster than a couple of Mars bars could replace it. My thermos flask was now empty, and I was running low on water. I needed to stop and get a proper hot meal inside me, and replenish my flask and water bottles. It was just starting to get dark when I spotted the corner of a plantation I was looking for, way off in the distance. The RV was a couple of kilometres beyond it. I decided to hit the plantation, and find a good spot with some running water and have a proper hot meal. We had all been briefed to allow ourselves at least one short break during Long Drag, and my body was telling me that now was exactly the right time. I was feeling very, very tired. I had been marching for about thirteen hours in daylight, had climbed two of the highest mountains in the Beacons, and had already covered about twenty five kilometres with forty-five pounds strapped to my back. I hadn't a clue how much more there was to trek, but the rest of Long Drag would have to be completed in darkness. Distance times are much, much slower in the inky blackness of night. No, overall, now was the time to take a short break. It was almost completely dark when I found the right spot I had been looking for. I dumped my bergan, and refilled and sterilised my canteens. I found that even that chore was done very slowly. It took me a little longer than I would have liked to prepare my meal and eat it, but I felt so much better when I had finished. I allowed myself five more minutes rest, and then with considerable effort re-packed my bergan. Having checked that I left no sign of my temporary presence, I set off for the last part of the journey to the next checkpoint. I found it easily enough, as it was on one end of a massive dam. I asked the instructor how I was doing, and he answered my question with just two words.

"Keep going!"

134

The next RV was a long way over a ridge and down to yet another dam. I hadn't walked over this area before, but it in the darkness it seemed just as bad (if not worse) than the last leg. There was no doubt in my mind now that the Regiment had saved the worst they had to offer until last. All the nastiest bits of country had been saved up, and then tacked together into a very long, difficult night march; which they had so accurately named 'Long Drag'. I set off into the inky darkness and spent the next three hours stumbling through a nightmare of moon grass and bogs. With all the filthy swamp water in my boots, I felt as if I had blisters on my blisters. My knee was OK; it had stiffened slightly during my short break, but had soon settled down again, once I kicked things into gear and started moving. Eventually, I got close to the RV and checked myself. I wasn't going to let those bastards give me any more press-ups. The Training Wing instructor warned me that the next leg was the worst of all, and that time was getting short. Wearily, I checked my watch; it was nearly midnight. I had just over seven hours left. It was a long way, and the obvious straight route showed a massive quarry intersected with cliffs here and there, which cut my route neatly in two. I could march around the scattered cliffs, which would mean another five or six kilometres, across more terrible moon grass country, or I could try to find a way through the cliffs, down into the quarry and up the other side. I was close to utter exhaustion by now and decided that the quickest route between two points was a straight line. The map suggested that the cliffs formed the quarry sides but there were plenty of large gaps between any sheer drops. If I could find one of these big gaps in the dark, I could be through this obstacle in front of me with ample time to spare. I marched on through the darkness for another hour and half. The ground in front of me slowly began to dip. I must be getting close to the quarry. The angle of the ground continued to become steeper and steeper, until I had no alternative but to slide down on my butt. It seemed that I must find the bottom of the quarry soon, as I spent what seemed like ages sliding down towards it. I wasn't descending too fast and managed to stop dead when the bottom half of my legs suddenly dropped over the edge. 'Oh Shit!' The slope I was sitting on dropped away into nothing vertically in front of me. I didn't have time to turn around before the earth ledge I was sitting on gave way, and I was pitched forward into the inky black void. As I fell, I frantically twisted myself around to try and grab onto something...anything! There was nothing there, except the smooth cold cliff face of hard granite rock.

I don't know how far I fell. It probably wasn't more than twenty or thirty feet but without warning, my boots abruptly hit a scree slope, and I pitched backwards. My bergan took most of the impact when I hit the ground; almost immediately followed by the back of my head. I remember suddenly seeing hundreds of brilliant exploding red and blue stars, then nothing........

135

I woke up, lying in the dark where I had fallen. All around me were solid, sharp blocks of granite, bigger than my bergan. If the back of my head had hit any one of them, there was no question, I would have been killed instantly. Purely by chance, however, my head hit a relatively soft patch of earth. I appeared to have landed on a ledge, which stretched away into the darkness along the side of the quarry. I had one hell of a headache, but the only real casualty appeared to be the inner glass lining of my thermos, which had shattered into a million tiny pieces. I wandered around still dazed for several minutes, looking for my rifle. I found it lying on a little ledge, about seven feet above where I had landed. I climbed up and retrieved it. I looked at my watch. Jesus! I'd been out cold for nearly three hours! The sudden shock left me verging on panic. I had to get going now, or fail selection. I pulled myself together and started to walk unsteadily along the ledge, which was actually a narrow path. I marched to the end of the quarry, as I certainly was not going to repeat my mistake of trying to find a short cut across it. The path eventually found its way down to a service road, which led up and out of the huge quarry. Having checked my map, I now knew exactly where I was.

The RV was about two and a half kilometres to the right of the road junction, which lay just ahead of me. It was now 06.05hrs on Friday morning. I had used up a full 23 hours, and now had less than an hour to go. If this was the last RV, I could still make it, if it wasn't, I was stuffed! Selection rules forbade using roads, but as far as I was concerned, this was now a real emergency. If I didn't cover the last short leg as fast as I could I would fail. I spotted a couple of recruits ahead of me, as I jogged up the road. I recognised them as two 'B' Squadron boys. We all doubled up that damned road as fast as our exhausted legs could carry us. Like me, they felt sure that this had to be the final RV. As they had both been released after me, at the start of Long Drag, we agreed that I would go in first. They dropped back a bit, as I carried on.

The sky to one side of me was glowing with pre-dawn light. My heart was pounding as I approached a bend in the road, close to what I prayed was the last checkpoint. Suddenly, there it was! The wonderful sight I wanted to see at that moment, more than anything else in the world. A military four ton lorry, an ambulance and a couple of Land Rovers, parked in a field beside the road. I checked myself for loose buttons and put my hat on. This had to be the end... It had to be.

I walked up to the instructor who was clutching a millboard, and gave him my name. He passed the millboard to 'Spud' O'Leary, who, standing ramrod straight, looked hard at it, then scrutinised his watch. He looked up at me and said.

"You have passed selection, get on the truck." ...

That was it. End of conversation… Sweet Jesus! What did you have to do to get a pat on the back in this Regiment? OK, no brass bands, no cheering adoring crowds energetically waving Union flags, but a slug of rum laced tea and a 'Well Done' would have been nice.

I didn't care though........I'd done it! Only thirteen minutes left. Pretty close, but a pass is a pass in anybody's language. I would have arrived hours earlier, but for my free-fall down into that bloody quarry. I walked around to the back of the lorry. There were several guys resting on their bergans inside. As I heaved my bergan onto the lorry, one of them grunted. "Pass?" I looked into the gloomy interior and smiled;

"Damn right!"…

Chapter 10
Continuation

It is impossible not to change, having just passed the mountain phase of SAS selection. After months of rigorous, immensely physical work, I now stood on the brink of a new military world ... An exclusive, secret world.

Ahead of me, lay the next part of the Regiment's selection process - Continuation training. By passing selection, I had now proven to the Special Air Service Regiment that I was a suitable candidate for further intensive training. There would be months of exciting, specialised training, which was exactly what I wanted to do. Before I begin recounting the next stage however, it is well worth reflecting on what had happened to me physically, and what had changed in my personality. Getting past the enormous hurdle of the mountain phase of selection, I had actually burnt off an extra stone of body mass during the final selection week. When fat reserves are gone, the body begins to feed on muscle. That didn't matter, I was fitter than I had ever been. More importantly, I had completely altered my attitude towards adversity. Suddenly, anything seemed possible. I had learnt a great deal more about myself, and devined that the mind controls the body, and definitely not the other way around. Pain and discomfort are things which the mind deals with. Marching alone for countless miles across the rugged terrain of the Black Mountains and Brecon Beacons had shown me that painful blisters were really just an irritation during the marches. Wet, chaffing clothing sometimes rubbed my skin raw, adding to the misery, but could be controlled and ignored. Twisted ankles and injuries caused by falls, might reduce my speed, but did not stop me from completing the course. Cramps, dehydration and exhaustion could all be overcome, simply by following the training I was given, and by gritting my teeth and getting on with the job in hand. By design, I did not receive an atom of encouragement from the Regiment's Training Wing staff; motivation to pass was 100% self-generated. I passed, because I made myself pass. Not being a man of letters, or a natural athlete, I would personally class myself as being a fairly ordinary, normal sort of bloke. Of course, physical fitness and stamina were vitally important aspects in successfully completing such a demanding selection course, but there are, however, two more important factors to consider, willpower and determination. Any healthy, intelligent man should be capable of passing, providing they have prepared their bodies to a much better than average physical condition, and then got into the right mental mindset to make themselves pass. Marching alone, over numerous mountains, and fighting through terrible, ferocious weather by day and night made the course, naturally, much more difficult but ultimately made success taste that much sweeter. I had overcome everything that they, and Mother Nature had thrown at me so far. The Regiment had exactly what they wanted, a successful candidate, who had passed by making a determined, individual effort. Selection had forced me to look deeply within myself, and I had not found myself wanting. It was a good feeling.

What about the eye injury, that had set me on this path?
After what I'd recently gone through, it had become nothing more than a mere insignificance. Having achieved so much, frankly, it just didn't matter anymore.

On reflection, the nearest equivalent lifestyle in civilian life might be a talented young football player, who was utterly dedicated from a very young age to his sport. Having trained hard, and played in a professional junior league, he might naturally progress to a 1st Division team. If he was really good enough, he might come to the attention of the English football selectors, and be picked to play for England. He'd then, of course, enjoy the natural adulation of his fans, and all the lucrative spin-offs associated with professional football endorsements. Ironically, although my military circumstances ran along similar lines, my goal had been achieved in secret, without any of the fanfares of a national hero. However, that didn't matter. I had made it to the pinnacle, and was in my own way, now, playing for England.

PHASE THREE

Chapter 11:

A fresh beginning

I sat in the back of the four-ton lorry feeling smug, sore, exhausted, but utterly elated. Outside, moments before, 'Spud' O'Leary had told me that I had passed SAS selection. He was the regular Regimental Sergeant Major in a Territorial Army Special Air Service Regiment. He was also the senior Non-Commissioned Officer, responsible of our final selection. His decisions were law, and remained absolutely final. Throughout the run-up to Long Drag, during selection week, he had chopped plenty of good lads who had failed to make the times required, during our continuous week of remorseless daytime marches. His cold, humourless attitude towards us was simply his way of being strictly impartial. He showed no favouritism to officers, ex-regulars, in fact, to anyone. We were all just faces to him. If someone failed, he chopped him without any emotion, end of story. Anyway, he had passed me, and that was the important thing.

The journey back to camp passed in a haze of exhaustion and adrenaline; I was too excited and chuffed to sleep. When we arrived back at camp, we were ordered to get our weapons and ourselves clean, grab some breakfast, and then be outside on parade at 09.00hrs. I wandered into the basher, and was met by a chorus of 'How did you do?' from the other successful candidates who had not fallen over a cliff, and as a result, made better times during Long Drag. They had been ferried back from the mountains before me. Several slaps on a sore back later, I sat down on my bunk and began to sort myself out. When my rifle was spotless, I showered, and dressed into my clean, dry uniform. It was always a relief to shed the filthy, sweat soaked gear I had worn on a march. Several lads that I had shared the return journey with were also ready, so we wandered over to the armoury together, signed in our rifles, and went across to the cookhouse for breakfast. The short parade at 09.00hrs was quickly followed by a trip straight to the lecture room. One by one, a final, formal confirmation of pass or fail was given to each of us. There were quite a few failures, where lads had been removed from Long Drag, because of injury or failure to make various cut-out times between individual legs of the march. Personally, I felt a huge wave of sympathy for the unsuccessful candidates. Having got so far, and then to have fallen at the last hurdle was a crushing, miserable end to their otherwise valiant attempt.

Of the ninety-three who had started the course three months earlier, there were now only nine successful recruits left. We were moved into another lecture room. Each man who had failed was interviewed by 'Spud', and his performance analysed. Clearly, the Training Wing staff had looked very closely at each man during the entire course, as they offered only two unsuccessful candidates the opportunity to re-select. The sting in the tail, however, was that if they wanted to try again, they would have to do the entire selection course all over again. 'Spud' told them to both go away and think about it, and to give him their decisions the following day.

When the new continuation course was seated in front of the Major Brook, (officer Commanding - Training Wing), he immediately gave us a stern warning about not becoming complacent.

"You have only passed the first phase of selection Gentlemen," he said. "But don't fall into the trap of thinking its plain sailing from here on in; because it most definitely is not! You can still screw up and fail during the next three months. You are now officially continuation recruits, but still have not been accepted into the Regiment, until you successfully complete the remainder of the course. In recognition of the fact that you have passed the mountain phase however, you may now wear the Regimental Stable belt."

The 'Stable belt' is a unique feature to each Regiment in the British army. The belt's colour varies, and most have their particular Regiment's cap badge embossed on the metal clasp. Our Stable belt was blue, complete with the Regiment's Winged Dagger, emblazoned on the circular silver buckle. We all grinned broadly at each other. We could purchase a belt later. Major Brook went on to outline the coming Continuation Training. He explained that because this was the first taste of military life for some of us, it was necessary to cover both basic and specialist training during Continuation. We would be taught some basic infantry tactics and field craft, but would quickly move onto combat survival, where we would learn to 'live off the land'. We would trap animals for food, build shelters and learn how to safely cross dangerous river obstacles, and so on. We would take part in Mobility training; driving Land Rovers, lorries, motor bikes, etc. We would be taught how to hot wire vehicles and steal them. We also had to learn how to rock climb and abseil. On our first weekend, we would use the dark arts of resisting interrogation if captured during operations. We'd learn about explosives, and would fire British and foreign weapons on the range weekend. Our Continuation course would end in a tactical Test Weekend, where we would finally put it all together. If we made it through the next phase, then, and only then, we would be presented with our sandy berets and be officially taken onto the strength of the SAS. Our O.C. went over the general scheme of things; the roles of the Territorial SAS, and how we fitted into the order of battle within NATO.

In concluding his lecture, Major Brook told us that our real training with the Regiment started when we finally joined our respective Squadrons, after we had been officially accepted. The first important hurdle after that was to pass the basic parachute course, run by the Royal Air Force, at RAF Brize Norton. When we had gained our SAS 'parachute wings' badge, we would go back to our squadrons, and choose our primary and secondary skills. They would be of real use within the patrol we were ultimately put into. Medicine, demolitions and signalling were the core elements of future training, and they would be studied at both basic and advanced levels; however, that would come later. Right now, we had to begin working on our Continuation training. I let his words sink in for a moment. This was exactly what I wanted out of soldiering. The opportunity was there in front of me to take on new challenges within the military and learn the skills, which, until now. I had only dreamed of. Major Brook finished his address, and handed us over to one of our Corporals. He unfolded a blanket lying on the table behind him, revealing a number of murderous looking firearms. He told us that his lecture was an opening introduction to foreign weapons. He would show us several assault rifles and light machine guns, so that we could begin to familiarise ourselves with them, prior to firing them for real, later during the course. He started his lecture with the Russian AK47 and an American M16 Armalite assault rifles. He explained them in detail, and demonstrated their workings to us. Because the course was now so small with only nine men left, we all had plenty of 'hands on' with the various weapons he showed us. When we had finished his very interesting lesson, we were told to be back in the lecture room in half an hour, and that we could temporarily fall out, and go and get a mug of tea from the cookhouse. The excitement and adrenalin of passing Long Drag was beginning to wear off, and the stark fact that we had not had a wink of sleep for over thirty hours, and marched for well over forty five kilometres was really starting to kick in, and be felt by all of us. We sat huddled in the cookhouse nursing hot sweet mugs of tea, by now really feeling the effects of our recent labours. Conversation was down to the occasional grunt by the time the tea was finished. It was time to return for more lectures. We passed the twenty-odd lads that had failed selection during our Test Week. Some were to carry out fatigue duties around camp, and those who had just failed to complete Long Drag were heading back to the basher for some sleep. Not us though, we had classroom, classroom and more classrooms, before we were finished today. By lunchtime, the entire continuation course was fighting extreme and overwhelming fatigue. Heads were nodding among us, with plenty of sharp elbows in the ribs from each other, to help stay awake. Lunch was eaten in virtual silence, and we all got our heads down for what was left of our generous two-hour break. Someone had asked one of the people on fatigues to wake us, which thankfully he did, with fifteen minutes to spare. None of us shone during that afternoon, we were all bleary eyed and exhausted. When the last lecture was finally over, we wandered into the cookhouse, grabbed a quick meal and to a man, headed back to our basher for a very well deserved sleep.

The next morning, it was time to head back to the comforts of home. Selection week was over. Our basher had to be scrubbed until it gleamed, and our clothing and equipment packed, ready for the journey back to London. The new continuation course was at last permitted to buy our new Stable belts. One of the Corporals checked our names, to prevent any unsuccessful candidate from slipping in, and purchasing what would be no more than a souvenir of failing selection. These belts meant a great deal to us. When everything was done, and we were ready, everyone boarded the coach and I for one, was glad to be leaving.

When we finally arrived back at the Duke of York's barracks in the Kings Road, Chelsea, interviews were being held for the new intake of recruits. They would form the next selection course, which would start in a few week's time. We didn't speak to any of them. They would find out for themselves, what was involved in their next three months? We handed in some equipment, and were told to be in at the usual time on the next Tuesday evening. As I had passed my driving test a month or so earlier, I threw my bergan into the boot, and climbed into my little blue Triumph Herald. I took a slow drive home, enjoying the freedom of being away from the intense nature of the course, and the rigors of what I had just been through.

Life went on outside the Regiment, my knowledge of London continued to improve. When I had first approached the London Taxi authority at Penton Street, Islington, they had enrolled me. I was told to appear next in 56 days time, when I would receive my first knowledge 'test'. Unfortunately, I had not done very well, as I simply didn't know enough by the time of my second visit to the 'Carriage Office'. I was told to get on my bike, and work harder. They told me to appear in another 56 days, when I would be given a further examination on my knowledge of the streets of the capital. When I made my next visit, I managed to answer enough questions to be placed onto 28-day appearances. This was a real boost to my confidence, as it put me firmly on the path to passing all the complex taxi drivers exams, which lay ahead of me over the next eighteen months. I was very lucky that my dad had helped me pass my driving test. When he had given me enough lessons, he insisted that I drive him down to the coast and back, to polish my technique. This did the job, and I was ready when my test arrived. I should add that selection also played its part, as I had a heavy cold during one of the latter weekends during selection, which had developed into a nasty case of Bronchitis. By the time the morning of my driving test dawned, I felt so bloody awful during the examination that there was no room for nerves; I just wanted to get it over with. I was determined to pass, and just got on with it. The examiner was happy at the end of my driving test, and passed me. I celebrated by driving home, taking two aspirins and going straight back to bed.

Things began to change, once continuation training really started. We paraded at the Dukes as normal, but were segregated from the new selection intake. Our small group of Continuation recruits stood out, in stark contrast to the vast battalion of eager young hopefuls who were just starting their journey through the selection process. Wearing our 'Stable' belts clearly defined our new elevated status. They gave us a higher standing in Training Wing's recruit pecking order, for what it was worth. Our training team had shrunk down to one very experienced Sergeant, who stayed with Continuation, and taught us each Tuesday evening. It was a funny thing, but we kept away from the new intake on selection. It wasn't arrogance that divided us, but simply, that we had cracked selection, and they hadn't. We were now a close-knit team, who had a great deal to learn, in a very short space of time. Having experienced the huge dropout rate during our initial mountain phase, we didn't want to make it easy for the new recruits. The routes of the various marches were all well known to us, but there was no way we would pass on that information to the new boys. If they wanted to pass, they had to do it the hard way, and find out for themselves, just as we had done.

Chapter 12:
Interrogation.

There was a palpable air of expectancy among us all, as we sat waiting for our first evenings lectures to begin. Our new SAS instructor, Sgt King; was a lean, tough, uncompromising ex-Grenadier Guardsman. He would be our mentor over the coming months, and having introduced himself, came straight to the point.

"You are only half way there boys, and you have a lot to learn. You will have to work very hard to make the grade, and get badged into the Regiment." He paused for a moment to let these important facts sink in. "There are several times on Continuation, that if you screw up, you will be binned on the spot... Right. I want each of you to stand up in turn, and introduce yourself, and then tell me a little about yourself."

First up was Jonnie-van-de-Pol. Jonnie was an ex. Territorial Army officer from the Mercian Regiment, based in the Midlands. Tough and stocky, his parents were originally of South African Boer stock. Posted down to London by Midland Bank, he had assumed a position as a junior lending Manager, in their Regents Street Branch. Our next 'player' was Paul Wilson, an advertising executive, working for a firm in London's west-end. I was next up, an ex-regular NCO, training to be a London cabbie. The next one on his feet was Keith Morgan-Williams. Keith was not really a recruit as such, as he was actually a serving regular Brigadier from the Royal Army Veterinary Corps. A tough middle-aged Welshman, Keith joined selection under the old pals act. His rank (just below Major-General) meant that he was in an excellent position to be of great help to the regular Regiment, and both Territorial Regiments of the SAS. He was particularly useful when it came to learning about dog evasion (we would learn much on the subject later during Continuation training). The Royal Army Veterinary Corps, provided training and care for the army's tracker, guard and sniffer dogs, and having a useful contact like Keith meant that the Regiment could call for dog teams, whenever the need arose. Keith had been very helpful to the Regiment in the past, and was doing selection for 'fun'. His ultimate reward was to complete the parachute course after selection, and wear his 'SAS wings' during the rest of his military career with the R.A.V.C. No special favours were given to him throughout the selection process. He was Trooper Morgan-Williams to the staff, and simply Keith to us. The next member of Continuation was Dickie Rouse. Dickie was a young and very fit scientist, who specialised in chemical research. He had flown around Long Drag with wings on his feet, and had very nearly set a new course record. He was quite what you might expect from a scientist, glasses, a thick shock of unruly hair and a terrible stutter when he got excited. Ollie Sale stood up next. Ollie had not been in the military before, and he swore blind that there had been a mix-up in his paperwork. He maintained that he had volunteered for the cavalry, but had ended up on selection by mistake. Ollie was our joker. He was always cheerful, and managed to extract the funny side out of almost any situation. He worked in sales, for I.B.M. The penultimate member of our Continuation course was Dave Smith, a Metropolitan Police Officer. He had managed to get special permission to try and join the Regiment, and ultimately wanted to transfer into the Special Patrol Group; an elite police task force, who were well known at the time for their firm policing methods in the capital's hot-spots. The last man to introduce himself to Sgt. King was Billie Hind, a young professional stunt man. He was becoming well known on the international stunt circuit, and had recently finished work on the latest James Bond movie. Taking Keith out of the equation for a moment, the rest of us were all in our early to mid-twenties. We had all found the necessary strength to pass selection, and were going to get to know each other very well, in the coming months.

Sgt. King explained that our first training weekend would be resistance to interrogation. He suggested that we took very great care with this subject, because the weekend would involve a period of escape and evasion, followed by a long period of capture and questioning. During the 'captured' phase, we would be subject to physical and mental stress and rigorous interrogation. He added the warning that if we cracked under interrogation, we were off the course, with no chance of having another go. All of us leaned a little closer; he had our total attention. He began his lecture by telling us that members of the Regiment were prone to capture troops. He explained that this meant that because we could expect to be working behind enemy lines, in very small numbers during wartime, we were more likely to be captured. Air crews in the Royal Air Force also fell into this category, as they were also likely to be caught, if shot down, assuming they had bailed out safely. We were taught about the Geneva Convention, concerning the treatment and questioning of prisoners of war, and given numerous examples of the abuses which P.O.Ws had been subjected to in the past. He covered 'capture shock' i.e. the shocked, degraded mental state it was all too easy to fall into when suffering the initial trauma of capture at gun or bayonet point. Escape was important within the first hours of capture, as prisoners were normally sent to the rear of the enemy lines quickly. The further back the prisoner was marched, the greater distance an escapee had to travel to return to friendly territory. There was also the question of physical health and strength. Prisoners could not expect gentle treatment from their captors. Although food and water should be provided, the initial captors might be hardened front-line troops that were short of both, and would be unlikely to be too generous, or gentle, with their charges. Given that a prisoner's strength would wane as time ticked by, the best chance of escape had to be early on after capture. When Sgt. Kings introduction to interrogation was over, various other detailed lectures continued for several hours, and finished off with an introduction to plastic explosives. Our minds were buzzing by the time Sgt. King stopped our first-evening training. We sat in the bar in 'B' Block afterwards, nursing a pint, letting it all sink in. If this was typical of Tuesday evenings for the next few months, Sgt. King was right; we had an awful lot to learn.

Our new instructor's treatment of us was quite different from the remote, detached attitude of the selection N.C.Os. Although he maintained an authoritarian distance from us, he was still friendlier, and much more approachable. Occasional jokes and stories about his own experiences kept us interested and focused during his training periods. We were now on nodding terms with the selection instructors and felt that the great divide we had first experienced with the staff on selection was quickly ebbing away. There were still the occasional twenty press-ups for making a mistake, but these were rather more light- hearted than before. Sgt. King had a nasty habit of firing off a question about some subject taught in an earlier lecture that evening, to keep our minds sharp. A slow response, or an answer of "Oh! Err. Um," would automatically qualify someone with a quick twenty. After numerous lectures, our knowledge on resistance to interrogation had become comprehensive as our first weekend drew near. We were ordered to parade on a Friday evening at the Dukes, without our bergans. This had an ominous ring to it, as, until now, we had always carried them with us, whatever our weekend training involved. We were to be dressed in combat uniform, suitable for patrol conditions, and be wearing our belt kits. If the need arose to dump our bergans during a patrol, we could live off the reserve rations in our webbing belt kits for several days. We were going to a secret training area used by the Regiment, and would have to evade capture until 11.30 hours on the next Saturday morning. There would be an active hunter force on the ground, whose mission was to find and capture us. We would then be passed down the line to an interrogation centre, where tactical questioning would begin, in earnest.

We climbed onto the lorry, having been told that we would be driven to the secret location in a closed down state. That meant the lorry's canvases would all be secured, so we would not see where we were ultimately going. The journey took hours. It must have been about midnight, when the lorry's brakes slammed on, and the tarpaulin flaps were thrown open. We were briefed earlier that there would be a rapid departure from the lorry, and that we must work alone during the night, and avoid capture at all costs. If we were successful, and stayed free throughout the night, we must make our way to a point at the Northern corner of the training area by 11.30 hrs. where we would receive further instructions. When the shout came to disembark, we all jumped out of the back of the lorry, into the bitterly cold night. I landed with a thud in the tarmac surface of the road, and broke hard to my left. Everyone scattered on contact with the ground. I ran as fast as possible, towards the shelter of a broad clump of trees, which I could just make out silhouetted on the hill ahead of me. As I reached the cover of what was actually the edge of a forest, I stopped for a moment and listened. Apart from the wind, I could hear nothing. An owl hooted somewhere in the distance behind me, and the trees creaked in the wind. There was nothing else; no other noise ruptured the peaceful, natural sounds of the night. I had struck lucky, as there was plenty of cover ahead of me in the forest. It was extremely dark, as I moved very slowly, deeper into the trees. I had no way of knowing how broad the forest was, but moved further into the dense cover of the wood, moving cautiously forward for ten more minutes. I would think that I actually only covered perhaps two hundred yards. I didn't want to make any loud sudden movement or sounds, and alert any possible ambushers as to my location. I did not have to get anywhere in particular, for the time being; just avoid being captured. If the hunters had night vision enhancing starlight scopes, they would see me wandering about, and catch me. What I needed was a good hiding place, where I could rest, and avoid capture. I found a ditch, and cautiously followed it. After a minute or two, I found a culvert, covered in nettles. I eased the nettles and brush aside, and wriggled my way feet-first into the pipe. It was dry inside, but a tight fit. I wriggled further into the narrow culvert, until I was about ten feet inside. Now I was secure; I hoped there would be little chance of the hunters finding me. At least now, I wouldn't blunder into them in the dark. I was tired and managed to get some fitful sleep during the night, but woke as dawn was braking. A military DMS boot, and camouflaged trouser leg suddenly appeared at the entrance to my hiding place. I froze, Hunters! The leg moved off, and was quickly replaced by another pair, which passed my hideaway without pausing. They must be blind, if they hadn't seen the culvert's entrance. I heard someone barking out orders. I hardly dared draw breath, and feared that the hammering of my heart would betray my location. The patrol commander's voice grew quieter, as he moved his men away. It had been a close run thing, but they were probably so intent on scanning the middle and far distance, that they had simply overlooked my hideout, which was literally at their feet. As a patrol had swept my area, it was unlikely that they would return too soon. I checked my watch; it was only 05.30hrs. I had to stay put, and wait it out.

I was stiff and very cold when it was finally time to move. My watch said 10.30hrs, and I had to get to the Northern section of the training area. Nothing happened during the last five hours, not a sign or sound of anyone. I cautiously eased myself out of the culvert, straining my eyes and ears for any sign of the hunter force. I stood up slowly. Nothing moved within my area of vision. I checked my compass and headed north, watching all the time for signs of movement around me. As it was broad daylight, my movement through the forest was easier, although the risk of being seen, was, of course, much greater. I dived for cover after twenty minutes, when a flock of birds suddenly took to the air ahead of me. I lay in the dry bracken, but saw and heard nothing suspicious. I continued after several minutes of watching and listening. Having reached the Northern edge of the forest, I had an excellent view of the target location I needed to get to. I lay under cover of the tree line and watched the area, as I had been trained to do. I noticed someone creeping very slowly towards the chain-link fence, which marked the perimeter of the training area. It had to be one of our guys. A white civilian van was parked on the perimeter road, just inside the fence. A figure wearing nonmilitary clothes was leaning against the van, casually smoking a cigarette. The runner edged closer and closer to the van, using any cover that was available. As he stood up and crossed the track, the rear van doors suddenly burst open, and out jumped four very big paratroopers. They had the runner down on the ground in a flash. They quickly secured his hands behind his back, and blindfolded him. Dragging him to his feet, he was thrown headfirst into the van. The Paras climbed in after him, closed the doors, and the trap was re-set. I lay quietly in my hidden observation point, feeling rather resigned to the fact that whatever I did, I was shortly going into the 'bag'. The hunters were busy all night, capturing any unwary (or unlucky) runners. This must be their final hoovering up point. I had to get caught, and go through the interrogation phase; there was nowhere else to go. It was now 11.20 hrs. I shrugged my shoulders, stood up, and started to walk down towards the van. I was about two hundred metres from it, when, to my complete surprise, the van began to drive away. This was starting to get silly. I was now running after the van, in order to get thumped by a gang of hairy paratroopers; and then be interrogated for God knows how long. The van drove on for fifty metres, and stopped suddenly on a bridge, which ran over a small river. I assumed they had seen me, and continued to jog towards them. My casual air must have annoyed them, or maybe I was just the last to be captured. When the Paras jumped out of the van, they grabbed me and threw me head first, not as I expected, into the back of the van, but into the slow-moving river. It was the end of January, and the water was absolutely freezing. I surfaced, coughing and spluttering, feeling as if a million frigid needles had been hammered into my body. One of the Paras splashed into the water and grabbed me by the hair. "What's your Regiment?" He yelled into my frozen ear. I mumbled some incoherent reply. The freezing water completely robbed me of the power of speech. The Paratrooper shoved my head back under the water for a couple of seconds, pulled me up, and repeated the question. I coughed up several pints of water, and grunted something equally unintelligible, as he

149

dragged me back to the riverbank. I was handcuffed, blindfolded and yanked backwards to the van, then unceremoniously slung into the back. I landed on the other captive with a heavy thud. I heard one of the hunters say. "Right, that's it; he's the last," as they all climbed back into the van. Four pairs of heavy boots thumped onto my soaking body as they sat down, and the van began to move.

The drive to the interrogation centre only took a few minutes. The vehicle stopped; the engine was switched off. The back doors opened. None of my captors said anything, as they dragged me out. My feet hit the ground, and I was pulled upright. They gripped me firmly and painfully under each arm, and frogmarched me across what I assumed was a car park. My guards yanked me to a stop, and I heard a door immediately in front of me creaking open. They pulled me forward again and marched me along what sounded like an echoing corridor. Doors were banging and slamming around me, but suddenly, I was walked straight into a wall. Tightly blindfolded as I was, it came as a complete shock. The impact of my face hitting the brickwork dazed me, but I remained conscious. We had been trained to exaggerate injuries when captured, and I groaned loudly, and sank to my knees. My playacting had no effect whatsoever on my captors; I was grasped even more firmly, and dragged away. Without warning, I was stopped suddenly, and my handcuffs were removed. My hands were forced against a cold stone wall in front of me. They were placed in line with my shoulders. I was roughly grabbed in the small of my back, and my feet were kicked outwards and backwards. I was now leaning forwards, still blindfolded, with my weight pushing against my fingertips. It was a very uncomfortable position, and I eased myself forward slightly. Immediately, my feet were kicked further backwards, and I fell face forwards, flat on the floor. Almost before I knew what had happened, I was grabbed once again from both sides, lifted up and kicked back in the wall standing `'stress' position. Clearly, at least two guards were watching me closely. They did not make a sound, but I could feel them standing close behind me. I'd got the message, and held my position this time. It felt very awkward, but there was no point in annoying my jailers... at least no yet! My wet clothes quickly reduced my temperature, and I began to shiver. As I was being forced to stand still, my muscles were trying to warm my body by shivering. I dropped one hand after twenty minutes, to gain some relief, but also to see if my guards were still behind me. Within seconds, my arm was pushed firmly back into position, and my hand slapped higher on the wall. OK, they were still there. My shivering was becoming more violent. Without any warning, my sodden jacket was pulled off me, and my shirt tail was pushed up my back. I was returned immediately to the stress position, where I stayed for several long and uncomfortable hours. Without the wet clothes on my back, I began to warm up a little, and my shivering eventually subsided. Sometime later, I was grabbed without warning once again by both arms, and marched away from the wall. The blindfold was tight, and I could see absolutely nothing. I heard a door opened in front of me. I was dragged forward, and then pushed firmly down onto a wooden chair. When the blindfold was removed, I found myself sitting in front of the Regiment's Doctor. On his right arm, he was wearing a white armband.

"You know who I am?" he asked.

I stared back at him, without saying anything. He fingered his armband and continued.

"This armband makes me an umpire. I'm neutral on this exercise, and cannot be impersonated. Are you OK to continue?"

I nodded slowly. He stared back at me for a moment.

"Very well. Guard!"

My blindfold was firmly replaced and I was dragged to my feet. The guards marched me around for several minutes, and eventually; I was forced down onto another chair. My blindfold was pulled from my head. I was now sitting in front of a man wearing what looked suspiciously like a Russian Officers uniform.

"Name?" He demanded.

I paused, before answering. "Uh,....Black". We were trained to stop before answering, and think carefully about each question, however harmless it appeared. We should never rush an answer, but look stupid, but try to appear helpful. That was fine, as long as we only gave name, rank, number and date of birth.

"What is your number?"

I paused, looked like I was trying hard to remember it, and then answered him.

"Is that an army number? He demanded. I didn't have to tell him that, so I replied slowly,

"I'm sorry Sir; I can't answer that question."

"What is your date of birth?"

I tried to look like I knew the answer to that one. I told him my birth date, but he tried it on again.

"Does that mean you were born in May?"

Of course it did, but I wasn't going to admit it. I furrowed my brow, looked hopelessly out of my depth at such a tricky question and answered.

"Err, I'm sorry Sir; I can't answer that question...."

"What is your rank?"

"Um....Private." He did not look impressed.

"You seem pretty stupid, even to be a private in the army!"....It was working.

"I'm sorry Sir; I can't..."

"I'm not asking you a question; I'm making a statement of fact, you idiot!" He thundered.

151

I could see that he was clearly becoming frustrated and angry with this half-wit sitting in front of him. He stopped, composed himself, and suddenly changed tack.

"You're name is Black, is that spelt B..L..A..C..K?"

I was obliged to tell him my name; but not how to spell it. I looked hopelessly lost at such a difficult question, although I really tried to look like I wanted to help, and slowly replied.

"I'm sorry Sir; I can't answer that question."

Interrogators try to get any deviation from name, rank, number and date of birth. Once they create a tiny chink in the prisoners' defence, they are quick to exploit it. If I gave him an inch, he would take a mile. His interrogation continued for what seemed like hours, but he was getting nowhere. He tried one more line of attack.

"What is your Regiment?"

I definitely didn't have to answer that one.

"Err, I'm sorry Sir; I can't answer that question"....

"Why can't you answer?"

"I'm sorry Sir; I can't"...

He'd had enough. Pounding his fist on the table, he bellowed.

"Guards! Take this idiot away!"

We were briefed before the exercise that we must, on this occasion not attempt to escape. We had to stay in the 'bag' and take whatever they threw at us. Hours slowly went by, spent mainly holding up the wall in what got steadily more uncomfortable positions of stress. Every now and then, I would be grabbed, and marched into a different interrogation cell. We already knew that we would face a number of different types of interrogator, the intimidating shouter, who screams in the prisoners' face, and hurls foul and horrible verbal abuse at him. Then there is the friendly guy, who wants to make things easy for you, and doesn't really want to do the interrogators' job at all. He only wants the prisoner to; for example, confirm the grid reference where the prisoner was captured. Nothing important, but it will get the poor interrogator's boss off his back. He might offer coffee or a cigarette, nothing wrong with taking a 'treat' as long as there are no strings attached. It makes the prisoner feel mentally better and stronger, because he has got something for nothing from his captors. Then there is the bumbling, clumsy interrogator, who knocks over his coffee, drop his pen, and appears to be in completely the wrong job. It is all too easy to forget that this bloke is a highly trained officer, who is trying to trick the unwary prisoner into letting something slip. Every interrogator had to be closely watched. They really were a mean, tricky bunch. The next technique was the use of a man and women interrogation team. The prisoner would be dragged in, his blindfold removed, and he would be ordered to strip naked. The pair then asked a few questions, and spend the rest of the period taking the mickey out of the prisoners physique, manhood and anything else which may make him crack. It was rumoured on a previous course that one naked prisoner had got an erection, which certainly put the interrogation team off their collective stroke.

After what I could only guess at fifteen or sixteen hours, I was starting to feel pretty stiff and tired. Throughout my 'wall standing', my captors played very loud 'white noise' at me. It sounds like something of a mixture, between a very loud vacuum cleaner and the deafening electronic hiss of radio static. The sound disorientates, making the mind confused. It is common to start hearing music mixed in with the racket. It is not there really, but I was damned sure I heard it. One of my interrogators ordered me to sign for my equipment, or it would be confiscated. The rule is simple; never sign anything, so I didn't. He got very angry, but my stupid act got me through it. Later, I had the lower part of my blindfold pulled clear, and a piece of dry bread forced into my mouth, while I remained holding up the wall. I received a mouthful of cold water shortly afterwards.

We were not tortured in the old-fashioned sense. There were no hot irons, or finger nails pulled out. Physical torture can make the recipient more determined to resist, or make him say anything; however, inaccurate, to stop the pain. Psychological torture, with isolation and wall standing in extremely uncomfortable positions, can break down strength and morale, and overall, have a better and more accurate rate of success. Clever questioning is the real key. There is no such thing as a 'Truth drug'. Injecting truth serums like Scopolamine or Sodium Pentothal don't make the prisoner tell the truth, they just relax him, and make his less cautious, and less defensive. Much the same effect really, as half a bottle of good Irish whiskey.

Several hours later, as I listened to the mind-game music, I became aware of another prisoner holding up the wall beside me. I was still firmly blindfolded, but couldn't miss several blatant clues. Over the 'white noise', I heard a groaning prisoner being dragged into my cell. I felt the impact of his hands slapped against my wall beside me. The dead giveaway, however, was when he vomited copiously down my left leg. Someone was playing the 'ill' prisoner tactic very well. Play acting, with plenty of groaning, moaning and rolling of the eyes. It can play havoc with a professional interrogator's game plan. Whoever it was; they had me convinced. I just wish he had thrown up in another direction. My next interrogation was a piece of everything, thrown at me by a panel of five interrogators. I had relentless questions screamed at me from all sides. After twenty minutes of fruitless yelling, there were promises of money and women if I helped them and threats of a firing squad if I didn't. They kept changing tack and told me that I would be paraded on television as a traitor, who had told them everything. If I co-operated with them, they offered to release me, in fact, they tried everything. I stuck firmly to my Private Stupid routine. For me, the highlight of that particular interrogation was when one of them leaned over me and yelled.

"God! What's that awful smell?"

Given that my leg was still covered in a thick coating of fresh vomit, it took enormous willpower not to laugh, when I gave them the slow, mumbled. "Err, I'm sorry Sir; I can't answer that question".

Although of course, they all knew exactly who I really was, I stuck to the same dopey attitude, and they finally gave up, and shouted for the guards to take me away. I was frogmarched around the inside of the building for several minutes, and then forced to sit down on another chair. My guards released their vice-like grip on me. Nothing happened for several seconds. I was half expecting a hard punch in the mouth, but still, nothing happened. A voice ordered gruffly.

"Take off his blindfold."

Someone ripped it away. There in front of me, sat Major Brooks, and the Doctor. Both were wearing white umpire armbands.

"Do you know who we are?" enquired the Doctor.

"I'm sorry Sir; I can't answer that question." I replied.

"We are umpires, Black, and cannot be impersonated under any circumstances. Your interrogation exercise is over!"

I felt disorientated and confused; was this a final trick? I couldn't be sure.

"It's all right Black; it really is over. You can go and get a cup of tea in a moment. How do you feel?"

I looked at their armbands again. Should I trust them? The exercise briefing had said that anyone wearing an armband should be trusted and accepted as genuine. OK, fair enough. I smiled.

"I'm fine Sir, thank you."

"How long do you think you have been captured, Black?" Major Brooks asked. Good question, but difficult to answer. I took a shot and guessed.

"Eighteen, twenty hours, I think Sir."

Major Brooks looked at his watch.

"Not a bad guess, about eighteen and a half hours, its 06.40hrs, Sunday morning. The interrogators are pleased with how you did. We will de-brief you fully later, on the coach going back. Right, off you go and get some tea."

I stood up and followed one of my Paratrooper guards, who were also now wearing a white armband. He led me into a makeshift cookhouse on the other side of the building, where most of my friends from Continuation were already sitting, busy eating bacon sandwiches. I grabbed some tea and a hot bacon sandwich and joined them. I looked around their tired faces.

"Sorry about throwing up on your leg David," said Keith. "Bit of a bad shot, I'm afraid. The Doc. told me it was you, I hit."

I laughed, and replied. "Yeah, cheers, you wanker." Everyone laughed, and we swapped stories about our experiences for the next few minutes.

"Where's P-P-P-Paul?" stuttered Dickie. No one had seen him, since the start of the exercise. Sgt. King appeared at that moment, complete with armband, and joined the queue for tea.

"Have you seen Paul Wilson anywhere, Staff?" Asked Jonnie.

Sgt. King shook his head slowly.

"He's failed; I'm afraid!" Was all he said. We were thunderstruck.

"Bloody hell!" Said Ollie. It turned out later that they had broken Paul, when they ordered him to strip. The male interrogator had acted as if he fancied Paul, and made several comments, which Paul couldn't handle. Paul lost control, cracked up and started shouting at the interrogator. Once they had an in, the interrogators made short work of him. He should have kept his mouth shut, and stuck to his own resistance plan. That was the whole point of the exercise. It wasn't just some silly children's game; it was deadly serious. They were not kidding about getting the chop either. Paul was removed from the exercise during the night. He was sent straight back to London on an admin. lorry. When he arrived at the Dukes, he was immediately discharged from the Regiment. Unfortunately, we didn't see him again; shame really, he was a decent bloke. Our course lost another member though; we now we were down to eight.

Chapter 13.

Mangle, Strangle and Dangle

Things continued to get more and more interesting.

Our next two Tuesday evenings were filled with lectures about communications, unarmed combat and advanced weapon training. We also had a lesson about dogs. Military dogs are a potent weapon in themselves. Fast, powerful and capable of inflicting fatal injuries, they were not to be treated lightly. We learnt that due to the specialised nature of our various roles in wartime, we were very likely to encounter enemy guard, tracker and attack dogs. If we were tasked to destroy a forward airbase, for example, we would certainly be crossing the path of these animals. Silenced weapons would take care of them, but dogs are rarely left to work alone. Each guard dog would normally have an armed human handler. He would need to be dealt with as well. Weighing in at up to ten stones, and able to maintain speeds in excess of thirty miles an hour over short distances, these dogs had to be considered a potent and very real threat to us. German Shepherds and Doberman Pincers were used throughout the Warsaw Pact Alliance.

Because of their ability to deliver a series of savage bites; they were to be avoided wherever possible, and neutralised, as necessary. When the immediate canine threat had been taken care of, and the task completed, we were likely to be hunted, using tracker dogs. These animals, were trained to follow our human scent trails, and could then lead the Hunters to us. We might be miles away from the target, and in order to avoid them; we needed to learn exactly how the dogs tracked us. A dog's sense of smell is believed to be up to two million times more acute that humans, and it is also thought that dogs 'think' in smells. As a four-man patrol moves quickly across country, they not only deposit their unique human scent trail, but also break grass and foliage underfoot, adding to the potpourri of odours for the dog to follow. There is little point in trying to disguise a human scent by walking in petrol, for example. This just adds a pungent 'extra' for the dogs to follow. Assuming that the dog teams are out of sight, following some miles behind, the trick is to destroy the confidence of the handlers in their dogs. Laying strong false trails, which might perhaps, lead the dog teams into danger, would be a first line of escape for the hunted. Laying powerful smells such as urine around rabbit warrens or the base of trees, might lead the handlers to believe that the dogs are more interested in rabbits or squirrels, than their real human targets. Use any trick, which delays the hunters, and adds distance between them, and their human quarry. Slowing the pursuit also weakens the scent trail, which will evaporate into nothing, as time goes by.

Sgt. King rounded off his lecture by explaining that a large dog's skeleton is almost armour plated, and the old story of forcing its forelegs apart until it dies was utter nonsense. To grab the front legs would mean exposing our necks and throats to a set of vicious, slathering jaws, filled with big, sharp teeth. If we were alone, unarmed and cornered by a dog team, better to surrender to it, avoiding injury, and try to escape later. We were to have a demonstration of a dog's prowess at tracking and attacking on our next weekend:

Combat Survival.

We would be going back to the same general area that we had used during the interrogation weekend. We were warned, not to bring anything edible with us, and we were thoroughly searched, before we left for the training area. We were allowed to carry water in our canteens, but nothing else to eat or drink. We arrived safely later that night, and were given a section of woodland to put up our poncho tents. Sleeping bags were not to be used; we were to 'rough it' for the next couple of nights. It meant trying to sleep on the ground, in February. I doubt any of us got more than an hour of sleep that night. It was very, very cold and uncomfortable. When Sgt. King arrived at 06.00 on Saturday morning, Continuation was looking rough. He told us to strike camp, and then we followed him down to a wide lake nearby. When we were arranged in a huddle before him, he explained our next practical lesson.

"River crossings" he said. "When we cross the countryside at night, we will sometimes have to cross river obstacles. As you are all aware, bridges are out, because they will be guarded; and you will be caught if you try to cross them. We never use bridges. The alternative is to swim the river. We lash all four bergans with each other, and use them as a floatation aid. This keeps the four-man patrol close together, and stops anyone from drowning in a strong current."

Like the others, I had a strong feeling that we were about to get wet. He told us to confirm that everything was safely waterproofed in our bergans, and lash two groups of four of them together. Once our 'rafts' were firmly attached, we took off our outer layers of clothing, packed them in waterproof bags, and stashed them, in turn into our respective bergan pockets. While we were finishing our preparations, Sgt King launched a big rubber Gemini assault boat into the water. He had an assistant from Boat Troop, 22nd SAS, to help him. The exercise scenario was that we were two patrols which had to covertly cross a wide water obstacle, in order to proceed with our mission. The Gemini would be there as a safety boat, in case anyone got into difficulties during the crossing. The other group went first. As this was our initial attempt at a river (lake) crossing, we were doing it in daylight, when we joined our Squadron, we would have to do it covertly, at night. The patrol carried the bergan raft to the lake's edge, and carefully lowered it into the water. It was clearly difficult, as the raft probably weighed in excess of one hundred and twenty pounds. When it was finally in the water, it floated surprisingly well. All the air trapped within the bergans did the job nicely. Now it was time for the patrol to enter the water. When the first toe hit the water, we could all see that it was very, very cold. Several hissed comments of "Oh Jesus!" and "Christ!" spoke volumes. The boys gradually lowered themselves all the way in, and each grabbed a corner of the raft. They swam steadily and quietly away from us, towards the opposite bank, approximately one hundred metres distant. The safety boat slowly circled the raft and its crew, as they made their way across. It took quite a time to finish the crossing. Clearly, the cold was affecting them all. It took some effort for two of them to climb out, check the area, then return and help the remaining two, and haul their bergan raft from the water. When they were clear of the waters edge, they moved into cover to dry and dress. The Gemini chugged quietly back to us on the other side of the lake, and Sgt. King signalled us in. It had been quite funny seeing the look on the first patrols faces as they entered the freezing water, but it wasn't quite so funny when our turn came. I had the same million frozen needle experience as two weeks earlier, but this time, I also had to swim for it. It was surprisingly difficult to move the raft, and the cold water quickly sapped our strength. We were all shivering violently, by the time we managed to make it safely across. We hauled our lifesaving raft out onto the muddy riverbank. When we were in cover, we quickly dried ourselves, and put our warm dry uniforms back on. Sgt. King debriefed us when we were all back together.

"OK, not bad for a first attempt. Both patrols took too long getting in and out of the lake, and you all made too much noise in the water. Remember lads, this job has to be carried out quickly and quietly. Next time you do this, you will probably be fighting a strong river current in the dark. If one of your patrol is wounded, three of you will swim, while the wounded man floats across on the raft." He paused for a moment, then continued. "Crossing rivers is a dangerous task; we lose more guys in river crossing accidents, than any other type of training."

Sgt. King's assistant from Boat Troop nodded his head in confirmation.

"Right lads, give us hand to haul out the Gemini, then we're off to learn some poaching."

Our next lesson was taken by two late middle-aged civilians, dressed in Tweed jackets and green Wellingtons. They were both gamekeepers from a local country estate. They had learnt their craft many years before, from their fathers; who they told us with a twinkle in their eyes were both notorious local poachers. We learnt how to catch rabbits and hares, using wire snares. They explained where and when to place the traps. How to catch roosting birds and how to pull more unsuspecting rabbits out of their burrows, using nothing more than lengths of bramble or barbed wire. There were tricks for catching wild fowl on a lake or river; and how to catch fish using simple bottle traps and gill nets. One of the gamekeepers showed us how to skin and gut a rabbit, and how to clean a fish. It was a terrific lesson, but no place for a hard-core vegan or vegetarian. When they had finished, we were given one dead rabbit between two of us, for later.

A very old witch gave the next lesson. Well, she didn't say she was a witch, but that's what she looked like. She taught us about mushrooms, toadstools and fungi. All fungi have a very low calorific value, and their nutritional value is debatable. Among others, she showed us two deadly poisonous mushrooms; Death Cap and Destroying Angel. If even the smallest fingernail size piece of either was accidentally consumed, death was certain within three days. There is no known antidote for either of them. They were both to be found across Europe, and the Death Cap looked very much like the Common Field Mushroom, to our inexperienced eyes. The overriding lesson was, do not eat mushrooms or fungi of any sort, unless you are 110% sure exactly what they are. She went on to show us how to prepare and cook stinging nettles, dandelions, both of which were rich in iron and vitamins, and tender bracken tips, among other various edible 'greens' which proliferate in the countryside. When the morning's lessons were over, Sgt. King recommended several books, which we should buy, including 'Food for Free'. Lunchtime came and went, without any sign of anything to eat. We followed Sgt. King down a woodland path, to an interesting series of structures, which were collectively known as Survival Village. Various shelters had been erected, out of materials found in any forest. They looked solid and waterproof. Bracken had been dropped thickly on the floor to provide warm, dry bedding. One structure had a roof made of thick turfs; another, was thatched with riverbank reeds. There were several homemade ovens, and a small smoking 'lodge' for drying and preserving strips of meat. When we had had a good look around at the various survival structures, we were sent to a cleared area, where, on one side was a raised bank of railway sleeper seats. A small fire burnt brightly at one end of the cleared area, close to a large, heavy wooden tripod. Sgt. King walked into the cleared area immediately in front of us. When we were seated and quiet, he began his next lecture by saying that so far, we had covered the capture of small animals for food. What, he asked, about larger animals like deer, wild boar and so on? They would provide good nutrition, and plenty of protein and fat. They were also a valuable natural source of salt. We exchanged glances with each other. We knew from experience earlier on selection, that the

159

Staff never said anything lightly. What did he have up his sleeve now? What would happen next? The answer was not long in coming. Two instructors dragged a rather dog-eared looking sheep over to Sgt. King. They lay the sheep at his feet, and secured its legs with some rope.

"If you are starving, and manage to catch a sheep, you are going to have to kill it." Sgt. King stared hard at us all. "If shooting is out, it's no good trying to pole axe a sheep to stun it...You just have to cut its throat!"

We all winced at the thought, but knew our instructor was right. He continued.

"Remember to catch the blood, don't waste it because it's full of salt, and you already know how much your body needs that."

We all nodded. He produced a medium-sized bowl, and slowly knelt beside the sheep's head. He reached for the back of his belt, and drew a large, razor-sharp hunting knife. We all exchanged apprehensive glances with one another. Sgt. King pulled the sheep's head to one side, exposing its neck.

"The sheep won't feel too much when you kill it, but you will have to straddle it, to stop it thrashing around, while it dies."

It is probably true to say that, all of us recruits were swallowing hard at that moment. Sgt. King placed the bowl under the sheep's neck, and deftly sawed through its throat. The sheep kicked for several minutes, as its lifeblood poured out of the gaping wound in its neck. With a final shudder, it lay still. Sgt. King wiped the bloody blade on the dead sheep's fleece, picked up the now full bowl, and stood up.

"OK lads, not pleasant, but that's the most humane way of killing a large animal. If you want to survive in the wilds, and you have nothing else, you might have to kill animals to survive."

It was a grim lesson, but he was right, there just was not any other way. Our instructor poured the steaming blood into a metal billycan and hung it over the smoking fire. After a minute or two, the blood began to boil, and then quickly congeal. When he was satisfied that it had enough cooking time, he removed the steaming billycan and brought it over to show us the results. Inside, was what looked like flaky brown scrambled eggs.

"Cooked blood; that's what black pudding is made from, lads. It tastes OK, and it will replace vital salt and vitamins, in your bodies."

He pulled a big spoon out of his pocket. "So eat it!"

He passed the can to me, as I was closest to him.

"Yeah, thanks Staff." I said, because I couldn't think of anything else to say at precisely that moment. I had eaten black pudding a number of times before, and he had said it was OK. I trusted his judgement. I took the spoon from him and scooped out a large piece of the still steaming congealed mess. With a resigned sigh, I spooned it into my mouth. Hmm, not too bad.

160

"Take another, Black," ordered Sgt King. I swallowed the first mouthful and refilled the spoon. My mum taught me not to speak with my mouth full, but this was a special case.

"Gone on, 'ith all right!" I said to Ollie, as I chewed. He was eyeing the pot suspiciously, and looking a bit green. He looked at me, then at Sgt King, and with a resigned sigh filled the spoon. Closing his eyes, he pushed it into his mouth. He chewed slowly, and then swallowed with some difficulty.

"Yes, probably an acquired taste." He said, pulling a face at me. All of us had to munch our way through the contents of the can, until it was gone.

"Sorry Staff, none left for you," said Ollie with a grin.

"Christ! I don't eat that shit unless I have to," laughed Sgt. King. No one had thrown up, which was surprising, given the looks on some faces as the billycan went the rounds. "Right lads, now we have our animal dead, you need to know how to butcher it, before you can cook it."

Sgt. King pulled some thick cord from his pocket, and tied it tightly around the sheep's hind legs. We lent a hand to hang the dead sheep's carcass, clear of the ground, suspended from the wooden tripod. Our instructor spent the next half hour teaching us how to reduce the sheep into numerous chunks of raw mutton. The sheep's stomach, guts and head went into a big plastic bag.

"Don't eat those bits." He advised with a grin…..No really?

Finally, we were all presented with a bloody chunk of very fresh meat.

"That's your lot lads, time for tea."

We set up our bashers close by, and organised a wood party, to scavenge fuel for a fire. One of our earlier lessons in the day concerned fire lighting, using sticks, small homemade bows, and plenty of hard work. Several of us had a go at making fire, which after much effort and cursing, eventually produced a little smoking pile of glowing embers. Added to some dry tinder, and blown gently, our reward was a small ball of flame. When larger pieces of wood were placed over our burning ball, we soon had a decent fire burning. The wood party returned carrying and dragging various bits of tree and dead branches. We paired up, and Jonnie and I set to work skinning and gutting our rabbit. When they were ready, we skewered the rabbits and chunks of mutton on long sticks, and hung them over the fire. As none of us had eaten for at least twenty-four hours, the smell of the cooking meat quickly reminded us, just how hungry, we were. It was fully dark, by the time we thought the rabbits were ready. It was difficult to see if it was fully cooked, but we tried a small piece and decided it was close enough. There wasn't much meat on our rabbit, and the edible bits were soon gone. Now it was time to try the mutton. Jonnie cut a slice and tried it.

"Err, yuk! It's still raw on the inside!" We decided it needed a bit longer, and slowly rotated it in the flames for another twenty minutes. When we eventually tried it again, it was rather crisp. Actually, it was more like charcoal, but we ate it anyway, because we were so bloody hungry.

It was the thought, and look, of what we had eaten, which was the initial difficulty. Once we were over that; it was not a problem anymore. It was a good final and probably most important lesson during our initial combat survival training. If we were hungry enough, we could and probably would have to eat anything.

Another cold, uncomfortable night later, we were up and ready, before Sgt. King arrived at our base camp. We had set our wire snares during the previous day, and went out in the frosty morning in pairs, to check and clear them. Jonnie and I had identified what we took to be a likely spot in a hedgerow, and had set the snare a hand's width above the ground, as we had been taught by the gamekeepers. The snare was in place, and empty.

"Bang goes breakfast," said Jonnie. I nodded. We recovered the snare, and made our way back. Ollie and Keith were blessed with better luck. They returned shortly after us and held their prize aloft, for all to see. They had a fat and very dead rabbit. The other two pairs returned empty handed. Keith and Ollie made a great show of preparing and cooking their catch. The rule was simply: You catch it; you eat it. Fair enough. When the boys had finished their meal, they took great delight with comments like.

"I couldn't eat another thing" and "I'm stuffed." The rest of us loftily ignored them, finding our rumbling stomachs much more interesting.

Sgt King arrived, in a two Land Rover convoy. As he climbed out of the lead vehicle, we heard a dog barking and whining in the second. Two military dog handlers climbed out of the second Land Rover, and walked around to the back of their vehicle. Once the dogs were firmly secured on their leads, their handlers led them over to us. Both dogs were big, fierce looking Alsatians.

"Nice doggie," muttered Ollie with a grin.

When the handlers spotted Keith, they both snapped to attention. Keith was as scruffy as the rest of us, with two-day stubble on his chin, and dressed in a dirty uniform, which he had slept on the ground in for two cold nights. Clutching their leads tightly, with the dogs sitting at their feet, Keith's boys saluted him.

"Morning chaps. Has Sgt. King briefed you yet?"

"Yes Sir!" they both replied smartly, still standing to attention. This was big army stuff; I hadn't seen it for a long while, and some of our boys had never seen it. Keith told them to carry on, and came over and sat with us.

"One of the perks of being a Brigadier," he said to us with a wink. "I get lots of salutes."

We had two demonstrations from the dog teams. The first involved the dogs in attack mode. Sgt King asked for a volunteer, and suddenly, eight heads went down, as we made a close inspection of our boots.

"OK, fair enough, Hind, well volunteered."

Billie looked helplessly at us. With lots of gleeful encouragement from his relieved course mates, Billie was led away to the back of the Land Rovers. Sgt. King helped Billie dress in a thick, padded jacket and trousers. The jacket looked too big, with the sleeves covering Billie's hands. A strong wire mesh helmet finished his outfit. Billie waddled over to the edge of an open field next to us and stopped. We walked over and stood in a huddle, with Sgt. King. The two dogs were getting excited, pulling and straining at their leads. The handlers were winding them up; this was going to be good! It was Keith, who spoke.

"What you are about to see, lads, is a demonstration of what happens if you are seen on a guarded site, and they set the dogs on you. He nodded towards Billie, who took his signal and charged off for the opposite side of the field.

The dogs were yowling and barking as they watched Billie running for his life. When he was half way across the field, one of the dog handlers shouted.

"Halt!..Halt or I'll release the dogs."

As soon as he had finished the last syllable, both dogs were released. They bounded across the field like canine heat-seeking missiles. The handlers ran after them, but the dogs were opening the gap, as they swiftly closed in on Billie. Suddenly, there was no more space between the dogs and their prey. Both animals hit him at full speed; almost at the same instant, Billie was spun in a tight circle, as the dogs leapt on him, sinking their jaws into his padded arms. Billie went down, under the impact of their combined weight. The dogs were up first, and continued to hold onto him, shaking their heads, and him, violently.

The handlers arrived several moments later, both shouting "Leave!" to their dogs. The dogs reluctantly obeyed, but Billie, sensibly, stayed where he was, curled up in a tight ball on the ground. Only when the dogs were firmly back on their leads, did he slowly and cautiously stand up. Even then, one of the dogs lunged at him again, and bit his protected leg, much to our collective amusement. Keith was grinning broadly.

"As you have seen, when the dogs have line of sight, and are released, you are in big trouble!"

It was a vivid lesson. The speed, power and aggression of the dogs left a lasting impression on all of us.

"Anyone else want to try?" Keith might have been a Brigadier in his world, but right now, he was one of us.

163

The only answer he got was a couple of mumbled. "Yeah, bollocks!"

Dickie Rouse was 'volunteered' for the tracking demonstration. The dogs were locked into the back of the Landover, where they couldn't see what was happening. To our left, the ground sloped away, and led down to several wide fields, which were separated, by tall hedgerows. Because of our excellent vantage point, we would have a panoramic view of the tracking demonstration. Dickie was told to run down to the first field, and cross the style into the second. He would then follow the inside of the hedgerow all the way around it. Then he must climb through the hedges until he emerged into a small copse, which bordered the second field. It was up to him where he hid, as long as he stayed somewhere in the trees. One of the dog handlers took his hat, from which the dogs would pick up Dickie's scent trail. The dogs remained firmly locked up as Dickie set off at a steady trot, following the trail he was given. When his course was complete, and he was safely hidden in the copse, the handlers removed the Alsatians from the vehicle. They were both straining and yelping, but remained secured on their thick rope leads. The hat was held firmly to each of their noses for several seconds. The dogs were ordered to 'Seek', and they began casting their heads left and right, with their noses to the ground, looking for the scent. It only took a minute for them to find it. Suddenly, the dogs ears pricked up, and they frantically pulled their handlers forward, following the invisible odour trail. The dogs mirrored the exact path Dickie had followed, keeping their noses pressed to the earth. Across the first field, and around the second, they hardly deviated at all. When they reached the copse, they found the unprotected Dickie, having learnt from the first demonstration, sitting up a tree. Sensibly, he had absolutely no intention of being attacked, and savaged by the dogs.

When the dogs were once again securely locked up, we had a final de-brief on the weekend from Sgt. King. It was a tough but incredibly interesting couple of days. Now we had experienced some basics; he encouraged us to learn as much as we could about combat survival; as one day, it could well save our lives. He suggested that we ate something unusual if we went out to dinner in the future. If there was anything bizarre on the menu, it was well worth trying. Roast Chicken is just protein, but so, for that matter, is octopus, ostrich, shark, snails, wild boar and crocodile. In fact, anything that would get us used to eating whatever was available at the time was worth a try. Frankly, having recently eaten the fresh blood of an animal killed in front of us, it shouldn't be too difficult to comply. If it slithered, crawled, walked or flew, and you were hungry enough, it was food, simple as that; lesson learnt.

Chapter 14:
More Good Things

The Continuation phase of selection taught us more than just military tactics. During the mountain phase, the Regiment stripped away the comfortable fabric of working as a team. They needed to know that each man was fully capable of working and functioning alone, and was of the right 'stuff' to join. Having overcome that phase, we now had to move on, and train to work in small four-man patrols. Each member of a patrol had to rely on its other members, when things got tough. We were all highly motivated, fit and had determination in abundance, but now needed to practice working together in small teams. The Regiment had found through experience that four-man patrols were ideally sized, for the type of operations it was tasked to fulfil.

Information gathering on the enemy is vital, prior to fighting and defeating him. It may not be a glamorous form of soldiering, but our Generals rely on the Mark.1. SAS eyeball when gathering information about enemy dispositions and movements, while they make their plans to fight the coming Corps. battle. It is true that the General Staff have satellite and aerial photographs; radio intercepts and information from prisoners and 'spies' to colour the overall intelligence picture, but they are well aware that the art of disinformation is used by all armies of the world. Careful camouflage, dummy radio transmissions and 'double agents' can all lead to a subtle and co-ordinated false picture being painted of the enemy's plans. Determined, resourceful men on the ground, armed with a pair of powerful binoculars or image enhancing night scopes can provide 100% accurate information, which at the very least will corroborate other intelligence sources, or alternatively blow the whistle on the enemy's attempts at deception. The main difficulties with this arduous and dangerous type of intelligence gathering, is getting behind the enemy's 'front line' and onto the necessary location in the first place, and then remaining alive and free to gather it. Who better than the SAS, to do the job? With their tough attitude and superb training, they are the ideal troops to successfully complete this type of mission. Getting into a position to gather information is difficult. A method of entry must be planned first.

Flying in by helicopter, or parachuting in from a transport aircraft are quick and efficient, but what of the enemy's anti-aircraft capabilities? On-route, if the aircraft is shot down, the mission will fail. Are there any suitable dropping zones if the parachuting option looks possible? Is vehicle entry an option? Can the patrol be inserted using motorised transport or boats? Land Rovers or even motorbikes might be used, if local conditions are right. Does the terrain or situation render unsuitable all these choices? If it is, then a covert forced march across enemy territory may be the only way in. Crossing minefields, fast rivers, and heavily patrolled enemy country add to the problems when considering a ground entry. Given that the patrol does arrive safely, they must then survive for days, or even weeks in a static, hidden base, if one can be found. They must carry enough food for the duration of their mission, plus weapons and ammunition, explosives, water and medical supplies, plus their own clothing and personal 'gear'. Furthermore, they must have been trained to use the latest high tech. Communications systems, because once information is gathered, it must be quickly sent back to friendly forces, or it becomes outdated, and useless. Radios and batteries add to the weight burden of the patrol, but are vital in order to communicate. The troops must be highly trained in camouflaging their position, to avoid discovery from roving patrols, who may be using dogs to assist their search.

Once the mission is over, and the patrol receives the order to ex-filtrate, are there other tasks to be completed on the way back to friendly territory? Should they mount a random campaign of attacking targets of opportunity using ambush, improvised mine laying and explosive demolition? This sort of action causes chaos behind enemy lines. The destruction of fuel supplies, ammunition dumps and key personnel means the diversion of huge numbers of enemy troops to try to find, and stop the perpetrators. In a number crunching world, it is a very cost effective use of a tiny number of men, who cause the enemy enormous problems in relation to their small numbers. Keep in mind that this is all happening where the enemy should feel at their safest, many miles behind their own front line.

All our training was geared to achieving these sorts of goal. Nothing had been overlooked so far, but there was still an enormous amount to learn. Our next weekends were Mobility, Tactics and Weapons.

Mobility weekend taught us all to use vehicles to our best advantage. There were three types of vehicle to consider, at this early stage of our training. The ubiquitous Land Rover was the Regiments first choice, rugged and reliable; the Rover was superb in difficult off-road terrain. The military version had the benefit of adaptations, which served the military role very well. The regular 22nd SAS Regiment had its own version, called the Pink Panther. Its unusual name came from its desert camouflage paint colour. Back in the 1930's an Intrepid British female aviator crash-landed in the North African desert during one of her record braking international flights. Despite an extensive aerial search within the normal flight corridor where she had crashed, her body (and plane) were not found for many years later. Her aircraft was painted in a dull pink, which unfortunately for her, blended into the desert background perfectly. Someone in the

Regiment heard this story, experimented with the colour, and the 'Pink' Panther was born. Although heavily armed, and fitted with huge internal, self-sealing long range petrol tanks, the 'Pinky', as it was known, suffered from an underpowered engine, and weak half-shafts. As a result, we used standard military Land Rovers, which fulfilled our requirements in the European theatre. We were also taught how to drive the 4-ton Bedford army lorry. The best vehicle we trained on was the army's Canard Motorbike. Normally used for dispatch riding, the Canard was a big powerful beast, which took some handling. As I was still riding around London on a little Honda 50cc bike, learning the knowledge, Sgt. King volunteered me to demonstrate my riding technique to the others. I had never ridden anything bigger than my little Honda before. The leap from 50cc to 750cc is considerable, as I found to my cost, when I let the clutch out. The bike surged forward with a mighty roar, with me hanging on for dear life. The last anyone saw, was me hurtling through a hedge, about 50 metres from my start point. I hit a ditch on the other side, and was catapulted over the handlebars. I landed hard and fast, about twenty feet in front of the bike. As I lay on the ground, trying to remember what day it was, my buddies jogged up to me. When they saw I was still alive, Sgt. King summed everything up nicely "Black, you really are a first class wanker!"

We learnt how to extract a Land Rover from a bog. Sgt. King explained that when a heavily laden Rover sank to its axels, no amount of over revving, pushing and shoving would extract it. To prove the point, he drove a Rover into a small lake. Making sure that it was stuck fast up to its axels in the mud, he invited us to try to get it out. Our attempts proved fruitless. After thirty minutes of revving, pushing and copious amount of swearing, the Rover remained stuck in the muddy lake bed. Sgt. King sat on the bank, chewing a blade of grass, watching our efforts. His cadre were all now soaking wet, tired and very frustrated. "OK lads, that's enough. Out you get, and I'll show you how it's done." He stood up, and walked into the water. Strapped to the side of the Rover, was a large bundle, wrapped in a dull green tarpaulin. He removed it, and laid the contents on the bonnet for our inspection. "This will do the job," he said with a grin. He explained that this was a Turfa winch. He ordered two of us to attach the thick steel hawser that came with the kit, to a sturdy tree which stood close by on the riverbank. When it was firmly attached to the tree's base, the other end of the cable was fed into the briefcase size winch. Another shorter cable was attached to the front of the Rover, and its end fed into the opposite end of the winch. Snapping a large catch on the side of the winch shut, he inserted a strong steel rod into the winch's body.

"It's taken all of you thirty minutes to achieve absolutely nothing, but with this winch, I can pull the Rover out, on my own. The Rover

167

weighs a couple of tons with all the gear on board, and I think you will all agree it is stuck fast. Rouse, knock it out of gear, and make sure the handbrake is off."

We all grinned; this we had to see. Sgt. King started to rock the steel rod backwards and forwards. The cables began to move through the winch, until they were both quite taught. Sgt. King continued his rocking motion and slowly, incredibly, the Rover began to move. As our intrepid instructor pumped the rod forward and back the Rover was slowly dragged out of the lake. When the Rover eventually stood free, and dripping on the bank, Sgt. King unhooked the winch and cables. He started the engine, and reversed it back into the lake. Making sure it was well and truly stuck again, he climbed out, put his hands on his hips and simply said....

"Right, now you do it." We waded back into the cold muddy lake, and complied. It worked a treat, and we had soon extracted the heavy Rover.

"The moral of this lesson lads, is if you have to use Rovers on a mission, always make sure you have a winch on board. You have ten minutes to change into some dry kit, before we start the next lesson on helicopter drills... Get Away!"

Our lessons continued throughout the day, concentrating later on vehicle maintenance, changing tyres and stealing vehicles. We were taught how to break into, and 'hot wire' a vehicle's ignition system. If we needed to escape during a mission, and an enemy or civilian vehicle could be stolen, we needed to know how to effectively and efficiently pinch it.

When our training was over, Sgt. King gave us a treat that evening. "I'm pleased with your progress lads, so we are off for a meal and a couple of beers at a local pub." There were no weapons to worry about, and none of us were wearing any insignia, so we set off in both Rovers to a quaint little village pub, a mile outside the training area. The publican nodded to Sgt. King as we trooped up to the bar, and began pulling nine pints. This was a very special occasion; the only evening we had off, during the entire selection/continuation course.

Our night off passed all too quickly. After a hot meal, and several more pints, we drove back onto the training area and quickly set up camp.

Early the next day, our training concentrated on cross country driving, and using the different low ratio gears on the Rovers. We learnt how to drive across incredibly difficult ground, and up seemingly impossible gradients. We ended the weekend with some practice of reversing the vehicles with a trailer attached. Not the easiest technique to master, but eventually, we all managed to reverse and park both the Rover and trailer in a reasonably straight line, between some bright orange bollards which Sgt. King had laid out.

Chapter 15
The End of the Beginning

We had two more weekends training before our final Continuation 'Test Weekend', where we would put it all together, and show that we were up to a sufficient standard to be officially 'badged' into 21 SAS Regiment.

One of the remaining weekends concentrated on teaching us the artful art of setting up a series of carefully hidden and heavily camouflaged hides. These are used by the Regiment to observe an enemy static point, or an area of strategic interest, such as a bridge, road junction, air base and so on. In their simplest form, hides can be just a one-man affair, located under cover, on the surface. Each man in the patrol stays in the hide for several hours at a time, and reports anything interesting back to the patrol, via a field telephone. The patrol then radios any important information to H.Q. via their radio equipment. This can be transmitted at routine times, unless the information is of an urgent nature, when a 'Flash Message' is sent. If a nuclear missile delivery convoy drove down the road we were observing, that was defiantly a 'Flash'. If nothing happens, and nothing is seen from the hide, it is still important to report non-activity. The simple rational is that if there is no movement in a particular sector, then our Generals needed to know that sector was quiet.

Hides or O.P.s (observation points) as they are also known, could also be very large, formal, four-man affairs. In order to make them proof from the effects of Nuclear, Biological and Chemical warfare, it was necessary to locate them underground. This involved several days of digging and camouflaging, before the O.P. was ready for use. The four-man patrol's workload was phenomenal, involving the removal (and camouflaging) of 30-40 tons of soil and rock. The spoil had to be removed from the immediate site, transported hundreds of metres, and hidden in the folds of the earth. As the soil was of a different texture and colour from the original top soil, it had to be covered with a scrape of original top soil, and camouflaged to be hidden in plain view. Digging began with the very first, faint rays of dawn, and finished only when it was too dangerous and dark to continue, as night fell. Three of four days were usually needed to extract enough soil to dig a hide, big enough to safely hold four men. When the underground O.P. was finally finished, complete with several feet of earth compacted above our heads, we had to check, and double-check the camouflage, before we entered our hide, and sealed the hatch. A periscope was used, to observe the point of interest, and this had to be cunningly hidden with an old tree stump, for example. Only when the patrol commander was absolutely satisfied that the job had been done to his complete satisfaction, the patrol, with all their food, water, weapons and equipment,would climb down the ladder inside the O.P.s hatch, and it would be sealed. Living for days in incredibly cramped conditions inside a four-man hide was difficult, to say the least. Apart from eating and sleeping, all other normal bodily functions had to be performed within the confines of the hide, in extremely close proximity to the other member of the patrol. Although universally hated within the Regiment, this type of O.P. was unfortunately a vital tool of the trade, and was used when the need arose, by a patrol that drew the short straw.

The penultimate weekend's training was weapons and tactics. We spent the entire time firing all the weapons we had trained so hard with thus far. We needed to be very slick with our weapon drills, and be able to hit the target and clear jammed weapons quickly. It was vital that we could use captured weapons, and we fired the Russian AK47, and several other foreign assault rifles and machine guns.

We learnt how to cross minefields. The enemy would deny access to various areas by laying anti-personnel and anti-vehicle mines. These deadly booby traps were a very dangerous obstacle, but could be traversed with the right training, and plenty of nerve. Knowing the different types of mine, and how to avoid detonating them was another part of the concentrated training we were immersed in. Patrolling, ambush and anti-ambush drills had to be practiced until they became second nature, both by day, and night. Meeting agents, who would pass on vital information, and the drills to carry out such a meeting were all crammed into the weekend.

We had to prove finally to the Regiment that we were good enough to join our Squadrons, and the final exercise was where it happened. We were split into two four-man patrols. Before we were briefed, at the start of 'Exercise Final Fling', we were introduced to our new umpires. They were two seasoned sergeants from the Regiment, who would act as impartial judges of our individual, and patrol performances during the exercise. As they had no previous knowledge of us, they would give their assessments purely on what they saw. Sgt. King would act as a floating umpire, and would perform various administration tasks during the exercise.

We received a very thorough briefing, but the outline of the coming final exercise was that each patrol would be inserted by helicopter into the exercise area. Then tactically patrol into the target area, and set up an O.P. overlooking an important road. As we had not yet learnt to use the Regiments very specialised radio equipment, we could not send radio messages back to base. We were therefore tasked to keep an accurate log of events, and the times they occurred, to simulate radio traffic. We would meet an agent, who would provide us with the latest location of the mobile target which we would attack. There would be dog teams, and a highly motivated, active enemy patrolling against us. If all went well, we would ex-filtrate back to a secure friendly location at the end of the exercise, for a final de-brief, and would only then learn if we had passed the final phase of Continuation.

Preparation began on the last Friday evening we would be parading with Training Wing, at the Dukes. We split into our patrols, and began checking our equipment and weapons. We drew copious amounts of blank ammunition and thunder flashes, plus smoke grenades and dummy explosive charges. These were all stowed into our bergans, along with ration packs, sleeping bags, dry clothing and several house bricks, which would simulate spare radio batteries. We all had at least 60lb bergans, plus our heavy belt kits, water and weapons. Sgt. King reminded us that this was only a two-day exercise; bergan weights could well double on longer missions. When everything was ready, we checked each other for personal items and applied plenty of camouflage cream to the exposed surfaces of our faces and hands.

We boarded the lorry, and were driven to a Royal Air Force Base on the outskirts of London. Our Puma helicopter sat silently waiting for us, on a dark and wet dispersal apron. We climbed aboard, and the pilot started the engines. The massive blades began to rotate. The noise inside the helicopter rose to a deafening pitch. After several minutes, the pilot fed more power into the engines, and with a mighty roar, the heavy Puma lifted clear of the ground, and we rose slowly into the air.

We flew at low level for over an hour. The pilot hugged the ground, to avoid being picked up on anti-aircraft radar. He would occasionally climb briefly to miss high-voltage power lines, but generally, he stayed at under 100 feet. The Royal Air Force has a cadre of their very best pilots, who make up a Special Forces fight, dedicated to flying the SAS, anywhere in the world, by fixed-wing aircraft or more locally, by helicopter. Using their considerable skills, and very latest high tech. equipment, they guarantee to be on time, wherever they are needed. Their professionalism isn't always matched by their appearance, as our flight crew dispatcher was wearing a bowler hat, under his earphones.

The interior red warning light began to flash, which gave us a two-minute warning, before we landed. My patrol was to be first off the helicopter, and our tense faces were highlighted inside the helicopter by the warning lights eerie glow. We had loaded with my patrol nearest the door, which the dispatcher slid open as we neared our drop zone. The icy blast of the roaring slipstream filled the interior of the passenger cabin, and the noise of the massive blades thundered in our ears. My stomach lurched as the pilot suddenly reduced power, and flared the aircraft. The nose pitched up, and seconds later we felt the thud of the tail wheel bumping into the ground. The flashing light changed from red to a solid green, and clutching our bergans and weapons; we leapt from the helicopter. On contact with the ground, the drill was simple. Run as a tight group clear of the punishing wash of the rotor blades, and assume a prone position of all round defence. Although the move took us only moments, the helicopter was already clear of the ground, and heading towards its next drop point. Our ears had become accustomed to the roar of the Puma's engines, and as the helicopter increased speed; and was gone in what seemed only seconds, the resulting silence was truly deafening. We strained our ears for tell-tale sounds of an enemy follow up, but heard nothing, except for the wind rustling through the long grass on which we lay. We stayed still until we were certain we had not been compromised. With a sharp kick on each other's ankles, we rose and shook out into single file patrol formation. I had been nominated as patrol commander, and in turn had nominated Keith as my lead scout. He would be slightly ahead of me in the file, and I would watch him as best I could in the darkness for hand signals of something ahead. Dickie assumed the role of signaller, and took up a position close behind me. Bringing up the rear, Ollie acted as 'tail end Charlie'. He had to look left and right as we patrolled forward (as we all did) but he also had to constantly scan the area to our rear, in case we were followed. Our tight patrol was flanked by Sgt. Wills, who was our roving umpire. For the purposes of the exercise, he was invisible, and would play no part in it. His only role was to observe us. His final individual assessment would be critical to our successfully passing into the Regiment. Our bergans felt heavy after the cramped flight, but it was good to be out in the quiet, still night. After a mile or so of slow deliberate movement, we reached a small copse. I indicated our first rally point to the others. If we were suddenly split up further on, after contact with the enemy, this was the immediate point to try and return to, where we could reform the patrol. I changed the boys around, so that they had different positions in the file. We had been taught to swap jobs during a tactical night time move, to help keep everyone sharp, and focused. Our initial task was to contact a friendly agent, who would brief us to exactly where to set up our surface observation point. He would meet him close to a railway line, near an unmanned level crossing.

We had a tight time schedule, and had to pick up speed slightly. We crossed the next three miles quickly and quietly, and arrived at the meeting point thirty minutes early. This was not by chance, but in order to establish a hidden O.P., where we could watch the immediate area for signs of enemy compromise, before meeting the friendly agent. When we had found a likely spot, I brought the rest of the patrol into a tight huddle and whispered "O.P." They knew from my initial patrol briefing what we were doing, and silently slipped off their bergans, and lay beside them, so that each man watched a ninety degree arc. I eased my bergan to the ground and slowly and quietly removed a Starlight scope from it. Lying flat on the ground, I switched the Scope on, and was rewarded with a faint high-pitched whine. I placed the padded rubber eye piece over my eye. The panorama ahead of me was clearly visible, but bathed in a green tint. The passive Starlight scope took in the faint light from the stars above me, and magnified it thousands of times, to produce the ghostly picture I now observed. Nothing was moving, and there was no sign of the agent. After watching for a minute, I switched the Scope off, and used my ears, to scan of any sound, which was out of place. I repeated this procedure regularly, until I spotted a man riding an unlit bicycle on the other side   of the track. As it was now two o'clock in the morning, this had to be our man. When he reached the crossing, he got off his bike, and pushed it over to our side. Caution dictated that we must always suspect a trap, so we lay still for several minutes, and continued to observe in all directions. Each of us used the Starlight scope to carefully scrutinise our surroundings, before I judged it safe to break cover and approach the 'agent'. I tapped Ollie's shoulder three times, which was the pre-arranged signal that I was moving. He passed on the signal on, until the last man tapped me. Now that I knew that all the patrol members were aware of our next move, I slowly stood up, and crept quietly towards my contact. I was within a few feet of him, when the agent turned and saw me. He jumped with surprise, and let out a muffled gasp. We had been trained to expect a very nervous reaction from civilian contacts like him, as his life was very much on the line, and he had every right to be frightened. If he were to be caught by the enemy, he, and also his family could expect imprisonment or execution for helping us. I had to make sure he was the right man however, so I whispered my challenge.

"The Danube is blue." The agent (Sgt. King) nervously stuttered his reply.

"But cold and dark, my friend."

These pre-arranged phrases identified us both to each other, and I lowered my rifle, and offered him my hand. As we shook hands, I whispered.

"Good to meet you, you are a very brave man." Given how frightened an agent would be, anything to calm him was an advantage to us.

"I have a message for you from London," he whispered, nervously looking over his shoulder. He gave me an envelope. "I must go now, there are patrols in the area."

"Where?" I asked.

"Everywhere!" he replied, turning his bicycle and climbing aboard. "Good luck," was the last thing he said, as he disappeared into the dark shrouds of the night.

We needed to decode the message, so I moved the patrol away from the meeting place, and after a kilometre or so, we headed into deep cover.

Once we had decoded the message, we had been tasked to observe and destroy an enemy headquarters about eight kilometres away. Thunder rumbled ominously in the distance, as we patrolled through the darkness, towards the target. I swapped the patrol order around again to help everyone stay sharp, which with hindsight, turned out to be a very bad idea.

It began to rain heavily, and within minutes, we were all soaked to the skin. With our experiences in the Welsh mountains, it didn't bother any of us. The tempo of the storm increased steadily, and lightning flashed across the skies followed by deafening claps of thunder. Despite the fantastic light show and intermittent noise, we patrolled forward, until the end of my wet rifle touched an invisible electrified cattle fence. I let out an involuntary yell as the high amps surged through my body, and I was thrown backwards. Afterwards, laughing, the others swore blind that I lit up like a Christmas tree and smoked when I hit the ground. My short hair was standing on end like a stunted Afro.

"E-E-Electric fence!" I stammered to Ollie, fulfilling my duty as lead scout,   to warn the patrol of impending obstacles.

"No shit, Sherlock." he hissed with a grin. "You wanker!"

The mission continued, with a successful daytime O.P., and after meeting up with the other patrol, we completed a violent and explosive destruction of the 'Target'. We recovered back to the 'Dukes', and began sorting ourselves out. Sgt King spent a hour in with the O.C. of Training wing, the Sgt. Major and our two 'umpires'. Our ultimate fate was being decided. When he emerged, he gave us all a smile, and thumbs up. We were ordered into Training Wing's classroom, and the O.C. debriefed us on the final exercise. Then, we were officially given the good news, and our very first compliment.

"Well done lads, you have all successfully passed selection and Continuation. Welcome to the SAS Regiment. Fall in outside, and I'll present your berets."

Grinning like Cheshire Cats, we trooped outside, and lined up in a single rank. Sgt King ordered us to attention, and Major Brook went from man to man, shaking hands with each of us, and giving us a hearty well done. As he handed me my sandy coloured beret, I just couldn't get the big cheesy grin off my face.

"Well done Sparky. Stay away from those electric fences, now, there's a good lad."

"Bloody right Boss!" Was the best I could do. I replaced my hated cap comforter with my new beret, complete with winged dagger cap badge. At last, I'd done it. I was in. There was still however, one last stage before I was a fully qualified Trooper with my new Squadron. I had to attend a military parachute course, and win my SAS parachute 'Wings'.

I had a funny feeling that was when the adventures would really start.
I was absolutely right of course, but that as they say...is another story.

The End

Also by David Black

EAGLES of the DAMNED

It was autumn in the year AD 9. The summer campaigning season was over. Centurion Rufus and his battle-hardened century were part of three mighty Roman Legions returning to the safety of their winter quarters beside the River Rhine. Like their commanding General, the Centurion and his men suspected nothing.

Little did they know, but the entire Germania province was about to explode...

Lured into a cunning trap, three of Rome's mighty Legions were systematically and ruthlessly annihilated, during seventy-two hours of unimaginable terror and unrelenting butchery. They were mercilessly slaughtered within the Teutoburg, a vast tract of dark and forbidding forest on the northernmost rim of the Roman Empire.

Little could they have imagined, as they were brutally cut down, their fate had been irrevocably sealed years earlier by their own flawed system of provincial governance, and a rabid traitor's overwhelming thirst for vengeance. But how could such a military catastrophe have ever happened to such a well trained and superbly equipped army? This is their story...

http://www.davis-black.co.uk

Published on Amazon in Kindle Format & CreateSpace Paperback.

Also by David Black

The Great Satan

Shadow Squadron #1

In The Great Satan, the first of his compelling new Shadow Squadron series, author David Black has produced his own fictional nightmare scenario: What if the Iraqi weapons that were said to be dismantled in the late 1990s included the ultimate WMD? And what if the deposing of Saddam Hussein left one of his most ruthless military leaders still at large, and actively seeking a customer for Iraq's only nuclear bomb? . . .

Published on Amazon in Kindle Format & Paperback.

http://www.david-black.co.uk

Also by David Black

Siege of Faith

The Chronicles of Sir Richard Starkey #1

Far to the East across the sparkling waters of the great Mediterranean Sea, the formidable Ottoman Empire was secretly planning to add to centuries of expansion. Soon, they would begin the invasion and conquest of Christian Europe.

But first, their all-powerful Sultan, Suleiman the Magnificent knew he must destroy the last Christian bastion which stood in the way of his glorious destiny of conquest. The Maltese stronghold... garrisoned and defended by the noble and devout warrior monks of the Knights of St. John of Jerusalem...

A powerful story of heroism, love and betrayal set against the backdrop of the cruel and terrible siege of Malta which raged through the long hot summer of 1565. The great Caliph unleashed a massive invasion force of 40,000 fanatical Muslim troops, intent on conquering Malta before invading poorly defended Christian Europe. A heretic English Knight - Sir Richard Starkey becomes embroiled in the bloody five month siege which ensued; Europe's elite nobility cast chivalry aside, no quarter asked or mercy given as rivers of Muslim and Christian blood flowed...

Published on Amazon in Kindle Format & Paperback.

http://www.david-black.co.uk

Also by David Black
OUT SOON!

Dark Empire

Shadow Squadron #2

Sgt. Pat Farrell and Two Troop are back in action!

Sgt. Pat Farrell and his reserve SAS troop are on a training exercise in Kenya when they are suddenly ordered into the primitive jungle of the Congo on what should be nothing more than a straightforward and simple humanitarian rescue mission.

Unfortunately, nothing is straightforward in Africa. Pat and his men find themselves trapped and facing the disastrous prospect of no escape from the war ravaged blood-stained country. Hunted by a feral legion of savage, drug-crazed guerrillas, things don't always go to plan...even for the SAS!

To be published on Amazon in Kindle Format & Paperback by CreatSpace
.

http://www.david-black.co.uk

ALSO COMING SOON !

Inca Sun
Chronicles of Sir Richard Starkey #2

Sir Richard and his giant servant Quinn begin their next great adventure, aboard the Privateer 'The Intrepid', in the treacherous waters off the Caribbean and South America coastline. Their heretic English Queen Elizabeth I has secretly commanded Sir Richard to prowl the high seas in search of King Phillip II of Spain's fabulously wealthy treasure convoys. They sail from the New World for Spain laden with gold and silver ripped from the Conquistador's mines in Peru and Mexico; dug from the dark earth by their cruelly treated Inca and Mayan slaves.

What Richard doesn't know when he accepts his latest Royal commission is that his arch nemesis - Don Rodrigo Salvador Torrez has become Governor of King Phillip's Mexican province of Veracruz.

One thing is certain, mere gold cannot pay the debt of honour that exists between the two men, since their first encounter on Malta during the great siege. The only currency which will settle the terrible debt will be the loser's noble lifeblood....

To be published on Amazon in Kindle Format & Paperback by CreatSpace

http://www.david-black.co.uk